D0755403

ALWAYS A MARINE

ALWAYS A MARINE
The Return to Civvy Street

STEVEN PREECE

MAINSTREAM
PUBLISHING
EDINBURGH AND LONDON

First published in Great Britain in 2005 by
MAINSTREAM PUBLISHING COMPANY (EDINBURGH) LTD
7 Albany Street
Edinburgh EH1 3UG

ISBN 1 84596 005 X

A catalogue record for this book
is available from the British Library

Typeset in Apollo and Stone Sans

Printed and bound in Great Britain by
Cox & Wyman Ltd

CONTENTS

FOREWORD

When people join the armed forces and specialise as soldiers, they are trained to kill without hesitation and go into war at the drop of a hat. Amongst their repertoire of fighting skills is the use of targeted and devastating aggression. All soldiers are trained to be professional when on duty, and to withhold this aggression when it is not required. Most can control it in off-duty situations too, when there is no official enemy to be engaged, but for some, having no outlet for their abilities spills over into violence amongst the ranks and beyond. Extreme strength with no control is a dangerous combination, and some soldiers can't limit their fighting to the battlefield. They unleash their energy and wrath on others.

When people leave the armed forces, they immediately become civilians. Mentally, though, they are still soldiers. There is no training for turning a soldier back into an ordinary citizen. Only time can assist with this. For some this journey may be easy whilst for others it can be a living hell.

At the start of my career in the Royal Marines in the early 1980s I walked into a culture of violence and aggression as a young 18 year old. My personality changed from friendly and amiable to hard and unforgiving. Violence was common amongst the ranks and, if provoked, I personally never hesitated to use it. After a few years I became reputed for this kind of behaviour, which eventually led to a court martial. However, to my relief I was fully acquitted by the court, but realised that my days in the Marines were numbered. The culture of tolerating violence and scuffles was disappearing, and those of us who couldn't curb our aggression would eventually be phased out. Consequently, after seven years' service, I opted to leave the Marines to seek a new career in civvy street. What I didn't know then was how difficult I would find the transition.

INTRODUCTION

Leaving the armed forces is a big step for a lot of soldiers. They spend their careers working with colleagues whom they can trust with their lives. Teamwork is crucial to their job, as is the ability to work alone when necessary. When they walk into civvy street, they need to learn to adapt quickly to a different lifestyle in a world full of individuals.

I left the Royal Marines in 1990 after serving for seven years in various parts of the world. I'd been trained to live, work, think, react and survive as a Marine. What I hadn't been taught was how to stop being one. It wasn't something I could just turn off. The propensity for anger, aggression and violence hadn't gone away. This was something that only time could heal: in my case, 13 years of time.

This story portrays my journey through life as a civilian. I have worked in various locations throughout the world, where I have experienced many kinds of different challenges and emotions, including violence and desperation as well as warmth and laughter.

When I left the Marines, I expected to walk into a new job, but I found it hard to find work with my skills and background and had to register as unemployed. The respect I had grown used to from the people of my home town soon disappeared, as they began to realise that I was no longer a Marine. Suddenly I became a target for them to test their fighting skills on. They were even coming at me with baseball bats. Yet I was not defeated and I forged a life amongst them.

My aggressive reputation preceded me into the workplace and eventually I was forced to work abroad. What follows at this point is a blow-by-blow account of the situations I got myself into and the types of people I met and worked with. At times the survival skills I was taught in the Marines came in useful, when I applied them in violent and difficult situations. As you will see, what finally stopped me from unleashing my violent nature on those who crossed me was the love of my family and the healing non-aggressive philosophy of the ninja.

CHAPTER ONE

CIVVY STREET

On 8 May 1990 I walked across the open square of the Royal Marines' Stonehouse Barracks in Plymouth for the last time. I could hear the sound of Marines' drill boots crunching as they hit the floor and a sergeant drill instructor shouting out commands to them as they marched past. On the far side of the square I saw another troop of Marines dressed in battle dress, complete with heavy backpack bergens and a multitude of different kinds of weapons. Then I saw the flag, the Royal Marine Corps colours, flapping in the wind, high up on a long white flagpole. I looked towards the big stone arch and tall green gates of the main entrance to the barracks. The Marine sentry who guarded the gate removed the ammunition magazine from his SA80 assault rifle and came over to see me. I'd known him for a couple of years and he'd been on my last night out with the Marines a couple of nights before. He smiled and held out his hand, which I shook.

'Good luck, Steve.'

'Thank you,' I smiled.

Then I tightened my grip on my bergen and walked out as a civilian for the first time in over seven years, wondering what the big wide world had in store for me.

I had no intentions of going straight home and had arranged to stay in a rented furnished flat with another ex-Marine for a few weeks in a nearby area called Mutley Plain. The other ex-Marine was called Graham Dudley. He was a couple of years older than me, about 28-ish. He had brown greasy hair and wore square-rimmed glasses. He was short and stocky and his arms and back were covered in various Marine-based tattoos.

The flat was fairly sizeable, with two bedrooms, a kitchen, a toilet and a dining room. I no longer had a regular salary to support my needs so I took a job offered by Graham to work with him as a doorman in a nightclub. The nightclub wasn't in the usual rough areas I had frequented for years and attracted a higher calibre of customer, who usually dressed in a suit or tuxedo or a ball gown for the women. The atmosphere inside was warm and friendly and a seven-piece jazz band provided the entertainment. Everybody seemed to speak with a posh Queen's English accent and their manners were impeccable.

There was hardly ever any trouble. The hardest part of the job was making sure the customers didn't fall into the small outside swimming pool as they staggered towards their cars and then assisting them into them when they couldn't get their keys into the locks. Then we would watch them drive out of the car park. It was obvious they were drunk because they skidded, braked excessively and frequently used to indicate in the opposite direction to which they were turning.

One night another guy, who was referred to as Big Benny, joined us on the door. He was related to the club owner, who had given him the job because he was out of work. Benny was built like a brick shithouse. He was older than we were, somewhere in his mid-30s, and had fat chubby cheeks and short spiky hair that was shaved round the back and sides. He told us that he had been working the doors for years and that the boss had brought him here to keep him out of trouble. He talked about fighting a lot of the time and told us that he was as hard as nails and that we could learn a lot from him. I looked at Graham and smiled and we just took everything he said with a pinch of salt.

When the club closed, we sat together in the empty bar. A good perk of the job was that we were allowed to drink as much beer as we wanted at the end of our shifts. Big Benny continued to brag about how tough he was, while Graham started in on a personal sob-story about his wife, who had recently separated from him. After a while Graham and I caught a taxi back to the flat and picked up a Chinese meal that Graham had ordered for himself on the way. Back at the flat we opened a bottle of chilled wine and Graham continued to mope about his ex-wife. He pulled out a photograph of her and showed it to me. My eyes opened wide. She was as ugly as sin. I bet the midwife smacked the mother when she was born, I thought. And I bet her mother used to tie a lamb chop around her neck so that the dog would play with her.

'Yes, very nice, Graham,' I smirked. 'I can see why you get so upset about her.'

I suppose this was two-faced, but he looked as if he would crumble if I really told him what I was thinking. We sat and sipped our wine. I felt hungry as I talked to Graham and stared at his unopened Chinese meal. Suddenly he burst into tears.

'She's gone forever and now I'm going to kill myself,' he cried.

I watched the tears streaming down his distressed and reddened face.

'I am, Steve. I am and I don't want you to try and stop me,' he continued.

I stared at his Chinese meal and rubbed my forehead. I was very hungry and my stomach started to rumble.

'Give me a minute, Graham,' I said as I stood up and walked into my bedroom. 'I've got an idea.'

I pulled my bergen out of a cupboard and searched through the side pockets. I quickly located my survival knife. It was about 12-in. long with a jagged edge. I'd used it for years as part of my Marine fighting order. I walked back into the front room, where Graham was still threatening to kill himself.

'Here,' I gestured. 'Use this and make a fucking good job of it. I'll look after your Chinese and I'll clean the mess up in the morning.'

'OK, OK,' he agreed in a whimper. 'I'm going to do it. I really am.'

I picked up his Chinese meal and went back to my room. I devoured the food in minutes to satisfy my hunger and then got into bed, where I quickly fell asleep. Next morning I could hear something tapping on my bedroom window. I opened my eyes and looked out into the daylight. It was windy outside and the branches of a tree tapped lightly on the windowpane.

I wonder if that silly bastard has killed himself and made a mess in the front room, I thought, before getting out of bed and going to check. I saw Graham lying asleep on the sofa. He snored mildly. My survival knife was placed on the table in front of him along with a suicide note he had managed to scribble. I picked the knife up, placed it back in my bergen and then put the suicide note in the bin. I made two cups of coffee and woke my friend from his deep sleep. He sat up and smiled at me before sipping from the cup.

'I see you haven't killed yourself,' I smiled.

'No. I changed my mind,' he replied. 'Did you enjoy my Chinese, Steve?'

'Yes. It was quite tasty, thanks. Look, I'm sorry you feel so strongly about your ex-wife. I guess she is quite a pretty woman,' I lied tactfully, trying not to upset him.

He smiled at me. 'You're a lying bastard, Steve. She's an ugly motherfucker and you know it.'

'But why were you crying about her last night and threatening to kill yourself?' I asked with my eyebrows raised.

'Because the ugly bastard ran off with seven thousand pounds of my money. My life savings.'

'Bloody hell!' I exclaimed.

'Yes,' he nodded. 'And you can keep your survival knife away from me and buy me a fucking Chinese tonight.'

'Yeah, no problem, mate,' I grinned.

The following week an ex-girlfriend of mine turned up. She was called Samantha and came from Somerset. I'd finished with her some months before, but she said she wanted to talk to me and to possibly try to make things up. Graham agreed to let her stay with me in the flat for a while. He was impressed with her figure and stunning good looks, but I assured him that she had the temper of a gorilla with a sore head, which was why I had binned her previously.

One Saturday evening Graham and I went to work in the nightclub and Samantha went into Plymouth city centre with her friends for a night on the town. Graham and I stood together as Big Benny entered the club.

'All right, lads,' he smiled. 'Hope you weren't panicking and thinking that I wasn't going to turn up. Don't want you boys getting beaten up.'

Bloody dickhead, I thought, as I exchanged glances with Graham.

The three of us stood side by side inside the entrance and bid people good evening as they started to arrive in their flash cars. After a while the flow of guests seemed to calm down and we stood listening to Big Benny telling us how tough he was once again.

Suddenly the entrance door burst open and a young man with short jet-black hair and a bloodstained face stood looking at us. He seemed out of breath and was gasping for air. Graham instantly recognised him.

'Badger,' he said with a big frown. 'What the hell's happened to you?'

'It's the local mafia,' he replied. 'They've beaten me up because I was coming here. You had better get out of here quick. They're coming to smash the place up.'

The three of us stared at each other and I could feel the hairs standing up on the back of my neck. We looked out through a window that faced towards the entrance in the grounds and saw a group of about six rugged-looking men walking towards us.

'Well,' chirped up Graham, looking towards Big Benny. 'This is your big chance to prove yourself.'

Big Benny looked petrified. I could see the sweat dripping down his forehead. He took another quick look out of the window and then ran out through a side door. I really did feel like following him, but Graham stood fast and I didn't want to leave him to face them alone. I looked out of the window again. They were only a few feet away.

'Well, I don't know who you are, but it looks like we're all in this together now,' I said to Badger.

Graham burst into laughter and so did Badger. For a moment this baffled me. Then the door opened slowly. The group of rugged-looking men stood staring at us. One of them had a shaved head. He looked mean.

'Evening, lads,' smiled Graham.

'Hiya, Graham,' replied the rugged man. 'I was beginning to wonder if we'd got the right place.'

'Yes, you certainly have. Please go inside. It's free for you tonight.'

The group of six men stepped inside. They said hello and walked into a nearby lounge. I looked at Graham, who was in fits of laughter.

'Come on then, tell me,' I said.

'Steve, meet Badger. He's a bootneck [a Marine]. The other guys are from the local rugby club. I invited them as guests.'

'I see,' I nodded. 'You've set Big Benny up.'

'Yes. I did. I got sick of the crap that tosser kept coming out with and decided to put him to the test. I guess you find out who your real friends are when the chips are down.'

We all laughed together and patted each other on the shoulders as Badger rubbed the fake blood from his face. It was now apparent that Big Benny was all talk and no action and when the going got tough, the tough got going! The rest of the evening went without incident. By 2 a.m. most people had left and we sat together to drink a few beers in the bar. A couple of loose women joined our company. They were waiting for Graham and Badger to leave with them.

'Aren't you on the pull?' asked one of them.

'No. My ex-girlfriend is waiting for me back at the flat.'

'And the flat is all yours tonight,' grinned Graham as he threw the door keys to me.

I smiled as I got up to leave and one of the loose women kissed me on the cheek. Ten minutes later Graham dropped me off near the flat and drove off with his woman. The night was quiet, except for the sound of Graham's tyres faintly screeching around a distant corner.

I put my key in the front door, opened it and stepped inside. I blinked my eyes and was startled as the hallway light was switched on. It momentarily dazzled me. Samantha was stood facing me. She looked angry and was dressed in her pyjamas.

'What time do you call this?' she shrieked at the top of her voice.

'Bloody hell, Sam. Keep it down. What are you shouting for?'

'I've been into town tonight. They're calling you a hanger-on.'

I frowned. A hanger-on was somebody who stayed put in the town they were stationed in when they left the Marines.

'You're late and you've got red lipstick on your face,' she continued.

'Oh, that's off one of Graham's tarts. It's not what you think.'

'You bastard,' she yelled as she lunged at me with an ornament in her hand.

I reacted quickly by grabbing hold of her and pushing her backwards into the sitting room. I kept her relatively safely at arm's length as we moved and tried to explain myself to her.

'Calm down,' I shouted. 'Calm down.'

For a moment she stopped fighting me and I released my grip. Then she lunged at me with the ornament again so I pushed her backwards. I had to do this a few times because she kept coming back at me. I became very worried. If she falls and knocks herself out, it'll look like vicious murder, I thought.

'Bollocks,' I snapped. 'I'm getting out of here. I'm no hanger-on.'

I grabbed my bergen and packed it with my things before stomping out through the front door.

'Don't go, Steve,' she pleaded. 'Please don't go.'

I wasn't listening. She's bloody crackers, I thought, and closed the front door behind me. I headed straight for the train station and caught a very early train to Newcastle. I was still dressed in a tuxedo, so I removed my clothes in a toilet and got changed into a tracksuit and training shoes.

I sat back in my seat and stared out the window. It is time I went home, I thought. I've left the Marines now. It's time I left the area. The train chugged away and I nodded off to sleep.

When I woke up, it was daylight outside. My mouth was dry and I needed a drink. I got up and purchased one from the on-board cafeteria. I sat back in my seat and stared out the window again. I recognised the area we were passing through and watched as the train crossed over the River Tyne.

'Next stop, Newcastle,' said a voice over the train's loudspeaker.

I stood up and slung my bergen over my shoulder. I got off the train and sucked in a few lungfuls of air. It was cold and I could smell the fuel from the train. I actually felt like I was going home on leave. I'd done it so many times before.

When I arrived home, the house was quiet. I found that all the curtains at the windows were drawn shut. It was almost spooky. I pulled my door key from my pocket and pushed it into the lock. I pushed the door open and stepped inside. A strange smell filled my nostrils. It smelt like a dead body. My father had died here less than a year ago and I could almost sense his spirit. I wasn't afraid; I felt sad. Although he hadn't been a good father to my two brothers and myself, I actually missed him terribly. I rushed around the house and opened all the curtains and windows. Then I went upstairs to the room where he'd died and sobbed.

My mother was still convalescing at my eldest brother Martin's house after a severe road accident and my other brother Peter no longer lived here. He had left a couple of months earlier and had moved into a house with his girlfriend. After a short while I calmed down and put my running kit on. I ran onto the nearby beach and along the coastline. It was my way of gathering my thoughts.

The following day I went to the jobcentre. I needed to sign on as unemployed and to get some information about getting a job. I felt bewildered when I stood in the queue with all the unemployed people. It wasn't a very nice feeling. I guess I'd been used to a regular income for quite some time now.

When it was my turn to be seen, I sat in a plastic chair and gave all my credentials to a gorgeous-looking woman called Anne. She had short blonde hair and a lovely slim figure. I told her I'd just left the Marines and hoped that this would impress her. However, she didn't bat an eyelid. She asked me to write down all the skills that I had, so I set about writing a resumé of my military skills. I thought they'd be queuing up to employ me after reading this. I handed the completed forms over and eagerly awaited her response.

'Well, this is all well and good for a soldier boy,' she frowned, 'but what can you do now?'

'Err . . .' was all I could say, and I shrugged my shoulders. It was the biggest culture shock I had ever had. My years of experience as a Marine were literally no good to me now and employers wouldn't be queuing up to give me a job like I'd thought.

I'd studied computers for a while in my last year in the Marines and Anne told me that these things were starting to take off now and that this might help me to get a job. I quite fancied Anne and asked her out on a date. She turned me down flat and said that she didn't know me well enough. There was nothing much I could do about this other than to accept the rejection, sign on the dotted line for my unemployment benefit and leave as casually as I could.

I spent the next few weeks working hard on maintaining my physical fitness, training during the day and socialising throughout the night. I mixed with the locals more than ever before. At first they gave me the respect I'd been used to for some years, but after a while they seemed to realise that I was no longer a Marine and that I was here to stay. Their respect started to turn sour and I began to receive offensive comments from a lot of them.

One night, when I had been out on an all-day drinking session around my home-town centre, I was standing with some friends in an upstairs wine bar called Las Vegas. Two men whom I knew from my school days joined me. One of them was called Chaz and he bought me a pint of cider. He was renowned for street fighting and had a reputation with the locals for being a bit of a handful.

'Is it tough in the Marines?' he asked me.

I nodded my head. We talked for a while and I finished my drink and bid them farewell. I was very drunk by this time and decided to call it a day. My legs suddenly gave way at the top of the stairwell and I tumbled head first down the stairs, landing with a thump at the bottom. I sat up and was helped to my feet by two doormen. It was strange because I hadn't hurt myself at all. I brushed myself down with my hands and stepped outside into the high street. I staggered around the corner and saw an old friend of mine called Barry across the other side of a busy road. I called his name and waved as I ran across the road to meet him. Suddenly I heard a loud screech of car brakes and felt a thud in my side as a taxi hit me slightly side-on from behind. My foot tripped on the curb in front and I fell down hard on the pavement. The momentum carried me forward and my face scraped across the floor.

I groaned as I came to a halt and was helped onto my feet by Barry. I ached all over, but the worst pain was coming from my face.

'Bloody hell, mate, are you all right?' shouted the taxi driver through his open window.

I nodded my head. The driver shook his head and drove off down the road. Barry stood looking at me.

'Steve, your face is a mess. All the skin has been scraped off it.'

At that moment I heard a group of females talking. I recognised one of their voices. It was Anne from the jobcentre.

'Are you OK?' she asked, sounding concerned. 'Your face is a mess.'

For a moment I paused for thought and hoped that she was describing my injuries and not what she thought of me in general.

'Yes, I'm OK,' I slurred.

Barry told her he would make sure I got home all right as she left with her friends. I could hear them asking who I was and she just said I was someone who signed on as unemployed.

Barry and I walked for a while and turned down a dark alley. My old school acquaintance, Chaz, and his friend appeared out of nowhere. I looked towards them and was confused because they looked very serious.

'Do you think you're a hard man, Steve?' Chaz asked, standing just a few paces from me.

I wished I had a pound for every time somebody had asked me this question prior to taking me on over the years. At the same time I was a bit disappointed in him, to say the least. Surely he could see what state I was in?

'I've been on the drink all day,' I slurred. 'I'm in no fit state to fight with you. I've just been knocked down by a car and skidded across the pavement on my face.'

'Yes. I saw that,' he grinned, with his friend standing behind him.

He knew I was an easy target and that I had no chance if he carried out his intentions.

'Are you going to beat me up?' I asked. 'I'm in no fit state to defend myself.'

Chaz stared at me for a while, sizing me up. Then he laughed wickedly, trying to humiliate me, before walking off with his friend.

Barry helped me along to my uncle Raymond's house. He was a boxing coach and he dressed my wounds and put me up in his spare bed. The next day my head, face and body ached all over. I thought about Anne and the fact that, if I'd ever harboured any hopes of winning her over, I'd most definitely blown it now. Those strips of flesh I had hanging from my face when she saw me must have reminded her of Godzilla or something.

I spent the next few weeks training hard in the gym and on long runs through the countryside. It was a great release for me. I still felt like I was on home leave. When somebody asked me a question about the Marines, I always explained it as if I was still one of them. I honestly still thought I was.

One Saturday afternoon I went into the town centre, where I browsed through the military books in a WH Smith store. I looked up and saw Chaz. He was standing a few yards away looking at the pop records. I felt the anger erupt inside me. I was very annoyed about his offer of violence: more so because of the drunken defenceless state I was in when he had approached me that night.

I stood behind him. He was alone so I waited patiently for him to turn around. After a couple of minutes he turned and saw me. He looked startled.

'Not so big now, are we, Chaz?' I snarled.

He looked towards the door and frowned. I didn't wait any longer. I just hit him hard under the chin with a fast upper-cut punch. The blow lifted him off his feet and onto the nearby sales counter. For a moment he sat staring at me, so I just pushed him back over the counter. He fell into some empty cardboard boxes next to the shop assistant, who screamed loudly.

I turned and casually walked out of the store. You've got to fight fire with fire, I thought. The civvy got what he was looking for.

The following Monday I went back to the Unemployment Agency to sign on again. I peered over the top of the other people in the queue to see if I'd be getting Anne. My luck was in. When my turn came, I smiled and sat opposite her on the plastic chair.

'You're looking in better shape now,' she smiled.

'Yes, but I'd feel even better if I took you out on a date.'

'Are you asking me out?' she asked.

I paused and smiled at her. For a moment I thought she was going to tell me to get stuffed. But she smiled and said she'd love to go out on a date with me. I felt elated. I don't know why but she seemed different from anybody else I had ever set eyes on. I thought she looked absolutely beautiful.

CHAPTER TWO

BASEBALL BATS

I started to see Anne on a regular basis. I guess I fell head over heels in love with her. She did think I was a bit strange, though, because I liked her so much that I didn't try to kiss her for the first two weeks. Also, thanks to my Marines drinking experience, I kept telling her to get the beers in when I occasionally bumped into her when she was out on the town with her friends.

One night she saw another side of me. A friend of mine came to visit. He was a Welshman whom I referred to as Taff. We'd been good friends for a number of years now and had always kept in touch by telephone. I'd first met him when I was serving at the NATO Allied Command Channel in Northwood in 1987, whilst he was working there for a construction company. He later stood as a defence witness for me at my court martial in Plymouth in 1989, when I was acquitted by the court.

It was great to see him again, and we sat laughing and joking at the bar of a pub called Cloisters in the town centre. Taff got some banter going with the barmaids, but one of them started looking down her nose at him.

'Do you have to swear all the time?' she commented.

'I only use swear-words that will go into one sentence,' Taff replied sharply, with a wicked-looking grin on his face.

'And what does that entail?' she queried.

I looked at Taff. He was already in full flow. 'Piss, bugger, bastard, shit, fuck, fart, wank, twat, arse, cunt, tits.'

Her eyebrows raised and then so did mine as she wrote down her telephone number on a piece of card and passed it to Taff. We all burst into laughter. It was definitely the strangest chat-up line I'd ever heard.

Later during the evening we bumped into Anne in a different wine bar. She was with several of her female friends. I was very keen to find out where she was going for last orders and asked if I could meet up with her. A while later, whilst I was talking to her, I noticed a short guy with black spiky hair looking at me across the bar. He was stood with another serious-looking man who was tall and balding. He too was staring at me.

Anne noticed I was becoming agitated with this behaviour and told me to ignore them. She told me that the spiky-haired guy was a friend of her ex-boyfriend and that he fancied her. The other guy was her ex-boyfriend's brother. I ignored their stares as Anne had suggested and she told me that she was going back to her ex-boyfriend's mother's house to have a friendly drink with her. She had split up with this guy some months ago because he was abusive, but she had remained friends with his mother, who was called Beryl. She asked me if Taff and I would like to come with her and we gratefully accepted her invitation.

We walked together for a while and I cracked some of my best jokes to try to impress her. She laughed a lot, but I wasn't sure if she did actually get the punch lines. We arrived at Beryl's house at about 11 p.m. It was located in the middle of a council estate in what even I would call a rough part of town. The house was in darkness when we arrived, but Anne was able to let herself in because she had a door key. This surprised me at first, but she explained that she used to live here and had only recently moved into her own flat.

After switching the lights on, we saw Beryl lying asleep on the sofa. The sound of our entrance awoke her and she quickly stood up and stretched her arms. She smiled at us and shook our hands when Anne introduced us. She seemed a pleasant woman. She was slimly built with dyed ginger hair and small round glasses. I would have guessed that she was aged around 50. What I liked most about her was that she was quick to pour us some drinks and she proposed a toast to her new guests. Then we sat for a while and I continued with my flurry of bad jokes whilst we drank some beers and listened to quiet background music.

Suddenly a loud banging noise interrupted our quiet conversation. Someone was knocking on the door. The door handle rattled a few times and a few more knocks could be heard.

'Mum, Mum, open the door. It's me, Gary,' shouted a deep voice.

Anne looked towards me and frowned as Beryl went to open the door. 'It's Gary. He's the tall baldy lad who was staring at you in the wine bar,' she whispered, with a concerned look on her face.

I shrugged my shoulders and smiled at Taff, who returned the smile. We looked towards the door as he entered accompanied by his short stocky friend with the black spiky hair. They both stood and stared at us. They looked very serious.

'What are these two doing in here?' asked Gary, looking directly at his mother whilst pointing towards Taff and myself.

'They're Anne's friends,' replied Beryl. 'They've all come to visit me, so sit down and have a drink.'

The two men sat down and Beryl got us all another beer. We sat together and Anne tried to get a friendly conversation going between us. The two men just sat and stared at us. They looked angry and uninterested in anything that anybody had to say. My bladder ached and I desperately needed to go to the toilet so I stood up and left the room to relieve myself. I could hear voices being raised through the wall.

'What's he doing with her?' shouted Gary, presumably referring to me. '*He* wants to go out with her,' he growled, referring to his spiky-haired friend.

'He's not the type of person you want to mess with,' I heard Taff warn them. 'He's an ex-Marine and he's fucking mental if you upset him.'

'Bollocks,' spouted the spiky-haired man. 'He doesn't worry me.'

'Look, I'm fucking warning you, right?' Taff snapped. 'He'll fucking batter the pair of you.'

The men's voices became even more angry and raised. Taff continued to tell them to heed his warnings, but this just seemed to make them more agitated. I could feel the tension when I walked back into the room. I winked at Taff to let him know I knew what was going on, then I picked up my beer and sat down.

'Who do you think you are, soldier boy?' Gary snarled as he glared at me with angry eyes.

'Calm down, Gary,' pleaded Beryl. 'He's not looking for any trouble.'

By this time I'd had enough and my temper kicked in. I felt like grabbing hold of the pair of them there and then, but thought better of it because I didn't want to wreck Beryl's house.

'Fucking get outside now and I'll fight the pair of you,' I growled angrily.

'Oh no, I don't want any trouble in my home,' cried Beryl as tears began to stream down her face.

'Yeah, she's right,' Taff interrupted. 'Fucking get outside and he'll fight the pair of you.'

The two men stood up. Their eyes were full of hate and they were baring their teeth like animals.

'Come on then, soldier boy. We'll see you outside,' Gary growled as the two angry men downed their drinks and slammed their glasses down hard on a nearby table.

Tension filled the air as a fight between us seemed inevitable. I polished off the rest of my drink and stood up. Taff looked at me and nodded to acknowledge that I was ready.

'Do you want any back-up, Steve?' he asked eagerly.

I shook my head. 'No. If I get beat off these two clowns, I'll deserve all I get.'

'Steven, is this really necessary?' asked Anne.

She was frightened; I could sense it.

'Don't worry, sweetheart,' I smiled. 'I'm not as daft as they look.'

I took a deep breath and stepped outside into the darkness. It was cold and my thin T-shirt offered little protection from the cool night air. I felt a shiver run down my spine, but then I focused on my two opponents, who were standing a few feet away in the middle of the quiet road.

My anger grew immensely. I felt like I just wanted to rip them apart.

'Come on then, bastard,' one of them bellowed.

My temper exploded and I shouted loudly at the top of my voice, 'Come on then; fucking come on then. FIGHT ME!'

My aggression was ferocious and it startled them both. Maybe they hadn't experienced this kind of aggression before, but their anger seemed to instantly disappear and they looked startled.

'Fucking give them it,' shouted Taff.

I ran towards the two men, who rapidly dispersed and ran off down the street in different directions. I didn't bother chasing them because one of my knees was aching from an old injury I'd picked up during my time in the Marines.

I breathed in deeply and let out a long slow sigh. I saw Anne and Beryl, who was crying, looking at me from the other side of the road. I really hoped this hadn't put Anne off me.

'I'm sorry,' cried Beryl. 'I'm sorry about the trouble they've caused you.'

'Don't worry,' I replied. 'It's not your fault.'

'I think it'll be best if we leave now,' added Anne and I nodded my head to agree.

'They're lucky you didn't punch their fucking lights out,' said Taff, shaking his head slowly from side to side.

I smiled at him as I put my arm around Anne and we bid Beryl goodnight. Taff continued to tell me what I should have done to the two guys as we walked down the well-lit high street. Anne and I just exchanged glances and smiled at each other.

Suddenly the noise of screeching car tyres filled the air, followed by a motor vehicle revving excessively. We turned around and looked behind us and saw a dark blue van racing towards us. Its headlights were on full beam and the horn was sounding out again and again. Then it skidded from side to side and veered across the road towards us and up onto the pavement, where it screeched to a halt.

Taff had already jumped out of the way and I pushed Anne into a shop doorway. I saw that the occupants of the van were Gary and his friend. They both had a baseball bat in their hands and were waving them at me aggressively. I think they expected me to run, but my injured knee ached too much to do that. Instead I stood firm and tore one of the wing mirrors off the front of the van. I needed a weapon to match theirs and this looked like the quickest solution. The two men waved their baseball bats at me again from inside the van and my temper began to rage once more. I repeatedly struck the van with the wing mirror and tried to pull one of the doors open to get at them. Fortunately for the occupants the door was locked so I continued to shout and vent my aggression by smashing the mirror against the van window, which made a loud crashing noise as it shattered into thousands of fragments. Then I saw fear in their eyes and one of them started to shout, 'Quick! Reverse, reverse! Put the van into reverse.'

Gary threw the gear-stick into reverse and revved the engine wildly. I stepped back from the van and watched as it rapidly moved back onto the road. It made a loud clunking noise as they put it into first gear and sped off back down the street and eventually out of sight.

In the weeks that followed I was told that this particular family consisted of Gary and another two brothers who were reputed as being local hard men. I was told that they were looking for me with the intention of giving me a good hiding. When I heard this, I just laughed and wasn't too bothered about them. One of my so-called best friends, Jeff, heard about the incident and told me that he was worried about these people and would no longer be socialising with me. This annoyed me immensely because I'd looked after him for a number of years whilst I was home on leave and had always made sure that nobody bothered him.

One Saturday night I walked into a wine bar in the town centre, where I saw Jeff and the three bad-boy brothers sitting at separate tables opposite each other. Jeff went white when he saw me enter the bar. He glanced towards Gary and his brothers and then looked down at the floor. This annoyed me so I tapped Jeff on the back.

'Hey, you: shithead,' I snarled and he turned around. 'I've looked after you for years and now you're putting your head down when I walk into the same pub as you.'

'You've picked on the wrong family,' he replied sheepishly. 'They're going to beat the shit out of you.'

I vented some anger on him and clipped him across the back of the head before stomping over to the table where the three brothers were sat looking at me.

'Do any of you want to fight me?' I snarled.

They exchanged glances with each other and then looked back at me.

'Well? Is that a yes or a no?' I continued. 'Because I've been told that you're looking for me. Well?'

The three men looked at each other again and then shook their heads to turn down my challenge. I turned and walked towards Jeff, who was sipping from a full pint of lager. I grabbed the pint glass from his hand and poured the liquid over his head.

'Fucking wanker,' I snarled as I slammed the glass down hard on the table and walked out the door.

A couple of days later Anne asked me to move into her flat with her. I gratefully accepted her invitation, but told her that I didn't have much money because I hadn't managed to find a job yet. She wasn't bothered about this, so I collected my things from my mother's house and officially took up residence with her.

Initially she found my Marine frame of mind hard to understand. Some nights I sat for long periods in silence just staring out of the window watching the rain as it thrashed against the windowpane. I actually felt like I should have been out there in the elements. I constantly talked about the Marines and frequently watched Marine videos. As I walked along the streets each day, I still looked at my surroundings as if they were fire positions (somewhere to take cover if I came under enemy fire). I couldn't help it; it seemed like second nature. Anne even woke me up a couple of times during the night because I was fighting in my sleep.

Finally my luck changed for the better and I was interviewed for a job working for an oil company. They wanted someone to operate their computer, which was used to track the fabrication of steel pipes in a local steel mill. The computer courses that I'd taken in the Marines appeared to be satisfactory to them and they offered me the job immediately. The cash wasn't bad either. I was earning over three times the weekly salary I had been accustomed to.

I continued to drink heavily and always drank just to get drunk instead of for enjoyment. My favourite drinking session was always a Sunday lunchtime, when I went over to the headland where I grew up and drank with men I had known since childhood. A session usually consisted of around ten pints. On one occasion my brother Peter came into a pub for last orders. His girlfriend's cousin, who was called Aaron, accompanied him. He was a tall thin man with short black hair. We sat together and Peter asked if Anne was coming to pick me up in her car. I told him that she was and he asked if we would give Aaron a lift home to a nearby village. I said we would and Aaron gratefully accepted the offer.

A car horn tooted outside. I looked out of the window and saw that it was Anne. I smiled and told Aaron to drink up because our transport had arrived. A few minutes later we were sat in the car and Anne happily agreed to drop Aaron off near his home. To reach the village where he lived we had to drive along a few scenic country roads. En route Aaron tapped me on the arm.

'Can we pull over so that I can take a leak?' he asked in a slurred whisper.

I nodded my head and looked at Anne. 'Can we pull over, Anne, so that we can take a leak?'

'Yes, of course,' she smiled and applied the brakes before slowly pulling into the side of the road, opposite a small set of roadworks. The left-hand side of the road was wide open field with no trees or bushes for us to hide behind, so we crossed over the road and walked through a broken fence into some thick leafy bushes. The pair of us sighed with relief as we emptied our bursting bladders. Aaron finished before me and started his journey back to the car. I finished a moment or so later and walked back towards the road too. I watched him step through the gap in the broken wooden fence and followed a few feet behind him. As he got to the side of the road, he looked down to fiddle with his zipper but kept on walking right into the road without looking left or right. I could hear a car coming as I reached the road and looked to my right. I saw a small grey sports car rapidly approaching and could see the driver through the windscreen. It was a woman and she was looking down towards her feet as she passed the roadworks. I quickly looked at Aaron and saw that he had stopped still in the middle of the road to continue fiddling with his zipper. The car was moving at speed and was now only a few feet away. I reacted on impulse and ran straight at Aaron.

'LOOK OUT!' I shouted as I pushed him forcefully away from the oncoming vehicle. He fell to the ground a few feet out of its path, screaming as he heavily made contact.

A split second later the car was about to hit me so I jumped up as high as I could to try to let it pass under me. Unfortunately the beer I had consumed affected my strength and judgement and the car hit my trailing left leg hard on the side of my calf muscle. The force of the blow knocked me over the outside wing of the vehicle. A searing pain shot through my leg and the whole of my calf muscle started to swell up and go numb. My face screwed up in agony as I held my leg and both Aaron and Anne came towards me. At that point the driver got out of the car. She had a confused expression on her face and I looked her directly in the eyes as she firstly looked at me and then at the front and sides of her car.

'Urm, which side of my car have you dented?' she questioned in a posh voice.

My eyebrows rose. I honestly could not believe my ears. I was in too much pain to speak and struggled to get myself onto my feet.

'Well?' she exclaimed. 'Who's going to pay for the damage?'

'Give your head a shake you stupid stuck-up slut,' I snapped. 'You were looking down at your feet. You never saw either of us until you actually hit me.'

'Don't talk rubbish,' she said flippantly. 'You stepped out in front of me. When I saw you, it was too late.'

'Bollocks,' I murmured under my breath. 'Anne, let's drop Aaron off near his village and we'll go to the hospital. My leg is killing me.'

She nodded to acknowledge my request and we all got into her car, leaving the woman in the sports car behind. I looked in the mirror on the sun visor and saw her image as we drove away. She was standing with her hands on her hips and was shaking her head.

My leg ached immensely and I felt like someone had just hit me with a sledgehammer. The alcohol I had consumed helped to numb the pain a little, but the swelling and pain were getting worse. After a few miles we arrived at the village where Aaron lived and we dropped him off. He told us that there was a hospital in a nearby town, but I instructed Anne to drive back home because I knew there was a hospital close to her flat.

On the journey back we passed the woman in the sports car. She was still at the same location and a police car was parked next to her. I noticed a police officer sat next to her in her car and informed Anne, who suggested that we stop and discuss the accident. The pain was now excruciating, so I declined Anne's suggestion and asked her politely to drive straight to the hospital next to where we lived.

When we arrived, I had a few minutes' wait and was then wheeled into casualty. Here a doctor inspected my heavily swollen leg and told me that I smelt strongly of alcohol. He also said that I had blood clots building up on my gastrocnemius muscle as well. I'd never heard the name of this muscle before and just agreed with him.

A short while later they wheeled me up to a ward and carefully put me into a bed. They had decided to let me sleep off the effects of the alcohol I had consumed before they would even consider attempting to look at my injured leg. Eventually they woke me from a deep sleep and gave me an injection, which sent me back into oblivion once more. When I awoke, my leg ached like mad. The only description I could think of to sum up the painful feeling in my calf muscle was that it felt like someone was dragging a load of razor blades through it. When the doctor came around, he told me he had cleared the blood clots but that I'd need a further operation on the leg to fix my ongoing knee problem. They carried this out within a couple of days, and told me that they'd used keyhole surgery to remove a piece of torn cartilage from the damaged knee. I was expected to make a full recovery, but was told I'd have to stay in hospital for a week and then rest up at home for at least another two or three.

Back home with time on my hands, I decided to start an autobiography about my personal life in the Royal Marines. I typed away on my computer keyboard for a while and put as many of my memoirs down in print as possible. After a few weeks I was ready to return to work and to clean the dust off the computer at the oil company office. Whilst there, a work colleague told me that I should pursue an insurance claim for loss of earnings. I discussed this with Anne and we decided to give it a go and sought the services of a solicitor. Later it transpired that the girl who was driving the sports car had somehow acquired a back-seat passenger who was allegedly a credible witness. This puzzled me because the police had turned up to the scene themselves. I wasn't worried about this, though, as Aaron's account would be an equal match here. I decided to give him a call and picked up the telephone receiver and dialled his number. The telephone rang at the other end of the line and was answered by a familiar voice.

'Hello?'

'Hello, Aaron,' I said anxiously. 'It's Steven, Peter's younger brother.'

'Oh yes. I remember you. How are you? What do you want me for?'

His tone of voice startled me. 'Do you remember my accident?'

'Oh, urm, yes, I do. The car accident.'

'Yes. Well, I need you to come to court with me and act as a credible witness.'

'WHAT? COURT!' he replied in a raised voice. 'No, sorry, not me; not court.'

'But I saved your life,' I said quickly. 'I got hit by the car instead of you. Surely you must be willing to return the favour and come to court with me as a witness?'

'No, no, sorry. I can't and won't do that. Not court; not me. I don't want to get into any trouble.'

Then the phone went dead as he put the receiver down. I stood still for a moment. I was gutted, to say the least. I'd suffered all this pain because I'd saved his life and now he had no intention of returning the favour. I tried calling his number a few more times but just received an engaged tone. If I could have got my hands on him, I would have strangled him, but unfortunately this was not to be. Because of this, there was no case to answer.

CHAPTER THREE

FORMER COLLEAGUE

My job at the oil company involved entering information into a computer tracking system that tracked the fabrication of steel pipes for oil and gas pipeline activities. I worked hard and gained a good reputation for my high standard of work.

My injured leg and knee continued to heal and the limp I had acquired through my injuries started to ease a little. I missed being able to go on the long runs I enjoyed but decided to take up weight-training at a local gymnasium to keep myself in shape.

One cold October evening I bumped into an ex-Marine called Tanner. I knew him from my time at 45 Commando and had occasionally socialised with him in a neighbouring town where he lived when I'd come home on leave. Tanner had left the Marines a couple of years before me and had joined the police force. We had a friendly conversation together and arranged to meet up on the following Saturday night in a pub called The Gateway in a nearby village. I felt very pleased when I discussed the chance meeting with Anne. I'd known this guy for a number of years and generally got on very well with him. Anne was looking forward to meeting his wife.

The following Saturday afternoon I put all my existing military kit into a Marine kit bag and went to the Army and Navy surplus store to sell it. I had two Green Berets and decided to hold onto one as a keepsake. The old gentleman behind the counter smiled when I placed the kit bag on top of a nearby table. I emptied the contents out and called out their descriptions. The last things I pulled out were my survival knife and coveted Green Beret. I felt dismayed when I handed these over.

I looked the old man in the eyes as I handed my beret over to him. 'It took a lot of blood, sweat and tears to earn this, mate,' I said with a big sigh.

He nodded in agreement and smiled, before giving me sixty pounds for the lot. It seemed a small amount of cash for what I had given him but at least it would be more than ample to pay for our night out.

At 7 p.m. that evening we caught a taxi to The Gateway pub and walked into a quiet bar to meet our friends. There was a crackling fire on the go inside, which created a nice feeling of warmth that filled the room. I saw Tanner sat at a table with two other men with short-cropped hair and his wife was nowhere to be seen.

'Hi, Tanner,' I smiled. 'This is my girlfriend, Anne. Which one of these two men is your wife?'

He smirked at me and I noticed he had a serious look on his face. 'They're coppers, like me. My wife wasn't feeling too well. She couldn't make it.'

Somehow I knew he was lying. But I didn't understand why. I purchased a couple of beers for Anne and myself and we joined the company of the three policemen. The conversation throughout the night was all about police work and who had nicked the most people for the most offences. Anne and I were getting bored with it so I decided to try to change the conversation.

'What about the Marines, Tanner?' I interrupted. 'Should we create a bit of banter about what the lads used to get up to?'

Tanner stopped in mid-speech and stared at me. 'What about the Marines? I'm not interested in the Marines,' he snapped. 'I prefer being a copper.'

Arsehole, I thought, and stood up and looked at my watch. 'Oh, is that the time already?' I sighed and looked at Anne, hoping she would take the hint.

She raised her eyebrows and stood up.

'We're going soon anyway,' Tanner added. 'We'll see you later. You could have come back to the police club with us if you were a copper.'

'Not for me, I'm afraid,' I answered sharply. 'See you all later. Bye.'

They bid us good evening and we casually left the bar. I knew Tanner wasn't interested in the Marines or me. I was very disappointed in him. I felt like he had let me down.

The next day Anne bumped into a female friend of hers. She said she had also been in The Gateway the night before but had only noticed us on our way out. She had then looked around to see who we were with and had overheard the conversation that took place between the three policemen. Apparently one of the policemen had asked Tanner who his friend was and Tanner told him that he was just some common criminal whom he knew as a child and had joined and served in the Marines with. This annoyed me a lot. I used to play with him when I visited my auntie who lived in the same town as he did and we'd later joined the Marines at the same time. The only civilian criminal record I had was something very minor, which he knew nothing about. When I was a kid I once stole some lead piping from a demolished building to make lead sinkers for my fishing line. Even if he had known about this, it hardly made me a common criminal. In reality I was a former Royal Marine Commando the same as he was. I didn't understand his attitude but I had heard about it from other people who also knew him.

A couple of weeks later I was drinking with a couple of friends in a pub called The Black Horse. Whilst there, I was introduced to another policeman whom I found to be a lot more amiable than the others I had sat with. He asked me about the Marines and also asked me about Tanner. He made it very clear in no uncertain terms that Tanner was full of himself and would stand on anybody's toes to progress his career within the police force. He said he hated him. When he muttered these words, my eyes lit up. This was the perfect opportunity to take my revenge for the way Tanner had treated both Anne and myself.

I recalled a night back in 45 Commando in Scotland in the early 1980s when one of the Marines had brought a loose woman back from town. The loose woman agreed to have sex with as many men as the Marines could muster and the number that queued up to satisfy her demands was 13. After they had finished, they had left the girl lying naked and half-asleep on a bed. At that moment Tanner came back from a night on the town and saw the girl lying naked in the darkness. He put his head between her legs and used his tongue to lick her gusset. When he had finished, he stood up and one of the Marines switched the light on and the rest of us started to applaud. Nobody told him what he had been licking until the next day. When he found out he turned green and vomited. From then on his unofficial name was Man-Fat Head.

When I told the policeman the story, he seemed really pleased and ordered four pints of beer and put them all in front of me. He thanked me for the information and left the pub with a huge grin on his face. An eye for an eye, I thought.

A week later my brother Peter asked if Anne and I would baby-sit for him, whilst both he and his girlfriend went out for the evening. We granted his request and went around to his house to look after his seven-year-old son. When we arrived, Peter opened the fridge and showed me its full stock of beer.

'There you are, Steve,' he smiled. 'There are 20 cans of beer in there. Just help yourself.'

'I will,' I grinned.

After Peter and his girlfriend went out for the night, I started to help myself to the beer in the fridge like he'd suggested. Anne said she didn't mind if I had a good drink because she was just going to drink coffee and look after the young child. It was like leaving candy for a baby. I eventually drank the whole 20 cans and was quite drunk.

'I'm hungry,' I slurred towards Anne, who was busy playing on the floor with the child.

'Have a look in the fridge to see if there's anything in there to eat.'

'There isn't,' I frowned. 'There was just beer in there and I've drank all that.'

'Go to the chip shop and get yourself fish and chips,' she suggested.

'Now there's an idea,' I hiccupped as I walked into the kitchen.

I looked at the long clear goldfish tank that Peter took great pride in. I reached inside and pulled out one of the ten goldfish with my hand.

'What are you doing?' Anne asked as she walked into the kitchen behind me.

'There's no chips, but I'm having some fish.'

I opened my mouth and put the wriggling fish inside and swallowed it. Anne frowned and shook her head from side to side as she walked out of the kitchen. I laughed and continued to eat the rest of them. The last one wriggled like mad and slipped out of my hand and under the fridge. I struggled to get at it as the front door was opened with a key and Peter and his girlfriend entered the house.

'Hello, Anne,' I heard him say. 'Where's our Steve?'

'He's in the kitchen. He's drank all your beer and now he's eating your goldfish.'

Peter walked into the kitchen and saw me crawling around on my knees trying to get at the wriggling goldfish that was still under the fridge.

'Steve, what on earth are you doing?' he questioned.

'I'm still hungry and I've dropped one of your goldfish under here,' I answered with a heavy slur.

'Don't worry about that. I'm fed up with them anyway. Here, I've got some fish and chips for you from the chip shop.'

'Cheers, Peter,' I hiccupped. 'That'll be better than eating these. I can feel them wriggling inside my stomach.'

Peter smiled and shook his head.

CHAPTER FOUR

PETER'S WEDDING

'Hello,' I said into the phone.

'Hello, Steve, it's Peter. There's something I want to ask you.'

'What's that?' I asked curiously.

'I've proposed to Rebecca and she's agreed to marry me.'

'That's a recipe for disaster,' I joked. 'You're both always arguing and fighting.'

'Yes, I know, but we love each other and we want to get hitched.'

'Oh well, I suppose I should say congratulations then.'

'Yes, and I want you to be my best man.'

'Yeah, sounds good to me. It's a pity I'm no longer a Marine because I could have worn my Blues uniform like I did when I was our Martin's best man. It looks good on the photographs.'

'No worries, Steve. We'll wear tuxedos,' Peter laughed.

'OK. When are you getting married?' I asked seriously.

'Tomorrow.'

'Bloody hell, Peter. What about a stag night?'

'I can't go out tonight,' he replied. 'I've promised Rebecca that I won't.'

'Hmm. Let's go for a few quiet beers this afternoon. Surely she can't whinge about that.'

'Yes, OK,' he agreed. 'Call around my house around lunchtime.'

'Will do. See you later, bye,' I smiled and put the phone down.

I looked at the clock on the wall. It was 10 a.m. Time for a run, I thought. My left knee ached a little as I ran. It had recovered from the cartilage operation but tended to ache whenever I ran on it. Sweat dripped down my face as I stepped up the pace along the sandy beach of the headland. My thoughts drifted back to my basic training at the Commando Training Centre in Lympstone, near Devon. I pictured myself running down the home stretch of a speed march in the build-up to the commando tests. The end of this run was down a road called Heartbreak Lane. I remembered a painting that was attached to a tree there. It was of a cartoon-character Marine with a fat belly and lots of sweat dripping from his forehead. It had the words '200 yards to go. IT'S ONLY PAIN' written on it. This memory always helped me to keep going when I felt tired. I ran for about seven miles and stopped outside Anne's flat to stretch my tired leg muscles.

After a quick shower I got changed and headed for Peter's house.

'Hiya, Steve,' he smiled as I walked into the back garden through an open gate.

Peter was mowing his lawn. He switched off the motor when he saw me and tipped the attached grass collector into a plastic bin bag.

'I won't be a minute,' he said as he casually climbed over our Martin's fence at the bottom of the garden, bin bag in hand.

'You're not going to leave it in his garden are you?' I asked curiously. 'He'll go crazy when he sees it.'

Peter shook his head as he dropped onto the patio on the other side of the fence. I watched him as he walked towards an adjoining neighbour's fence and tipped the contents of the bin bag into the garden.

'What are you doing that for?' I asked with a puzzled look on my face.

'I don't like him,' he replied with a frown. 'I saw that bastard's cat shitting on my front lawn yesterday and the cat shit is amongst this grass.'

'But he'll think our Martin has dumped the grass in his garden.'

'Don't worry about it. Come on, let's go and drink some beer.'

'Where's Rebecca?'

'She's out shopping, so I've left her a note to let her know I've gone for a few quiet beers with you.'

'OK,' I nodded. 'Let's get a taxi to the Navy Club in town.'

We arrived at the club a short time later and I signed Peter in because I was a full member.

The bar was quite small, with a few sets of tables and chairs, and there was a pool table in one of the corners. The atmosphere was noisy and fairly busy. Many of the punters were filling the air with smoke from cigarettes and pipes.

'You all right, Royal?' said a familiar voice.

I passed Peter his pint of beer and looked around. I recognised the voice and saw that it was an ex-matelot (sailor) called Johnny. He was a short fat guy with a balding head who had recently retired from the Royal Navy after serving for 22 years. Royal was a term used by the Royal Navy when they referred to a Royal Marine.

'Who's this guy you've brought in?' he asked.

'Why do you want to know that?'

'Because I'm the new chairman and I don't like strangers. Is he another Marine? I don't like Marines either. You know that,' he smirked.

'It's a good job I've got a sense of humour,' I replied with a prolonged stare.

'I'm not a Marine. I'm his brother,' Peter interrupted.

'Well, any trouble or bad language and you're out,' Johnny warned before walking away into an adjoining room.

'What's his problem?' Peter asked.

I smiled at him. 'He's a nobber. He makes it common knowledge that he hates Marines.'

'How does he get away with his bad attitude?'

'Because he's the chairman. If I hit him, I'll get barred out.'

'Why doesn't one of the other ex-Marines hit him?'

'Because most of them are old men and they just put up with him. They don't want to be barred out either.'

Peter shrugged his shoulders and drank his beer. He didn't like the reception we had received from the chairman and neither did I, but I guess there was very little we could do about it.

Much later in the afternoon we drank the final drops of our tenth pint. Peter looked at me. His eyes were glazed and his cheeks were glowing red. He looked up at a clock on the wall.

'Oh shit, look at the time. It's four o'clock. I'd better get a taxi home,' he slurred heavily.

'Your future wife won't be upset if you're a bit tipsy, will she?' I asked with a hint of sarcasm.

'Tipsy? I'm pissed out of my skull,' he exclaimed with his eyes wide open.

'Does that mean our drinking session is over?' I asked with a sense of disappointment.

He nodded his head. 'Yes. I'm getting married in the morning.'

'OK, we'll get a taxi,' I agreed. 'I'll come with you and nip over the fence to see if our Martin has any beer in the fridge.'

A short while later I called a taxi and made the short journey back to Peter's house. Peter, incidentally, had fallen asleep as soon as he sat in the back seat and fastened his seat belt. He snored mildly and the taxi driver gave me a look of concern.

'What's the matter, mate?' I asked him.

'If he vomits, I'm going to charge you an extra twenty pounds,' he warned.

'Don't worry about it, mate. He'll be all right. He never vomits.'

In reality I'd seen Peter throw up in the back seat of taxis many times before and sincerely hoped that he wouldn't repeat this here. We were soon just a couple of blocks from Peter's house so I pulled down my visor so I could use the mirror housed inside it to see how Peter was getting on. Oh bollocks, I thought, as I saw him being sick on the back seat. Neither the driver nor myself could hear him vomiting because we were passing the town football ground and the crowd were singing and chanting. I watched Peter sit up on his seat and wipe the residue of his stomach acids from his mouth with his sleeve.

'Right, mate, that'll be five pounds, please,' said the taxi driver when he pulled up outside Peter's house.

As I paid him his fare, I heard Peter climb out of the back and slam the door shut behind him. I stepped out of the taxi and watched Peter as he staggered up his garden path towards the front door. The taxi sped off into the distance and then I too walked up the garden path. Peter opened his front door, walked inside and closed the door shut behind him. I smiled to myself and walked down the side of his house and into his back garden. I could see our elder brother Martin. He was sat in his garden drinking beer on the other side of Peter's fence.

'Hiya, Martin,' I shouted and watched him cough and splutter on his mouthful of beer.

'Bloody hell, Steve,' he coughed with his eyes full of water. 'You scared the shit out of me there. I wasn't expecting you.'

'No worries,' I grinned. 'Have you got any more beer?'

'Yes, of course. Climb over the fence and sit down and I'll get a few more beers out of the fridge.'

We sat together and I told Martin about our drinking session. I told him about the attitude of Johnny the Navy Club chairman and about Peter throwing up in the taxi.

'Sounds like a right nobber that chairman, Steve.'

'Yes he is,' I agreed.

'There's never a dull moment with our Peter,' he continued. 'Him and that future wife of his are always fighting one another.'

'Does he hit her?' I asked, with a sinking feeling in my stomach.

'Hit her? Hit her, you say.'

'Yes, hit her,' I frowned.

'It's more the other way around.'

'What do you mean?'

'She's as hard as iron. You probably don't know because you've been away all these years. But I'll tell you, she's a nasty bugger when she wants to be.'

I felt a bit confused about what he had said. Then, just as I sipped from my can of beer, I heard a woman shout, 'You drunken bastard! I'm going to bloody kill you!'

It was Rebecca, in an extreme bout of anger. Martin and I looked at each other and then at Rebecca and Peter, who had run into their back garden and were now rapidly exchanging blows.

'Bloody hell, Martin. She's a better boxer than me,' I exclaimed, referring to my boxing days in the Marines.

'Piss off and leave me alone, you silly cow,' Peter screamed at her as he ran back inside the house.

Rebecca stood there screaming blue murder with her fists clenched. I was a bit startled with her performance but knew she at least had a reason for it. Her anger seemed to intensify.

'I'm going to stab you, you bastard!' she shrieked.

Suddenly Peter appeared at the doorway. He was holding a sewing machine. We looked on as Peter raised it above his head and ran towards Rebecca, who was shouting at him. He threw the sewing machine at her and she screamed loudly as it bounced off her shoulder.

'You bastard,' she bellowed. 'The wedding is off.'

Then she burst into tears and ran back inside the house and slammed the door shut behind her.

Peter staggered towards the fence in front of us. He was puffing and panting and had scratches all over his face. He leaned against the fence.

'The fucking wedding is off,' he slurred with a look of disappointment on his face.

Martin and I couldn't control ourselves and we rolled around laughing hysterically at Peter's comments. Peter frowned first and then he too burst into laughter.

'Sorry. But you've had us in stitches with that sewing machine,' laughed Martin.

Then we all burst into a fresh bout of laughter and drank a few more cold beers together. Later I called a taxi and went back to our mum's house to get some sleep. I have no idea what else happened that night, but at seven o'clock the next morning I received a phone call from Martin, who informed me that the wedding was back on.

At eight o'clock that morning I received a phone call from my friend Taff. He told me that he'd been having an affair with a woman in London and that her husband, who was some sort of gangster, had found out and was going to break his legs. I quickly gathered that he was very much afraid of this guy and suggested that he should catch the first train north and told him that he could stay at my mother's house. She'd moved back to her own home now and already knew Taff, so I knew it wouldn't be a problem. I also told him about Peter's wedding and invited him along. Several hours later he arrived and I met him at my mother's house, where I showed him to a room that he could sleep in.

'This is my old bedroom, which you can stay in whilst you're here,' I said.

'Very nice,' replied Taff. 'Have you shagged many birds in it?'

'No I haven't. This is my mother's house, not mine. And whatever you do, don't piss my bed.'

'As if,' he grinned.

By 1 p.m. we had changed into our suits and climbed into the car that arrived to take us to the wedding. Anne didn't really know my family at the time, so she'd made her own plans for the day. Peter was waiting inside the car for us. He smiled when he saw us both.

'Hi, Steve. Hi, Taff,' he said, greeting us both with a firm handshake. 'Have you got the ring?' he asked eagerly.

I looked at Taff, who stood up from his seat and dropped his trousers and underpants to show his bare arse. He grabbed the cheeks of his bum and pulled them apart.

'Here, Peter, tell her to shove her finger up this ring,' he joked.

We all burst into laughter and so did the driver of the vehicle.

'Yes, I've got the ring,' I assured my brother. 'Don't worry about it. Taff, quick, pull your trousers up. Here's my mother.'

Taff quickly pulled his trousers up and fastened his belt before our mother climbed into the car with us. She had made a full recovery from her accident now and was back in good health once again.

'Hi, Peter,' she smiled. 'Are you excited?'

'Very excited, Mum.'

'What are those scratches on your face?' she asked with a look of concern.

'Oh, nothing to worry about, Mother,' I intervened. 'Peter had a few too many beers yesterday and fell against the sewing machine at home.'

She just smiled at him as the car pulled away and drove off towards the church. On arrival our eldest brother Martin and his wife greeted us.

'Have you got the ring?' asked Martin.

'Yes, I've got the ring,' I smiled.

A few minutes later Peter, Martin and myself were standing together down the aisle waiting for Rebecca to arrive. Peter lifted one of his legs up and twisted the cheeks of his face as he squeezed out a loud fart.

'Behave!' snapped Martin.

'It's my wedding. If I want to fart, then I'll fart,' Peter replied and let rip with another blast of bad wind.

I smiled to myself and recalled Martin's wedding a few years previously when Peter broke wind constantly all night. At least this time it was his wedding.

The church organs burst into tune and played 'Here Comes the Bride'. Rebecca looked fabulous, apart from a couple of scratches on her face from the sewing-machine episode that she had failed to hide with make-up. It was her day though and she seemed overjoyed when she saw her future husband waiting down the aisle for her.

She stopped opposite Peter and raised the veil from her face. They exchanged glances and smiled at each other. Then she frowned.

'It smells a bit pongy in here,' she whispered in a faint voice.

Peter smiled. 'It's our Martin; he stinks.'

'Get stuffed. You're not blaming me, you dirty bastard,' snapped Martin with a look of disgust on his face, just as Peter broke wind once again.

Everybody giggled and the vicar came out from a room and stood in front of them. He smiled and took a few sniffs of the foul air, which caused him to start to cough. Then he cleared his throat and quickly opened a nearby window to let some fresh air in.

Following the ceremony we headed for a local working men's club where we were having the reception. Before long I was giving my speech, which seemed to be well received by the large number of guests. I told everyone that I saw Peter and Rebecca as two pieces of string that had been floating around in life and had finally come together to tie the knot. After my speech Taff, who looked to be quite merry, approached me. He was dressed smartly in a three-piece suit.

'Bloody quiet in here, isn't it?' he said.

'Yes, I suppose it is. But we're going back to Peter's house for a barbecue soon and I guess things will probably liven up by then, mate,' I assured him with a smile.

'Can we go now and light the barbecue?' he asked.

'Yes. I'll let Peter and Martin know where we are going.'

A few minutes later Taff and I arrived at Peter's house ahead of everybody else. It was literally just around the corner. The barbecue was standing at the foot of the garden and had all of the coals and firelighters already placed on it.

Taff tried to light it a number of times with a match but failed miserably. The firelighters just wouldn't catch fire.

'Here, you try,' he slurred. 'I'll have a look in the kitchen to see if I can find something to help ignite it.'

'OK,' I nodded and took the box of matches from him. I reset the coals and the firelighters and added some rolled-up newspapers. The newspapers helped me to get the fire going and the firelighters started to burn.

A couple of minutes later Taff returned from the kitchen carrying a chip pan.

'Look out. This will get it blazing,' he said, and swung the pan back and forth.

My eyes opened wide and I looked on in total disbelief as he hurled the contents of the chip pan over the smouldering barbecue fire like a pail of water. I quickly jumped out of the way as the chip-pan fat burst into flames. The barbecue was totally engulfed in a raging fire and I saw that Taff's suit had also caught alight. I ran at him and pushed him onto the ground before using an available tea towel to smother the flames. I then lifted him back onto his feet and removed his jacket. Fortunately the flames had not penetrated it and hadn't burnt his skin.

'That was bloody close,' Taff coughed. 'I'm going to get a drink of water.'

Whilst he was gone, I stood staring at the raging barbecue fire. All the grass around it was burnt black and smouldering.

'Look out,' Taff said again.

I turned around and this time saw him swinging a bucket of water at the fire. I'd learned about oil fires during my military service and knew that the last thing you should throw on them was water. This time I dived straight at Taff and knocked him down to the ground just as the water hit the fire. There was an almighty BOOMING noise and the barbecue flames raged once again.

Thankfully we had both got clear of the flames and were unhurt.

'Bloody hell, Steve,' gasped Taff. 'Are you trying to kill me or something?'

'No, mate. I think you're trying to kill us both,' I replied.

The fire continued to rage and gave off thick black smoke that poured into the air. There was a blanket hanging on the washing line so I took it into the kitchen, where I soaked it with water. Then I got Taff to assist me with smothering the fire and finally doused the flames.

When we removed the blanket, the fire was out and all the coals had been burned to a white ash. Suddenly we heard the wailing sound of a fire engine's siren and saw the engine pull up outside the front of the house. We explained to the firemen what had happened and they told us to be more careful and soon departed.

We still had a barbecue to rescue so I sent Taff to the shop for some new coals and eventually met with an element of success with relighting it before a trickle of guests started to arrive.

Soon the music was blasting out through the windows of Peter's house and everybody was in the party mood. Taff and I organised a game of shoot the can. This was played by piercing the lower part of a can of beer with a pen and shaking it hard with your finger over the hole. Then you had to place your mouth over the hole and pull the ring from the top of the can. If you didn't drink hard enough, you got a beer shampoo from the fizzing lager.

This game went down very well with a lot of people and Taff and I showed our experience by drinking it without spilling a drop. Obviously it was also a very quick way of getting drunk. The atmosphere livened up a lot during the late afternoon and everybody seemed to be thoroughly enjoying themselves. After all the earlier commotion with the raging fire we even managed to provide an acceptable barbecue.

Suddenly I heard Taff bursting into a loud rendition of 'Summertime', by Gershwin.

I looked around but couldn't see him anywhere. Then I followed the sound of his voice and looked upwards, along with everybody else. We saw him standing completely naked on the roof of the house. He was leaning against the chimneystack with a can of beer in his hand and was singing his head off.

'Come down, Taff, you silly bugger,' I shouted. 'You'll get locked up for flashing your naked body in public.'

Then he stood on the edge of the roof and started to urinate down into the garden. Everybody jumped back and burst into laughter.

'Now you are taking the piss,' I remarked. 'Come on down; we're going into town.'

This seemed to do the trick because he climbed down the drainpipe and got dressed back into his clothes. A little later we called several taxis and headed off into town. We were all very merry from the alcohol we had consumed but were still very much in control of our senses.

Taff continued to show that there was no end to his talents as he did a headstand with his back to the bar and his legs bent backwards, resting on top of it. Then he drank a can of beer upside down: a feat I personally had never witnessed before. We eventually ended up at a nightclub called Murton's and it was my turn to buy a round of drinks. I searched through my pockets for my wallet but quickly realised that I had lost it somewhere.

'Taff, I've lost my bloody wallet somewhere,' I said. 'Can you lend me some cash to buy the drinks with?'

Taff just smiled at me. 'You must have dropped it somewhere. No problem, I've got plenty. I'll lend you some.'

'Thanks, Taff.'

It was good to know I had a friend like him and that he was more than happy to help me out in times of need like this. I bought the beer and looked around for the rest of our group to give them theirs. I saw Peter on the opposite side of the dance floor talking to a couple of strange men. They both had short hair and were dressed in jeans and T-shirts. They looked like servicemen to me and I saw that Peter was laughing and joking with them. The disco music was loud so I nodded my head to indicate to Taff that I wanted to go over and stand with Peter.

I passed Peter his drink and he smiled at me. Then he introduced me to the two strange men he was talking to. He informed me that they were Royal Navy sailors and that their ship was docked in our port.

'This is our Steve,' he said to them. 'He's a Marine.'

'I'm an ex-Marine,' I corrected him.

'You're a bootneck?' one of them frowned.

'An ex-bootneck,' I replied.

The same guy grinned at me. 'We hate smarmy bootnecks, mate. My mate here beat one up a few weeks ago.'

The atmosphere between us immediately changed. I could sense that trouble was imminent and watched as both of the sailors put their drinks down onto a nearby table.

'Do you think you're hard?' one of them asked in a serious manner.

'I wish I got ten quid every time somebody asked me that question, mate,' I answered confidently.

One of them raised his hand to grab hold of my shirt so I dropped the pint of beer I was holding onto the floor. This startled the sailors and was the perfect distraction to hide the attack I made with a flying head-butt into one of their faces. Without hesitation I followed up with another rapid head-butt into the face of the other sailor. It thudded hard into his nose and was practically a mirror image of the first one I had launched.

Both of the men were rolling around on the floor holding their faces and blood was oozing through their fingers. Another guy who was with them ran towards me with his fists clenched and shouted at me.

'BASTARD!'

I ducked as he swung a punch that missed me and hit him hard under the chin with a powerful upper-cut. It was a perfect strike and one that I would have been proud of during the time I boxed in the Marines some years before. This guy also started rolling around on the floor, holding his jaw.

Then a couple of the nightclub's security men appeared. I knew one of them. I had grown up with him when I was a child.

'Come on, Steve, that's enough. We want you to leave,' he asked with a sound of desperation in his voice. 'We know you're a Marine. We don't want any more trouble.'

'I'm an ex-Marine,' I answered. 'Tell these nobbers that when they decide to get up off the floor.'

I left the nightclub with Taff, who'd come to my side for back-up the moment the commotion had started, although I hadn't known it at the time. Peter was presumably carrying on the party somewhere, and we'd become separated from him and the rest of the group, so we decided to cut our losses and walk back to our homes. The night was cold and dark and a heavy fog started to fill the air. After a couple of miles it was time for Taff and I to part company because I was going back to Anne's flat and Taff was heading back to the room I had prepared for him at my mother's house. Fields surrounded the area I was passing through and the fog was so dense that I could hardly see five foot in front of me. It reminded me of the many times I had been out in the field in my years in the Marines. I was certainly no stranger to this type of weather.

With this in mind I decided to take a short cut I knew across the fields. It was more or less a straight line and I thought I could cut out a huge chunk of my journey home. The fields were full of long grass and my trousers got soaking wet as I waded my way through it. I reached a fence that I knew wasn't too far from the road I was heading for. As I climbed over it, I could hear voices. It sounded like two men having a conversation. All of a sudden the ground seemed to give way and I fell forward into a complete somersault and landed with a thud on my buttocks.

'Oomph,' I groaned and could feel that the immediate area I was sat in was covered in wet squelching mud.

'Welcome to the trench of darkness, mate,' said a strange voice from somewhere nearby in the darkness.

'Did you try and take a short cut too?' said another, and he lit up the dark area with a lighted match.

The three of us burst into uncontrollable laughter. It was very funny really. I couldn't make their faces out clearly in the darkness but they were obviously in the same situation as me.

'Any idea how we can get out of here?' one of them asked. 'We've tried all sorts of stuff – like trying to climb the walls, but they're too muddy and now so are we. We're covered from head to toe in it.'

'Actually,' I replied with a slur, 'I think I know where we are. I once fell into this trench a few months ago. If we follow it for a couple of hundred metres or so, we'll come out near a service station.'

'But we can't see where we are going,' one of them said. He sounded worried. 'What if there are more trenches – deeper ones full of water?'

'No, no, there aren't. The trench runs in a straight line. Anyway it's the only choice we've got at the moment and it's bloody freezing sitting here.'

I told them to follow me and to tap on the walls with the sides of their fists as they walked. It was a tactic I had learned from a Royal Navy sea survival course I had once attended. It was used to move and feel your way around in a smoke-filled room. There was no smoke but the principles were the same.

After a while we could see that the trench walls were becoming shorter and then we could just make out the bright lights of the service station. We stood on the forecourt together and shook hands. We were all plastered in mud, but the two men were very grateful that I had helped them to get out of the dark wet trench. We shook hands again and bid each other goodnight before we went our separate ways.

A few minutes later I arrived at Anne's flat but was unable to gain access because I could not find my door key. I was wet and freezing and I shivered in the cold fog. I knocked on the door several times but was unable to get an answer. Bollocks to this, I thought. I'm an ex-Marine. I've never met a door I couldn't break down. I took a few steps back from the door and prepared myself to break it down. I inhaled a deep breath and ran hard towards it. For an inexplicable reason, or most probably because I was drunk, my shoulder wasn't where it was meant to be when I reached the door and I hit it hard with my face and head. It felt like someone had just hit me with a sledgehammer. The impact had no effect on the door, which held firm and hurled me backwards onto the ground. I sucked in another deep breath and looked up at the stars, just as Anne returned from a night out with her friends. She saw me down in the darkness and screamed loudly.

'Shush,' I whispered. 'It's me. I'm locked out and have fallen on the ground.'

'Oh, thank God for that,' sighed Anne. 'I thought it was a burglar.'

The next morning I was up bright and early and went for a run to help clear my head, which was aching more from trying to break the door down than it was from a hangover. It was cold and snowing slightly, so I slowed down my pace to avoid slipping over. Following this I showered and went to work.

At this point I had been employed by the oil company for several months and I always worked hard. I was used to giving 100 per cent at any task I was given to do. This was always something that was expected of a Marine. However, this did not always go down very well because it sometimes made other people look like they were slacking. One of these guys was a piping inspector called Benny. My boss often commented to him that I was more productive on the computer than he had been before I'd arrived and this tended to make him angry. Sometimes he would make sarcastic comments towards me, but this day I was feeling slightly under the weather and he just went too far.

'Morning, teacher's pet,' gestured Benny with his usual snide approach, as he entered the office. 'It must be nice sitting in this warm office instead of the cold inspection shed I have to sit in outside. Do you know what it's like to be cold?'

I frowned at him. During my service I spent a total of 15 months working in arctic conditions whilst training in arctic warfare. The coldest still-air temperature I had experienced was -46°C. Of course I knew what it was like to be cold.

'Don't start this morning, Benny,' I advised him. 'I had a heavy day yesterday at my brother's wedding and I feel a bit under the weather today.'

'You're supposed to be a Marine, aren't you?'

'What do you mean by that?' I asked.

'I thought you lot were meant to be tough and able to handle your beer. Really you're just a bunch of pussies.'

'You're talking a load of crap, Benny.'

'Horse shit,' he snapped. 'One of these days I'm going to stick one on you, you soft shit.'

Then he left the office and headed across the snow-filled ground and back into his cold inspection shed. I sat for a few minutes and mulled over what he had said to me. I'd put up with his sarcastic comments for a while now but was in no mood to listen to him any more. I felt my temper start to rage and got up and put my coat on. As I crossed the snow, I could feel my anger growing by the second. I wanted to beat the hell out of him to teach him a lesson.

I opened the door to the inspection shed and stepped inside. I could feel the warmth from the wall heater when I entered. It wasn't cold like Benny had said. It was in fact the total opposite: very warm and cosy. Benny was sitting at a table reading a newspaper. His face dropped when he saw me enter.

'What the fuck do you want?' he snarled at me.

I didn't answer. I turned and put the bolt in the door to lock it shut. Then I looked at Benny, whose aggressive expression drained from his face. He looked startled. I grabbed his newspaper and scrunched it up before throwing it on the floor. Then I grabbed him by the throat with both hands and thrust him backwards before releasing my grip. He fell onto the table and I grabbed him again with both hands on his jacket.

'Are you trying to piss me off?' I shouted several times at the top of my voice.

I knew he could feel the might of my aggression and I shook him wildly before throwing him to the floor. The chair behind him fell over and the contents of the table crashed down next to him. Suddenly there was a tap on the window. It was the boss. I told Benny to stand up and to say nothing. He looked frightened and nodded his head in agreement.

The boss walked back to the office with me and asked me what had happened. He told me that I was too aggressive for this job and that maybe I would be better off rejoining the Marines. I didn't agree with him and I didn't appreciate what he'd said. However, I did promise him that there would be no repeat performances of this event and I felt fairly sure that Benny would leave me alone from now on.

That night I went home and talked with Anne. During our conversation she told me that some money had been taken from her purse when Taff had been visiting and that she also thought he had stolen my wallet during our night out. Initially I totally disagreed with her. I didn't want to believe it was true, even if it was. To put my mind at rest I telephoned my mother and asked her if she had noticed any money going missing. To my dismay she said that some money had also been taken from her purse and that she was fairly sure it was Taff who had taken it.

I felt betrayed. We were good friends, but he had stolen from my girlfriend, my mother and myself. I felt unsure about what I would say to him as I got into my car and drove off towards my mother's house. When I arrived, I saw Taff in the living room. He was sat with his feet up on a stool drinking a cup of tea and watching the television.

'Hello, Steve,' he smiled. 'Are we going out on the piss?'

'No, mate, we're not,' I replied in a serious and firm voice.

'What ups?' Taff asked, sensing that I was upset about something.

'Someone has been stealing money from my girlfriend, my mother and me.'

'Oh, now, come on, Steve. Are you accusing me of being a

thief? I went to court for you, man. We're mates.'

'Yes, Taff,' I frowned. 'That's why I know you did it and that's why I'm going to give you two days to get your shit together and to leave here for good.'

He sighed deeply and nodded. I felt like hitting him and throwing him out, but decided against it. Instead I got up and left. Outside the house, I bumped into a friend of mine called Christopher. He also knew Taff and got on quite well with him. He refused to believe my story and said that he wanted Taff to pack his bags and stay with him for a while. I insisted that he let him leave the area in two days' time but he was quite adamant about putting him up, so I went back into the house and told Taff to pack his bags and to go with Christopher. As they left, I took the spare key from him and locked the door.

A few days later I received a telephone call from Christopher. He told me that Taff had left and that some cash and credit cards were missing. Consequently we contacted the police and reported the theft straight away. We never saw or heard from Taff ever again.

CHAPTER FIVE

FIRST AID

By the end of 1991 things were going quite well for me. Anne had fallen pregnant and we'd put a deposit down on a four-bedroomed house from a sum of money that I'd managed to save over the past year. The house was a dream come true for me. It was a long way from the cold damp council house that I grew up in as a child.

I continued to work hard at my fitness and still only drank at weekends. I was overjoyed with Anne's pregnancy and was looking forward to becoming a father. My goal in life was to provide a better lifestyle for my own family. I knew this was probably most fathers' intentions but unfortunately it was the last intention on my father's mind when I was a child.

The contract on my first job had expired and they weren't too keen to renew it because of the run-in I'd had with Benny. Fortunately I had impressed the boss enough with my high standard of work for him to recommend me for another job, working on the computer systems in a local fabrication yard. Thankfully the money was quite good again and I was very keen to get my teeth into this new job.

When I arrived, I met my new boss and I instantly found out why I had been offered the job without an interview. He was a guy called Barry who knew me and had grown up with my elder brother Martin. My job was to write and modify a computer database used to track welded pipes and to put together certification packages that validated the integrity of the welds. Unfortunately this was in a bit of a mess when I got there and the senior welding engineer who reviewed them was so unhappy with the standard of quality that he was contemplating moving the contract to another company. Barry explained the importance of improving the certification packages before they were reviewed by the senior engineer. He also asked me if I was skilful enough to improve the computer tracking system. I had gained a lot of experience at my last job and I told him that I was quite confident that I could achieve both objectives.

The fabrication yard consisted of a large pipe-building shed where all the welding took place and four portable cabins, which were used as offices. One of these was used as the company administration block, one by two welding foremen, one by the senior engineer and the other by myself and another guy called Mike Raymen.

Mike was about the same age as me. He had short black hair and a slim build. He'd been working there for about a year prior to my arrival and was a close relative of one of the senior managers. For some reason he made sure I was aware of his family connection within an hour of meeting me.

For the first time in my life I was learning about workplace politics. I found that people were given jobs by their friends and relatives even though they weren't always the best choice or even suitable for them. This was very different to what I'd been used to whilst I'd served in the Royal Marines. The difference there was that you respected senior rank because it was earned and you respected each other because you wore the same colour beret. That was, of course, unless you upset one another. In those circumstances, sometimes, even rank didn't matter. However, you never got a particular job because you were related to someone or were, for want of a better expression, an arse-licker.

Mike took me into the welding foremen's cabin and introduced me to the senior foreman. He was a short fat guy called Yacker. He was aged about 45 and had short brown hair.

'Hi, Yacker,' said Mike, in a broad Geordie accent. 'This is our new boy, Steve. He's an ex-Army fella.'

'Ex-Marine,' I added with a smile.

'It's the same shit, young 'un,' snapped Yacker and he glared at me. 'Now listen, kid. I don't like gobby young kids around here and especially ex-soldier kids. So keep your fucking mouth shut and do as you're told.'

Cheeky bastard, I thought. I might be only 27 but I bet I've seen a lot more of life than you have. I felt like telling him to shove his job up his arse but I knew I had too much responsibility at home now to even contemplate such a thing. Instead I just nodded my head.

Back in our cabin I reviewed the workings of the computer tracking system and was able to add the additional configuration changes that it needed to work properly. Unfortunately Mike wasn't too overjoyed about this, as he had previously told the senior management that these enhancements were not possible.

'Sorry about this, Mike, but if we're going to trace the pipes that have been welded then we need to ensure that the computer system works correctly.'

'Yes, OK, OK,' he frowned.

'I need you to explain to me how the certification packages work so that I can review them and see if we can improve them,' I explained.

This seemed to annoy him and I felt an atmosphere growing between us. Then he walked out of the cabin and into Yacker's cabin. This became a standard move of his for the next few weeks that followed.

The senior welding engineer was called Burt. He was a middle-aged Scotsman with short grey hair and a fiery temper. He was annoyed because the certification packages were still badly put together and said they were not worth the paper they were written on. He was right but I needed Mike to help me to understand their composition before I could try to improve their quality. Unfortunately Mike was not too keen to help me and told me to stick to working with the computer.

Barry entered our cabin. He looked fed up and sighed as he pulled up a seat next to me.

'What's up, mate?' I asked curiously.

'Burt has just been screaming bloody murder about the poor quality of the certification packs. He said he is definitely going to take the contract off us. This will mean that we'll all be out of a job.'

'Oh shit,' I sighed. 'I know I can improve them, Barry, but I need Mike to show me how they are put together and what the content needs to be. I also need to get the senior engineer out of the way for a few days to give me time to learn about the certification packs, review them and improve them.'

'You'll need a bloody miracle, mate,' frowned Barry. 'Mike's related to one of the senior managers here and is also well in with one of the senior foremen. He does what he pleases and there's no way you will be able to get the senior engineer out of the way for a few days because he's got no holidays booked.'

'Well it looks like we're up shit creek without a paddle,' I said, and Barry nodded and got up and walked out of the office.

I sat for a few moments and pondered on the problems facing me. As a Marine I was always taught not to give up, even when the odds were stacked against me. Just because I was in civvy street now, it didn't mean I had to look at life's issues and troubles any differently.

The first problem I needed to overcome was to get Burt, the senior engineer, out of the way. I literally had no idea how I was going to do that. Suddenly the door opened again and a tall strange man entered. He was dressed in overalls and wore big heavy boots. This made it obvious that he was one of the welders from the fabrication shed.

'Yes, mate, can I help you?' I asked politely.

'Have you got any water or fizzy drinks in here?'

'I've got a can of lemonade in my bag that you can have, but why do you want it?'

I was curious and thought this was an unusual request to make.

'I'm constipated and I need to take some of these laxatives,' he said seriously. 'I'm not going to ask the lads in the fabrication shed because they'll take the piss out of me.'

My eyes lit up as an idea entered my head. Laxatives, I thought, brilliant: this could be a great way to get rid of the senior engineer for a few days. With this in mind I made the welder a proposition that I would give him my can of lemonade in exchange for half of his laxatives and thankfully he agreed.

Next I headed for the senior welding engineer's cabin, where I found him sat quietly at his desk reviewing certification packages. He looked annoyed and was shaking his head from side to side and was quietly cursing and swearing. I tapped lightly on his door. I did this out of respect for his senior position and out of courtesy. It was a good polite habit I had learnt as a soldier. Burt looked up when he heard the knock.

'It's the computer whizz-kid,' he said in a broad Scottish accent. 'Come in, young man, and have a seat.'

'You sound like a Glaswegian,' I said.

'I am,' he smiled. 'Have you worked in Scotland?'

'Yes. I used to be in the Marines and I was stationed in 45 Commando in Arbroath in the early '80s. I also spent a fair bit of time in the mountains up by Fort William, doing mountain training. Nice place.'

'Yes,' he nodded. 'But they'll have to send more than the Marines in to sort this pile of shit out and if they don't do it very soon I'm going to have this contract taken off them.'

'Do you fancy a cup of coffee?' I asked him.

'Yes, but make sure you don't piss in it,' he laughed.

I made us both a cup of coffee and added the laxatives to his cup. Hope he can't taste these, I thought, because then I'll be in the shit instead of him.

We sat and drank the coffee together and he continued to curse and swear about the state of the certification packages. Later I watched him drive home for the night in his big flash car. I crossed my fingers for luck as he drove off into the distance.

That night I went to the gymnasium as usual and trained hard. I knew I needed an element of luck with Burt. If the laxatives didn't work, then my plan would fail. At the end of my training session I stood naked in the shower and the hot water splashed off the top of my scalp. My thoughts were about what to do next. I needed to get Mike to teach me about the packages. I wasn't sure how I was going to achieve this, but beating the shit out of him was definitely an option and heavily in my thoughts at the time.

Next day I arrived at work early. I did this because I knew Mike always came in early and I wanted to get hold of him.

'Morning, Mike,' I smiled as I entered the cabin. But what I really meant was 'Hello, tosser'.

'It was morning when I got up,' he grunted, shrugging his shoulders. 'Why are you in so early? Have you shit the bed?'

'Very funny,' I replied, clapping my hands. 'Why aren't you sat in the foreman's office, kissing his arse?'

'I don't kiss his arse. Anyway, he's gone on holiday for a week so it looks like I'll have to put up with you and your stupid stories about the Marines.'

I've never tolerated fools lightly and this made me so angry that I flew into a raging temper and slammed him hard against a wall. I told him in no uncertain terms that he either showed me how to assemble and check the certification packages or I would kick the shit out of him. The ferocity of my anger frightened him so much that he started shaking. I could sense his fear and further assured him that I meant what I said. Then he nodded and agreed to work with me.

Would you believe it, the senior welding engineer was off sick with a sudden illness, and the training I needed took a couple of days to complete. During this time my boss's younger brother started working with us. He had lots of experience of certification packs and really knew his stuff. Thankfully he was able to resolve the issues with the packages that had been annoying the senior welding engineer.

It was over a week before Burt returned to work. He told everybody that he had succumbed to a dose of the runs and was keen to get his teeth back into some work. Later he pushed the door open to our cabin and peered inside.

'Hi, guys,' he grinned, with a look of contentment on his face.

'I don't know what you've been doing since I've been away but the standard of these certification packs has dramatically improved.' He finished with 'Keep up the good work,' and closed the door behind him on the way out.

The new guy and myself shook hands to acknowledge our good work, then we looked towards Mike. He didn't seem too happy and slipped out through the door and headed over to see the foreman, who had recently returned from his holidays. Suddenly the door opened again and the welder whom I'd got the laxatives from peered inside. He looked worried about something.

'Does anybody in here know first aid?' he asked anxiously.

'I'm not a first-aider,' I replied. 'I was taught it in the Marines but I haven't used it for some time now. Have you tried the admin cabin?'

'I've tried everywhere, mate, and the only person I can find who is qualified is the secretary in the admin cabin and she's said that she doesn't feel confident about this.'

'What's happened? Has someone been hurt?' I questioned, trying to gain some information.

'Yes. One of the welders was busy working when he was hit by a large piece of pipe. It was hanging down off a sling. There's blood coming from the side of his head.'

'OK. Where is he? Is he in the fabrication shed?'

The welder nodded his head and I grabbed a first-aid box that was sitting on one of the shelves and walked past him and over towards the shed. I didn't run because I didn't know what I would be running into once I got inside. When I entered the shed, I looked around and saw about 20 people standing together. They were all looking at a welder who was sat down on the floor a few yards away. The first thing that surprised me was that nobody knew what to do and just seemed to be standing around in a state of confusion. I could see blood slowly dripping down the side of the welder's head. He was motionless. First I checked the area next to him to see if there was anything else that could injure me when I approached him or that could cause another accident. I noticed that his welding kit was still powered up to the electrical mains so I quickly switched it off. Then I approached the casualty and reassured him.

'Hello, mate. My name's Steve. You've been hit by a pipe on a sling and have got a head injury. I'm going to apply first aid to you. Can you tell me if you are experiencing pain anywhere else?'

He didn't respond. He was conscious, but just stared into the distance in a daze. He had the symptoms of being in shock. I pulled some of the things from the first-aid box I was carrying and cleaned a wound on the side of his head before applying a bandage. I didn't try to find any broken bones in his body in case I caused him any further injury. Instead I told one of the onlooking welders to call an ambulance. Then I wrapped a nearby fire blanket around him to keep him warm.

The crowd of welders stood staring at us, so I told them to take a tea break and not to worry because an ambulance was on its way. When it arrived, I briefed the paramedics about what had happened to the welder and asked if I could accompany him to hospital. They agreed and I climbed aboard the ambulance. En route to the hospital I continued to try to converse with the conscious welder. Eventually he started to smirk and shook my hand as they wheeled him into the hospital. After this I returned to work and found that the whole workforce had walked out on strike because of the lack of first-aid-trained personnel on the site.

I went back to the cabin to collect my things. As I prepared to leave, Yacker walked in behind me. Oh shit, I thought, it looks like Mike has told his welding foreman friend that I threatened him.

'Steve, son, can I have a word with you?'

I sighed deeply and rubbed my fingers through the stubble on my chin. 'You can say what you want about me threatening Mike, Yacker. As far as I'm concerned, it was the only way to get the job done.'

'No, no, not Mike. I mean, yes, Mike has been whinging about you threatening him, but I'm not bothered about that.'

For a moment I was confused. 'What's on your mind then,

Yacker?' I asked and was prepared to repel any attack he might throw at me.

'No, it's not what you think. That welder that you took to the hospital.'

'What about him?'

'He's my brother. I want to say thanks for your help. Did they teach you that stuff in the Army?'

'In the Royal Marines,' I smiled and accepted his offer of a handshake.

Three weeks later my contract ended. I tried a few places locally for work but unfortunately word had got out about my aggressive nature. The only option that was offered to me was to take a contract down in France. I didn't want to be away from Anne, who was now heavily pregnant, but I literally had no choice and accepted the contract.

CHAPTER SIX

FIRE IN FRANCE

A cool fresh breeze at the rear end of the car ferry we were travelling on blew in our faces as we watched the wake of the ship. We'd set off from Dover and were destined for Dunkirk in France. My new boss, who was called Greg, and two piping inspectors called Ian and Kevin accompanied me. Greg was a tall thin gentleman, about 48 years old with ginger curly hair. He was the site supervisor. Ian and Kevin were roughly in their mid-30s. Both of them were chubby and had balding heads. We'd all been recruited to work as a team on a pipe production contract for six months in Rouen.

I was responsible for maintaining the computer tracking system that was used to track pipe-mill production of steel pipes and their mechanical testing. Basically the French pipe mill produced the steel pipes on behalf of the oil company we represented. The pipes were destined for a pipeline project in the Far East and it was our team's responsibility to monitor their formation from molten steel to formed round pipes and then track their subsequent testing, which decided whether or not we accepted them.

Once we arrived at Dunkirk, we had about one hour's drive to the port of Rouen and then across the city to our hotel, which was called the Hotel du Chapeau Rouge. It was a fairly decent hotel with about 26 rooms. When we arrived at the hotel, we found that we were the only clients and were able to make a special deal with the landlord, using our lengthy stay as a bargaining tool. He accepted our offer and we were shown to our rooms, which were located at the end of a long corridor on the third floor. Generally the rooms were clean and tidy and each had a large double bed and en suite facilities. I felt quite content with my room. It was definitely a big leap from the four-man room that I'd had to share when I was a Marine. I put my suitcase on the bed and opened the window to let in some fresh air. When I looked out, I saw that there was a sheer drop of three floors. I felt a little uneasy, as I didn't recall seeing a fire escape at this end of the corridor. What if there was a fire? We'd have no chance of getting out. Using foresight was something I was taught when I served with the Royal Marines Police. We used it when we needed to document on our statements what we foresaw as the outcome of someone's actions when we caught them committing a military offence.

I alerted my colleagues to the potential risk we were facing, but they just laughed it off as some kind of joke. Next I called the landlord and asked him to review the situation with me. He too laughed and commented in broken English that there were smoke alarms in every room.

'Yes, and that's great,' I said. 'They'll make lots of noise if there's a fire, but they won't help us to get out of here.'

'It's no problem, monsieur. Don't worry,' he laughed. 'We have no fires in my hotel.'

'That's OK for you to say, but I want a room on the ground floor.'

'No more room, monsieur. All full.'

'No they are not,' I insisted.

I knew he had put us up in the far corner of the hotel to keep us out of the way of his regular guests and I was adamant that he moved us.

'What about the rooms in that annexe down there,' I asked, pointing out of the window.

The landlord rubbed the palm of his hand over his chin. 'Hmm, that will cost more money, monsieur.'

'Stop whinging, Steve,' interrupted Kevin. 'These rooms are fine.'

'Yes, he's right, Steve. Stop whinging. What are the chances of the hotel catching fire?'

I paused for a moment and looked at them and at the room. Then I thought about something else I was taught in the Marines, which was to always expect the unexpected, and not to think it will never happen to you. I remembered these words from a lecture on mountain- and arctic-warfare survival in a place called Gardermoen in Norway. A very experienced member of the Royal Marines Mountain and Arctic Warfare Cadre said them to us prior to us going out into the mountains. That same year in Norway we experienced a number of Marines dying from asphyxiation caused by carbon-monoxide poisoning. This was caused by a lack of fresh air in their snow-holes and by the fumes given off from their small gas-lit naphtha heaters. We also experienced a huge avalanche that took the lives of a number of our allies in the Norwegian forces and also a couple of Marines being crushed by the snow when their snow-hole ceilings collapsed.

'No, sorry, my friend, but I want you to give me a room on the ground floor or else I will find another hotel,' I said to the landlord, who was stood waiting with his back leaning against a wall.

He rubbed his chin with his hand again and looked out through the open window and then at my friends and myself.

'OK,' he nodded in submission. 'I have four special rooms for you all downstairs in the annexe.'

'Great,' I said with a sense of relief.

My colleagues were shaking their heads at my granted request but all of them agreed to move into the annexe.

The rooms downstairs were very much the same as the others, but I felt a lot more at ease than I did when I was upstairs. I walked outside into the courtyard and could see the window of my previous room high up on the third floor. I suppose the odds of the hotel catching fire were very slim, but I saw it as an unnecessary risk that my gut feeling told me I wasn't prepared to take.

The following day we went to the pipe mill, which was our place of work. Firstly I went for a walk around the mill with the two inspectors to have a look at how the steel pipes were made and what forming and testing processes they had to go through. Then I went to set up our office and the computer tracking system with Greg. He was a very experienced manager who was also good with computers. Generally we got on very well together.

During the first few weeks I was introduced to a Frenchman called Nigel Kronnen. He was about the same age as me and I learned that he was a former French commando. We exchanged many stories over a few beers during the evenings now and then and were surprised at how much we had in common. We also trained together and he regularly complimented me on my high level of physical fitness.

One day we sat in the works canteen with the other members of the team and ate our lunch together.

'Bloody Nora, lads,' exclaimed Ian. 'You two eat your food so quick that you could have seen sparks coming off your knife and forks.'

Nigel and I looked at each other. 'You know, I've never really thought about it before, but I do eat fast,' I said to Nigel, feeling as if I'd just discovered something.

He nodded his head, agreeing with what I'd said to him. 'Yes, me neither, and so do I. When I was in commando training, we had very little time during meal breaks and had to eat quickly.'

'Yes, it was the same for me in the Marines,' I commented. 'I guess you never really enjoyed your food or thought very deeply about its content. You just ate it because you were hungry and knew you needed the calories to work with.'

We both nodded in agreement. 'I guess we do the same with our beer,' added Nigel, and I nodded too, before we shook hands and both burst into a bout of laughter.

The people I worked with didn't do much on an evening and generally sat on their beds watching television. I personally spent most evenings in a gymnasium I had managed to find and trained hard to keep my fitness up to scratch. When I trained, I seemed to draw an amount of attention from the locals. The strenuousness of my routine made them keep asking me what I was training for. However, I was just maintaining the fitness level that I was used to and that the Royal Marines were famed for. I also continued to work on the book I was writing and finally completed the first draft after working on it for nearly two years.

I didn't eat much of an evening and chose to live cheaply so that I could save more money for my girlfriend back home and our expected child. I could have eaten better if I'd wanted to because we were very well paid. I was actually earning more money a day than I got paid for a week's work as a Marine and my daily paid expenses were more than a day's pay too. However, I was here to work and to make money and not really to enjoy myself.

Rouen itself was a great city. It was famed for its many churches and Notre Dame cathedral as well as its history. It was the place where Joan of Arc was burnt at the stake during medieval times. The churches were beautiful, but their bells made my head ache on a Sunday morning after drinking a couple of bottles of cheap cooking wine the night before.

We travelled home for a weekend once every month. We left on a Friday lunchtime and drove to Dunkirk to catch a ferry to Dover. If we missed this ferry, which we sometimes did, we drove further down the coast to Calais and caught a ferry to Folkestone. If we missed that ferry, which we sometimes did, we had to cancel our journey home. Aborted journeys were due to Greg always refusing to leave the office until exactly midday on the Friday, so any traffic hold-ups could cause us to miss our slot.

When we arrived at one of the ports on the other side of the English Channel, we had a long drive home to the north-east, which usually ended at 2 a.m. on the Saturday morning. Our return journey started at 8 p.m. on the Sunday evening and finished around 6 a.m. on the Monday morning in Rouen.

Greg did all the driving and occasionally I caught him asleep at the wheel on the return journey. This and the struggle to catch a ferry every month worried me and eventually I told Anne that there'd be no more monthly visits.

One weekend when I'd come home prior to this, Anne and I were invited around to Peter's house for a birthday party. Anne's pregnancy was nearing the end now but she agreed to go because I wanted to. When we arrived, we found everybody to be in good spirits, including my eldest brother, Martin, and his wife, Janine.

Martin shook my hand when he saw me. He smiled and gazed deeply into my eyes. The strange thing was I immediately got the impression that something was on his mind, but decided to shrug it off because I thought that it must have been just my imagination.

'Hello, Steve. Good to see you,' he said. 'I can see that Anne hasn't got long left before the little one arrives.'

'Not long,' I grinned.

'How's she coping?'

'She's finding it hard with me being away in France, but generally she's coping fine.'

'Oh good,' he replied, with the same gaze he had given me earlier. 'I can see you've calmed down a lot since you left the Marines.'

I nodded my head in agreement. I was sure he had something on his mind but didn't quite know yet what it was. I just smiled at him and said hello to his wife before moving on to talk to my other brother, Peter, to wish him a happy birthday.

The beer flowed freely throughout the evening and I socialised and joked with literally all of the guests who were present. One of the jokes I told was this:

'Three men wanted to join the Royal Marines. The first of them approached the instructor.

'"Here's a fully loaded handgun," said the instructor. "I want you to run through that door over there and fire six shots into your wife."

'"My wife!" exclaimed the man.

'"Yes," said the instructor.

'He cocked the weapon and ran towards the door, which he

kicked open. He pointed the gun at his wife and then stopped and burst into tears.

'"I can't do it. She's my wife. I love her."

'"Put the gun down," said the instructor. "You won't make it as a Royal Marine."

'Next the second man stepped forward.

'"Here's a fully loaded handgun," said the instructor. "I want you to run through that door over there and fire six shots into your wife."

'"My wife!" exclaimed the second man.

'"Yes," said the instructor.

'He cocked the weapon and ran towards the door, which he kicked open. He pointed the gun at his wife and then stopped and burst into tears.

'"I can't do it. She's my wife. She's the mother of my children."

'"Put the gun down," said the instructor. "You won't make it as a Royal Marine."

'Next the third man stepped forward.

'"Here's a fully loaded handgun," said the instructor. "I want you to run through that door over there and fire six shots into your wife."

'"My wife!" exclaimed the third man.

'"Yes," said the instructor.

'He cocked the weapon and ran towards the door, which he kicked open. The door creaked and then slammed shut. Six loud BANGS were heard as six shots were fired.

'The instructor ran inside the room and saw the third man holding the gun. His wife was lying unconscious on the floor.

'"Oh no. What have you done?" asked the instructor.

'"You'll never believe this," frowned the third man, shaking his head. "Some bastard put blanks in my gun so I had to strangle her."'

Everybody burst into uncontrollable laughter and literally had to hold their ribs. I laughed too and was approached once again by Martin.

'Hey, you really have changed since you were a Marine,' he said once again. 'You've really calmed down now.'

Suddenly I knew what he was getting at. Martin and I had had a fight several years before. It ended violently and I was the victor. I wasn't proud of it, but he pushed me into a position where I either fought him or he was going to kick the shit out of me. Unfortunately he left me with no choice and I ended up beating the shit out of him. Now I had put two and two together and got four. I had realised that this was still on his mind and at some point this evening he was going to try to take his revenge.

I watched him cautiously as he approached me again. I could see the intent in his eyes as he got closer. 'You're a lot less aggressive now, Steve, aren't you?'

His voice quickened and I saw his right arm come up at me with a clenched fist. I reacted quickly and ducked away from the punch. Unfortunately I fell against Anne, causing her to gasp for breath. This annoyed me immensely because his attack had nearly injured her. Aggression seared into my veins like a bolt of lightning and my anger intensified towards Martin.

'YOU BASTARD,' I growled at the top of my voice. 'I'M GOING TO FUCKING CRIPPLE YOU.'

Martin's face literally dropped and he looked terrified. He quickly turned around and ran out into the garden through the half-open door. I turned to make sure Anne was OK and, gladly, she was. Then I ran out through the open door in pursuit of Martin. When I got into the garden, I couldn't see him anywhere. He'd evidently made haste and had disappeared out of sight because there was nowhere to hide in the garden. My anger was bursting now and I really felt like I wanted to tear the limbs from his body. I ran to the bottom of the garden and climbed over the fence into Martin's garden. I looked around but couldn't see him there either.

'WHERE ARE YOU, YOU BASTARD?' I shouted furiously. 'I'M GOING TO FUCKING CRIPPLE YOU WHEN I GET MY HANDS ON YOU.'

My voice echoed through the air. I searched his garden and shed and then walked down the side of his house to his front garden. I tried his front door but found it locked. Then I walked down the path and opened the garden gate into the front street.

Nothing stirred and the air seemed to be filled with total silence. I looked up at the windows of his house and for a moment I wasn't sure if I saw something move at one of the upstairs windows. My anger raged again and I ripped the front gate from its hinges and hurled it hard at the front of the house.

'BASTARD!' I screamed and ran hard at his front door. It was still locked shut but it caved in under the force of my strength and sheer determination to get inside. The door literally broke into two halves and I surged through after Martin. I ran up the stairs and searched through all the rooms. All were silent. Then I ran back down the stairs and searched through the downstairs rooms. He was nowhere to be seen. I switched on the light and suddenly realised that the broken door had torn the skin from my hands, face and legs, all of which were dripping with blood. I shook my head and walked out into the garden once more. Then I saw Martin standing with two tall men next to Peter's back door. I was still bursting with anger and jumped back over the fence to meet them.

'COME ON THEN!' I screamed at them, beckoning them to come towards me with both my hands.

Martin stood still and the two tall men stepped into the light. I observed straight away that they were policemen and also that they were the biggest two policemen I had seen in my life.

'Calm down, Mr Preece,' one of them said softly. 'Just calm yourself down.'

I puffed and panted heavily as I fought to control my temper. I was very angry at Martin, but I wasn't stupid. I knew that these two guys would lay into me if I didn't calm down. I looked up at them both and smiled.

'What's caused all the blood on your face and clothes, Mr Preece? Have you done something silly?'

'No, I haven't. I slipped climbing over the fence and bust my nose. That's all.'

'Come on, Steve, calm down,' one of them said again, as both of them gripped their truncheons. 'We know you're an ex-Marine.'

'Yes, I am an ex-Marine, but who the hell were you expecting? Johnny Rambo?' I panted.

Both men eased off their truncheons and laughed with me. I noticed Martin slipping away out of sight in the background, but said nothing. It was probably the best thing he could have done anyway. Then Martin's wife Janine stepped forward.

'Do you want to press charges?' a policeman asked her.

'Not if he goes away and leaves Martin alone,' she replied in a soft but nervous voice.

'Oh, that's great, isn't it,' I snapped. 'It's all my bloody fault, as usual.'

'Do you want to press charges?' a policeman asked her again.

For a few moments there was pure silence. My anger had cooled off and my throat felt sore from all the shouting I had done.

'Press charges,' I croaked, shrugging my shoulders. 'I don't care.'

Janine frowned and took another couple of steps closer to me. She looked at my bloodstained face and clothes. 'No, officer, I don't want to press charges.'

'Are you sure? Because we'll lock him up if you want us to,' one of them replied, with his hand on his truncheon once again.

'No, I don't want to,' she insisted, with Anne now standing beside her.

The policemen nodded their heads and then told me that they wouldn't lock me up if I agreed to let them give Anne and myself a lift back to our flat. I accepted their offer, or took their advice, depending how you look at it. Later, back at the flat, I got showered and cleaned myself up before climbing into bed for the night. Thankfully Anne and our unborn child were OK.

The next day I got up early and sat with a cup of hot coffee. My body ached from head to toe but thankfully my wounds were only superficial. I telephoned Peter to apologise for the disturbance and he told me that Martin had called the police when he had run off. The two big gorilla-sized policemen who arrived were apparently sent by Tanner, my former Marine colleague.

At 8 p.m. that night Greg called to pick me up for the long drive back to France and I gave him the 'fell down the stairs' excuse when he asked me about the fresh scars on my face. I gave Anne a hug and a kiss and watched her as we drove off into the distance. I was already missing her, because I loved her immensely. I'd had lots of girlfriends when I was a Marine but Anne was the only one I had ever fallen in love with.

Back in Rouen the weather was cool and fresh. It had been a long drive back and I just wanted to get stuck back into work to take my mind off missing home. Greg and I received a phone call to inform us that a fax would be arriving shortly with the details of the ship that would be carrying some of our pipes to their intended destination. Greg asked me to go and collect it from the pipe-mill director's office. When I entered the office, I met the director's secretary. She was a short plump girl in her mid-20s and was wearing square-rimmed spectacles. She spoke very good English and was at times very rude and sarcastic about my ability to speak French. She passed me the fax and smiled.

'Is your French still crap, Steven?'

'Err, yes. Absolutely shite, to be honest. Where did you learn to speak English?'

'I learn it at school and I learn it from you and your friends,' she smiled.

I looked at her for a moment. This is the perfect opportunity to get my own back, I thought.

'You are twatty bollocks,' I said with a straight face.

She peered over her spectacles at me. 'Bollocks. That is a rude English word. I know that.'

'No, no,' I smiled. 'That is bollocks. Bollocks is different. It means humour in English.'

I fought back the urge to burst into laughter. If I laughed, I would give the game away and at this moment she really looked like she would take the bait.

'Bollocks means humour in English.'

'Yes, and twatty bollocks means in good humour.'

She looked at me over her spectacles again. She had a sort of half-smile on her face as she tried to figure out whether I was winding her up, but I kept my face completely straight. I thanked her for the fax and left. A couple of days later I had forgotten all about our conversation and was sat having a team meeting with Greg, Ian and Kevin. There was a knock on the door and the secretary entered.

'Good morning, my English friends. I am twatty bollocks,' she said in perfect English.

Everybody around the table burst into hysterical laughter and staggered around the room holding their ribs. The secretary's face said it all as she realised I'd been taking the piss out of her. She pulled a long face, stormed out of the office and slammed the door shut behind her. For some reason I never ever saw her again!

Several weeks later I was lying on my bed in the hotel. It was about ten o'clock in the evening and I was watching television. This was never an easy task because all of the channels were in French, but it did help with improving my language skills. Suddenly, I thought I could smell smoke. I got up and checked the back of the television to see if there were any loose wires, but everything seemed OK. I lay back on my bed and stared up at the ceiling. Then I noticed smoke coming through a small air vent that was high up on one of the walls. Shit, something was on fire. I got up and put my shoes on. I rushed outside and saw that the courtyard was full of smoke and the hotel was a blaze of flames.

'FIRE, FIRE, FIRE!' I shouted at the top of my voice and started to bang hard on the other guy's doors. They were all outside the annexe within minutes and were running like mad through an arched gateway that led to the main street.

'Where are you going?' Ian shouted.

'To raise the alarm,' I answered and ran inside the hotel lounge via an unlocked door. The fire didn't appear to be in the lounge, but I could hear it blazing from the stairway behind one of the closed doors.

'FIRE, FIRE, FIRE!' I shouted.

Suddenly the landlord and his wife arrived through another doorway. They were dressed in their pyjamas.

'Quick, outside,' said the landlord, pointing to the door I had just entered from. I looked at him.

'What about the guests?' I asked with a worried voice.

The landlord shook his head. 'No guests tonight. Outside, outside.'

We quickly ran outside and into the open street, where we were greeted by wailing sirens from two arriving fire engines. The firemen quickly got the fire under control and put out the flames coming from the upper floor and annexe roof. About an hour later we were allowed back into the hotel lounge, where the landlord made us all a cup of coffee. We found out that the fire was caused by an electrical fault and that, although there was some damage to the roof of the annexe, the only rooms that were really damaged were the ones initially allocated to us.

The landlord passed me a cup of coffee and gazed at me with a look of concern on his face. 'You were right, Steven,' he commented.

I nodded and looked at my work colleagues, who put their heads down. We were bloody lucky as well, I thought.

The next day I was walking around the pipe mill when I bumped into Kevin and Ian. Kevin didn't seem happy about something.

'What's up, mate?' I asked him.

He didn't answer and looked the other way. For a moment I was confused and looked towards Ian. 'What's the problem, Ian?' I asked curiously as I watched Kevin walk off in the opposite direction and disappear through a door that led to an office in a different part of the mill.

'Kevin doesn't think you should get paid the same money as us, Steve,' he answered.

'Why not?' I snapped.

'Because we're qualified pipe-mill inspectors and you're not.'

'But I'm an expert with the tracking system. Neither of you two have that skill.'

Ian shrugged his shoulders. 'I haven't got an issue with what you get paid, Steve; it's Kevin.'

I felt very disappointed. Not only did I raise the alarm the night before but I also thought we were fairly good friends. I went back to the office, which was empty, and I picked up the telephone and called the other office, where Kevin had gone to.

'Hello,' he answered sharply.

'What's your problem with my rate of pay?' I asked.

'You shouldn't get the same pay as us, Steve,' he snapped. 'You're not an inspector; you're just a brainwashed tick-tock soldier.'

I paused for a moment and looked at the telephone receiver as if I was looking at Kevin. I felt annoyed now, very annoyed. I needed someone to talk to about this so I dialled home and spoke to Anne. I told her how angry I was at Kevin's complaint and his grudging remarks and she assured me that the best thing to do was ignore him. I agreed with her and put down the receiver. Within a minute, though, I could feel my blood boiling and wanted to rip his head off.

I made my way down to the other office and saw Kevin walking around the mill. He saw me as I approached him and he started to run. I ran too and began to gain on him as we sped past the hot burning furnaces. I continued the chase and saw Kevin duck under a pipe that was rolling along a conveyer system. I ducked under it too and it narrowly missed my head as it moved down towards the water quenching system. Now I was just a few feet away from him. I could hear him panicking as I neared.

'I'm going to take my pay out on you,' I snarled at him.

He stopped and fought hard to fill his lungs with air.

'Steve, don't do it, mate,' Greg's voice called out. 'It's not worth it. You won't get another job in the pipe-mill teams for a long time.'

I looked at Kevin. I was angry and wanted to hit him hard. Then I thought of Anne and our expected child back home and realised that I had too much to lose.

'OK,' I nodded and walked away from Kevin and back to the office with Greg, who told me I had made the right decision.

Neither Kevin nor Ian spoke to me for the last few days of the contract and when it finished there was total silence as we made our way back home in Greg's car. Unfortunately there wasn't a job that I could immediately move on to so I returned home and had to sign on the dole for a while. That was a regrettable side of the contracting game. There was good money when you were in work and none when you weren't. The secret was to stay in work or, as we said in the game, make hay whilst the sun shines.

CHAPTER SEVEN

GERMANY

A few weeks later I went to a mill in Germany on another pipe-production contract. No one knew me in the new team, but I was selected for my computer and database skills, which were still relatively rare in the early '90s.

The site supervisor was younger than my previous boss. He was called Darris and was a tall thin man with jet-black hair. I'd heard he had a bit of a reputation for standing on people's fingers to get what he wanted. However, I had no interest in his reputation with other people and was just glad to be back in work again and earning good money.

I found Germany to be a great country and had never been there before. When I was with the Royal Marines, I was told that we couldn't go there in force during the Cold War period because our status as elite soldiers meant the Russians would have asked serious questions if we'd turned up near their border. This reminded me of a time in 45 Commando in Scotland in December 1983 when the Cold War was still active and the Berlin Wall was still intact. We were told that the Russians were no longer a big threat and that Russia would break up with civil war within the next ten years. We were also told that the next war would probably come from the Middle East. I don't know the source of this intelligence but it certainly proved to be very accurate in the years that followed.

The pipe mill in Germany was a huge complex and I was introduced to another inspection team from the UK, who were working on another project. The site supervisor of that team was a guy called Nigel Freeman. He was a 50-year-old Scotsman and was a former Special Air Service (SAS) Commando. I had a lot in common with him and we spent a lot of time socialising and training together at a local weightlifting gym. He warned me to be careful of Darris and said that he didn't trust him.

I spent the first two weeks reprogramming the computer tracking system to suit this particular pipe-making process. Darris showed a keenness to learn about the tracking system and asked me to teach him how to program it. I was glad to share my knowledge, because most people I worked with showed very little interest in it.

One night in our hotel bar I was sat with Darris. We talked about my years in the Royal Marines and he told me about a haulage business that his father owned. He said his father was having a lot of trouble with a competitor and he actually asked me if I would be willing to blow up the competitor's trucks if he paid me.

'Sorry, Darris, but I'm not and have never been an explosives expert. I really wouldn't be able to carry out this objective for you,' I asserted. He'd clearly been watching too many war films.

'But what if I can get you the explosives, Steve? Will you do it then?'

'Why don't you do it yourself, Darris?' I asked him.

'I wouldn't know where to start, Steve, but you would, with your background. I'm willing to pay you a lot of money to do this.'

I shook my head. 'No, sorry, mate. I have too much to lose back home. My girlfriend is very close to giving birth to our first child.'

Then Nigel came into the bar and joined us. He asked us if we wanted a beer and I accepted. Darris declined the offer and said that he needed an early night. Several minutes later he bid us both goodnight and left.

I felt as if I could trust Nigel and told him about Darris's proposition.

'I told you not to trust him,' he reminded me. 'He'll get you to do his dirty work and let you end up in prison instead of him.'

I nodded my head. 'I see what you mean now, Nigel.'

Nigel and I sat and chatted into the early hours of the morning. We talked about soldiering tactics, field-craft and survival skills. I found his knowledge to be very impressive and it was quite evident that his training and experience were superior to mine. Another quality I liked about Nigel was his quick wit and great sense of humour. Generally he was very sharp and turned a lot of dull situations into something quite humorous.

Somehow the conversation got around to brewer's droop and man's ability to keep his pecker up when he had consumed vast amounts of beer.

'Do you ever get brewer's droop?' I asked Nigel, who paused for a moment and smiled at me.

'When I was 21 years old, my erect penis was rock hard,' he said. 'When I was your age, Steve, I could bend it a little.'

'Yes . . .' I answered, wondering where he was going with this.

'Now, I can bend it in half.'

Was he really telling me he was getting past it? 'I'm sorry, Nigel, but what are you trying to say?'

'Well, I think I'm getting stronger!' he laughed and we both burst into fits of laughter. This was a typical example of his quick wit.

A couple of weeks later Nigel's team completed their contract and said farewell to us. Before he left, Nigel reiterated his warning about not trusting Darris. Darris, incidentally, never mentioned his father's business rival again. Instead he concentrated on learning from me how to program the pipe-tracking system and before long he became as expert as I was. It was then that Nigel's warning hit me like a bolt of lightning. Darris told me that he had agreed to set up a limited company with my previous boss, Greg, and that they would supply and maintain computer tracking systems for lots of other oil companies. At first I thought it was a great idea because I could picture myself being kept in work by his company. However, I did not feature in Darris's plans as he told me that he thought I could be seen as competition against his company. I tried to assure him that I was only interested in having a job, but he wouldn't listen and told me that my contract would be finishing at the end of that week. I couldn't believe my ears, but I now fully understood why Nigel had no trust or respect for Darris.

On the last night of my job I went into a bar for a few farewell drinks with Darris and a guy called Alastair, who was another member of our team. Alastair was a tall stocky man and was about 30 years old with brown hair. He was a pipe-mill inspector and was known to be a very close friend of Darris's. We sat and drank a few beers together. Darris told us to drink as much as we wanted and said that he would pay for it. It was his way of saying thank you for teaching him about the tracking system. Personally I was very annoyed with the way he had used me and also fed up because I didn't know where my next job was coming from.

Later in the night we were heavily under the influence of alcohol and Alastair decided to tell me a home truth.

'I'm also going to be a partner in this new company,' he slurred. 'Darris is going to teach me about the pipe-tracking system and I'm going to take over your job when you leave tomorrow.'

The beer was loosening his tongue and he went on to tell me more. 'Darris chose you for this job because he needed you to show him how to use the tracking system. Don't worry, though, I don't think you'll be out of work too long,' he sniggered.

I'd heard the term shithouse before, but never fully understood what it really meant. Now I knew what it meant because I was sitting with two of them. I looked at Darris and he put his head down. He seemed disappointed that Alastair had let the cat out of the bag. I felt like I was going to explode and fought hard to contain myself. I got up and went to use the gents' toilet. When I returned, I saw that Alastair was sitting alone.

'Where's Darris?' I asked.

'He's gone back to the hotel to get some sleep. He's bought us another couple of beers to drown your sorrows with,' he tittered.

For me, this was the last straw. I'd had enough of Alastair's attitude now. I grabbed one of the beers on the table and threw it in Alastair's face. I followed up with a hard right-hand punch, which made a thwacking noise when it hit his jawbone. The blow knocked him over the back of his chair. The half-empty beer glass he was holding flew out of his hand and smashed against a nearby wall. Alastair quickly jumped back onto his feet and ran at me. When he got close, I ducked his oncoming punch and launched a hard head-butt onto the bridge of his nose. I felt it crunch when I hit it, and blood started to drip onto the wooden floor. He held onto his face with both hands as a crowd of the local Germans started to form around us.

He didn't come back at me so I made my way through the crowd and out through an open door. Once I got outside I thought about doing the same to Darris and went back to the hotel to find him. When I got back, I asked the night porter if he had seen him and he said that he was sure he hadn't returned yet.

I was still very angry and went back to my room to pack most of my things, ready for the long journey home the following day. Suddenly the telephone rang and I answered it.

'Is that you, Steve?' Anne said in a soft quiet voice.

'Yes, it's me.'

'What's the matter? You don't sound very happy.'

'I'm not. This Darris is a shithouse and has got me to teach him about the pipe-tracking systems and has now put me out of a job. When I find him, I'm going to kick the shit out of him.'

'Forget about him, Steve. I want you to come home now because I'm starting to get contractions and the baby will be born soon.'

'But I'm going to be out of a job tomorrow,' I told Anne, expressing my disappointment.

'Don't worry about it. I need you to come home now.'

I knew she was right and I agreed to leave for home right away. I wanted to stay and settle my differences with Darris, but knew that Anne and our future baby were more important.

CHAPTER EIGHT

OUT OF WORK

I've never been one for tolerating fools and I've generally dealt with them in my own way. Unfortunately I seemed to find this kind of person in most jobs I'd worked on so far. I felt as if I attracted them like magnets. Regrettably I had now become reputed within the pipe-mill industry for my inability to control my aggression and was blacklisted by the inspection teams. Following this I spent the next nine months out of work and had to find other things to occupy my time.

In September 1993 Anne's contractions became more intense and regular, so we got into the car and drove to the hospital. A short while later my son Gary was born. I was overjoyed that I'd now become a father. Anne held him in her arms as he gave out a loud cry. She smiled at me.

'Is this the best moment in your life, Steve?' she asked, and looked deep into my eyes.

'It's an equal best moment in my life, Anne.'

'What do you mean?' she frowned and looked down at Gary and then back at me.

'When I passed out of training as a Marine was one of the best moments in my life, as well as the birth of my son. The funny thing is, they both took nine months.'

Anne scowled and shook her head. 'There's more to life than the Marines, Steve,' she said.

She was right, but at that time I just couldn't see it.

Fortunately I'd managed to save a few thousand pounds during the time I was in work and this helped to cover the bills during my long period of unemployment. I joined a local gymnasium and worked out there every day. I took great pride in my personal fitness and worked hard to maintain it.

I missed the Marines more than ever and sometimes wished that I had never opted to leave when I did. However, I'd left for good reasons: my court martial, which I was acquitted from, and also my tendency to resort to violence whenever someone crossed me. I had got away with a lot of things over the years I had served, but knew my days would be numbered if I continued in this vein after my court case. For a while after leaving I even wondered whether or not I wanted to keep on living. When I was a Marine, I enjoyed life to the full, but my personality and lifestyle didn't seem to just slot into being a civilian. I seemed to be fighting life rather than living and it was a case of one door shuts and another slams in your face. When I got fed up, I watched a couple of videos on the Marines from time to time or browsed through my photograph albums. This tended to remind me of who I was and helped to raise my spirits when I needed a boost. Also, my loving girlfriend and newly born son gave me a renewed sense of determination. I needed to work at succeeding at some form of employment because I had more than myself to support now.

I put the finishing touches to the first draft of my autobiography and decided to mothball it and to build up some much-needed qualifications to improve my chances of employment. Consequently, my energy went into studying. I remembered the remarks that were made to me in France about not being qualified as a pipe-mill inspector and decided to use this spell out of work as an opportunity to rectify this. I studied and qualified in welding inspection, pipe-mill and pipeline inspection and metallurgy. This took me about six months and cost me several thousand pounds in course and examination fees, which I borrowed from the bank. Now I had lots of qualifications but unfortunately very little experience to back it up. What I really needed now was for somebody to give me a break and give me the chance to get some experience under my belt.

On the weekends I drank in a local pub called the Black Swan and vented my frustrations on anybody who got in my way. The only conversation I seemed to have was about the Marines, but this was not always everybody's cup of tea. The locals nicknamed me the Mad Marine and tended to cross the road if they saw me coming down the street. I didn't like this and felt quite dismayed when one of the guys whom I had served with in the Royal Marines did the same thing. When I saw him, I asked him why he did this. He told me that he'd thought I was very aggressive and violent when I'd served with him as a Marine and that he didn't really think anything had changed yet. I felt disappointed at his criticism, but I knew he was right and I accepted it.

Anne introduced me to one of my potential future brother-in-laws. He was called Bill and was a couple of years younger than I was. He occasionally socialised and trained with me and we became fairly good friends. One night he called round to the house and I offered him a beer. I pulled a bottle from a box and bit the top off with my teeth and passed it to him. Then I spat the top into a nearby bin. I did this a few times and watched him gulp each time I did it. He seemed very nervous. I can't remember if I ever let him in on my little secret. I had brought a number of boxes of beer back from my trip abroad. The bottle tops looked like they were the kind that you levered off with a bottle opener, but really they were screw-off tops. I had loosened them before he arrived and let him think I was biting the tops off!

I started to frequent the Navy Club once again and Johnny the ex-matelot picked up where he left off with his continuous barrage of insults and abuse towards me. One night I'd had enough and decided that he had gone too far.

It was a warm summer evening and I caught a taxi to the Navy Club. I was alone, but this was nothing new for me, because I just tended to head for the bar and find someone to talk to when I got there. The Navy Club had organised a special function for ex-serving members of the Royal Navy and the Royal Marines. To suit the occasion I was dressed in trousers and a shirt and tie. I also took great pride in displaying my new Royal Marines tiepin.

The Navy Club was busy when I got there, but mainly with ex-sailors. Unfortunately, to my knowledge, ex-Marines were thin on the ground around here. I purchased a pint of beer and sipped it. Then I saw Johnny approaching me. He was drinking too, and he had the usual smarmy look on his face.

'Now then, Royal. What brings you here? You haven't shown your face in here for a while.'

'No, Johnny, I haven't. I've been working away in Germany.'

'Best place for you,' he sniggered as he looked into his pint glass and drank his beer. 'So what are you doing here?' he continued, with beer froth all over his face.

I looked at him carefully. He had a huge gut that hung over his trousers and a few protruding warts that stuck out of his stubbly cheeks. He looked like he needed a good wash. I never really knew why he had such a bad attitude towards ex-bootnecks; maybe he had once been beaten up by one of them, I thought.

'I can come in here any time I want. I'm a full ex-serving member,' I smiled.

'Yes, Royal, and just remember, I'm the fucking chairman.' He sniggered again and drank the remaining dregs from his pint of beer. 'If you're here for this function, keep your big trap shut. There won't be many of your lot here.' He stared at me seriously and banged his empty glass down on the bar before walking off into an adjacent room.

Fucking nobber, I thought. He's got a head like a baby's pram: full of shit and broken biscuits. I drank my beer and ordered another pint.

'I'll buy that,' a voice called out from the other side of the bar.

I recognised the voice and looked up. It was a guy called Ernie whom I knew. He was an ex-Para and very proud of it too. He displayed his regimental badge on the left side of his jumper. I smiled and waved Ernie over to join me. We'd been friends for a while now. I'd met him during that week I'd spent in hospital after my car accident. I thought a lot of him and respected the pride he showed in his former regiment.

'Don't take any notice of that daft nugget,' he said as he passed me a pint of beer. 'He's just a big fat nobody with a chip on his shoulder.'

'Hmm, sounds about right,' I replied. 'What's the big issue with him? He seems to hate Marines with a vengeance.'

Ernie started to laugh. I looked at him. Whatever it was that had tickled him, he certainly found it very funny.

'You obviously don't know, because you don't come in here very often,' he smiled and started laughing again. So much that he had tears in his eyes.

'Come on, Ernie, let me into the secret.'

'When he was serving in the Navy, he was mouthing off at some big hairy-arsed Marine, who then proceeded to punch him so hard in the face that he knocked all his front teeth out. One of the other committee members in here was with him at the time. He said the Marine hit him so hard that he was surprised Johnny's teeth didn't come out of his arse and bite him.'

We both burst into laughter and drank our beers. Now I understood why Johnny had such a bad attitude towards me. It still wasn't fair, though, because it wasn't me personally who he had been punched by. Ernie and I spent the next couple of hours playing pool, during which time we continuously took the piss out of each other's regimental badges.

Later in the evening we all assembled in a large upstairs room, where we sat around a large wooden table for a meal. There were about 20 people in all, many of whom were strangers to me. I noticed that several of them were shabbily dressed in very cheap suits, which looked like they had just been bought in a jumble sale. The men who wore them were elderly and I would guess were aged around 70. They all looked in my direction, smiled at me and raised their glasses. I couldn't hear what they were saying as a toast so I just raised mine and drank too.

Johnny tapped on his empty beer glass with a pen to get everybody's attention. He gave a long speech about the Royal Navy being the senior service in the British forces and raised his glass to propose a toast of his own.

'To the senior service, the Royal Navy,' he said and stood up to attention.

He was joined by most of the occupants around the table. The exceptions were all of the shabbily dressed gentlemen and Ernie and myself, who remained seated. I knew why Ernie didn't stand up, but what I didn't know was why these other guys didn't. Maybe they were ex-Army lads like Ernie, I thought.

After the meal I was introduced to these men, who all turned out to be former Royal Marines who had all served during the Second World War. They told me that they didn't come in very often because Johnny always gave them a hard time. The reason they were shabbily dressed was that they didn't have much money to live on and had bought the suits from a charity shop just for this occasion. I sympathised with them and bought them all a beer. I felt a little sad that they had to struggle in life and also a little bit dismayed that Johnny often insulted them. I saw him standing at the other end of the bar. He kept turning his head and was watching us. Each time he looked away he seemed to pull a face. I just ignored him.

I enjoyed conversing with the older Marines. I found their war stories to be intriguing and I listened with great interest to the arduous conflicts they'd survived. Then I told them how much I missed being a Marine and how difficult I was finding things in civvy street. They all assured me that they had missed the Marines when they'd demobbed from the corps, but they all agreed that things got a little easier as the years went by. One of them put his hand in his pocket and told me that he wanted to buy me a beer. I refused and insisted that I buy another round. After a few exchanges of polite words he agreed to toss a coin for it and I gladly won. I walked over to the bar next to Johnny and ordered another round of drinks.

'You're not buying the drinks again for that lot, are you, Steve?' he smirked.

'That's my business,' I replied in a polite manner.

'They're dressed like shit. I shouldn't have let them come in. We've got standards in here, you know.'

'They haven't got much money,' I snapped.

'Don't you talk to me like that or I'll bar all of you out,' he snapped back. 'Anyway, make that your last drink and piss off out of here.'

I was astounded by his remarks and lack of respect for the elderly gentlemen and finally my uncontrollable temper erupted.

'YOU HORRIBLE BASTARD!' I screamed loudly, and at the same time swung the back of my hand hard into Johnny's face. It made a loud smacking noise upon contact. The blow knocked him back against the bar and I grabbed him by the hair and slammed his head hard against the wooden bar top. I saw his false teeth slide across the wooden surface and disappear onto the floor on the other side. He looked pathetic without his teeth and I could hear the old boy Marines laughing at the other end of the bar.

Johnny initially struggled to find his teeth and quickly put them back in his mouth. He stood up on his feet, with blood trickling from his lips.

'Get out,' he insisted. 'All of you get out now. You're all barred out for good.'

The group of ex-Marines and myself swilled our beers and made a quick exit out of the club. The old boys asked me to join them in another social club that was close by. I accepted the invitation and gladly went with them. Once inside they were adamant that they bought all the beers for the rest of the evening and told me that they thought Johnny had got what he deserved.

The evening finished on a high. We all felt very proud to have served in the Marines at one time or another. Prior to my departure I shook the hands of all my new friends and wished them all the very best for the future, then I bid them farewell. It was a fairly mild night and my personal pride made me want to run home instead of calling a taxi. I felt very drunk by this time, but that didn't deter me. As I ran along, I could hear the faint noise of birds singing. I ran up and down a few steep hills and could feel sweat dripping down my face. I felt good inside and smiled to myself.

Suddenly I could hear the faint sound of footsteps hitting the ground in the distance. They seemed to be in step with mine.

Then I felt a hard crack under my chin as I hit the ground hard. The faint footsteps I could hear were my own. The alcohol I'd consumed had made me start to lose consciousness. I felt like I had just been hit by a sledgehammer and groaned a bit when I tried to raise my chin off the floor.

I could hear the sound of two or more men laughing in the distance. The volume became louder as if they were coming closer, but this closing-in was another trick of my semi-conscious mind. My body ached all over and I could feel blood dripping from my chin and around my neck. I looked up to see who was laughing and saw a white van opposite, just a few feet away, with two men sat in it. I fought hard to focus on the sign on the side of the van. It said POLICE.

Oh shit, I thought. It looks like I'm going to spend the night in a prison cell. Then I could hear the birds singing again. At first they sounded as if they were close by and then they became distant. All of a sudden I felt myself rising upwards and opened my eyes to see two police officers lifting me up from the ground by my arms.

'Are you all right, sir?' one of them asked me.

I tried to reply yes, but the words didn't come out of my mouth. My head and jaw ached and I felt like I wanted to close my eyes and go to sleep.

'That was quite a fall, sir. You've injured your chin and face.'

I looked at my bloodstained clothes and saw that my Royal Marines tiepin was bent and twisted and also covered in blood. It was still attached to my tie so I used the tie material to rub the blood from it, whilst the two policemen held onto me as I swayed a little from side to side.

'Oh, I see you're an ex-serviceman, sir. That tiepin badge looks like the Marines badge.'

I still couldn't find any words so I just nodded my head. My blurred vision started to clear a bit and I could see the two policemen reviewing my state of awareness. I saw one of them nod his head at the other as if coming to an agreement about something.

'We're not going to lock you up tonight, sir. We're going to give you a lift home.'

I nodded my head to let them know I was coherent enough to understand what they were saying to me. They helped me into the back of their van. I felt relieved at this. It reminded me of serving with the Royal Marines Police in Plymouth. Royal Marines were expected to get drunk when they socialised, especially after a tour abroad. We often used to pick some of them out of the gutter at the end of the evening and drop them off at their barracks without charging them for being drunk. Generally we would ask the duty guard commander to keep an eye on them until morning, just to be sure they didn't choke on their own vomit.

'Can you tell us where you live, sir?' one of the policemen asked.

I tried hard to answer his question, but still couldn't find any words. I raised my hand and pointed in the direction I had been running.

One of them started laughing. 'I used to be in the Army myself, a few years ago. I understand your situation: you can think at the moment but you can't speak.'

I nodded my head.

'I'll tell you what, sir. You point in the direction we need to go in and we'll drive you there.'

I nodded my head and smiled at him. Then I pointed down the long road to indicate the direction I needed to go in to get home. The driver turned the vehicle around and we began the journey home. The road was a few miles long and I sat back and reminisced about another time in the Marines Police. I was sat in a military police van in a small area of Plymouth called the Octagon. We were parked on a side road opposite a long street called Union Street. This street was infamous for the vast amounts of servicemen that drank there and in particular the Royal Marines, as well as other units of commando forces and the Royal Navy. This was a place where a lot of servicemen let off a lot of steam.

I was sat in the front of our vehicle with a Marine called Roger, and an attached Army rank from the Royal Military Police (a redcap) called Jerry Slater was sat in the rear. We watched the flow of servicemen walking and at times staggering up and down the street between the many pubs that were available. We saw two servicemen start to fight between themselves on the other side of the road.

'Quick,' gasped Jerry. 'Let's arrest them for fighting.'

'No, wait,' I insisted and turned towards Roger who had a big grin on his face.

'I bet the one in the blue jumper wins,' Roger smiled.

'No, it'll be the one in the red jumper,' I said. 'He's smaller but he's stocky and well built.'

'They're committing a military offence,' Jerry informed us. 'We should arrest them.'

'Look,' I snapped at him. 'We do things differently in the Royal Marines compared to what you're used to in the Army. We expect the men to go out and get pissed. We expect them to fight occasionally and to let off steam. We can't arrest them every time this happens.'

'I don't agree,' Jerry snapped back. 'I'm going to arrest them.'

He put his hand on the van door handle and went to push the door open. I turned around and grabbed hold of him.

'Stay where you are,' I said in a voice of authority. My rank was the same as his but I meant what I said. 'If the fight gets out of hand, then we'll intervene; otherwise we won't. Now sit down and be patient.'

We watched the two men exchanging blows and the man in the red jumper started to get the better of the man in the blue jumper.

'Now,' insisted Jerry as he grabbed the door handle once again.

'No!' I shouted. 'You don't run into a situation like this; you walk into it. You need to let it register in their minds that you're an MP [military policeman] and let them think MP, otherwise you'll get dragged in there yourself.'

With these words Jerry sat back in his seat and hesitated to get out. Roger and I smiled at each other and walked across the road together. The two men saw us approaching and looked at us both. They instantly knew we were policemen from our uniforms and armbands, and the man in the red jumper bolted off down the street.

'STOP!' I shouted at Jerry as he started to give chase. He stopped and walked over towards Roger and me.

We asked the man in the blue jumper if he was OK and he said that he was. His nose was bleeding, but that didn't seem to bother him.

'Go on, beat it,' Roger told him and pointed down the long street.

The man didn't need telling twice and ran off into the distance.

Later we went back to the Military Police control office and reported that all was quiet. Just before we handed over responsibility to some other policemen who were on the next shift, I was told to report to the sergeant-major's office. When I entered, I saw Roger, who was sat down, and Jerry, who was standing next to the sergeant-major.

The sergeant-major had a very serious look on his face. 'Lance-Corporal Preece.'

'Yes, sir,' I frowned, sensing that something was wrong.

'Lance-Corporal Slater has reported that you failed to arrest two servicemen who he has reported as being engaged in a fight. Can you explain this?'

'Err, yes, sir. A fight did take place between two servicemen, but it did not get out of control.'

'What else happened?'

'One of the two men eventually got the better of the other, sir, so we intervened and broke it up.'

'Why didn't you arrest them?'

'Sir, if we arrested every serviceman whom we judged to be drunk or everyone who took part in a fight, we wouldn't have enough cells in Plymouth to contain them.'

He smiled at me. 'Good decision, Preece.' Then he turned towards Jerry. 'Lance-Corporal Slater, pack your bags and piss off back to your Army unit.'

Jerry's face dropped. 'Yes, sir. Will do, sir.'

I never saw or heard from Jerry again.

'Which way do we go now?' asked one of the civilian policemen, jolting my thoughts back to the present.

'Uh, oh,' I grunted and pointed down the street where I lived.

'Point at the house,' the policeman instructed as we slowly drove along the last few metres of my street. When we arrived outside my house, I pointed at it and the van came to a halt. I tried to stand up to climb out through the back door, but fell against the side of the van.

My headache returned and I started to drift back into unconsciousness once again. Then I felt the two policemen pull me out of the van and back onto my feet. They held tightly onto my arms and steadied me as I walked down the garden path to my front door. When they knocked on the door, I knew they were hoping I had got the right house and that some poor unsuspecting neighbour was not going to be very disappointed at being woken up by a drunk and two policemen. The door opened and Anne stood looking at my bloodstained face and clothes. I smiled at her.

'Is this yours?' a policeman asked her.

'Yes, officer, it is mine,' she replied with a sigh.

The two officers handed me over to Anne, who assisted me into the house. The two considerate policemen bid us goodnight and left a few moments later. Back inside the house I fell to the floor in the hallway and into a deep sleep.

Next morning I awoke around 7 a.m. I could hear the sound of our son crying. My head ached and I knew I needed to get cleaned up and to apologise to Anne for my entrance the night before.

CHAPTER NINE

THICK AS THIEVES

Although I'd been out of the Marines for three years now, I still managed to maintain good contact with a number of men whom I'd served with. I drank heavily on a weekend and tended to phone them at all hours of the night and early morning. I didn't do this to annoy them. I missed them a lot. They were great friends and were the main thing that made it so good to be a Marine. Friends like these were few and far between in civvy street. By the time I made the telephone calls, I was usually well under the influence and had truthfully lost all track of time. They always answered the phone and always took the time to talk to me. I appreciated this and the good thing was that I often returned the compliment when they phoned me after having a lot to drink.

Our money was running low so Anne made a decision to go back to work whilst I looked after the baby. It was hard work. I fed and changed him as well as doing the cooking, pots, shopping and all the housework. I was fed up but I had to pull my weight around the house.

In the supermarket one afternoon Gary was sat comfortably in his pushchair as we queued up at the checkout. I watched the girl who was serving me scan my shopping into the till and place it down on the counter to her left. Gary started crying so I leant down over his pram and put his dummy back in his mouth. This did the trick and he soon quietened down. I smiled and stood back upright to pay my bill. Unexpectedly I saw a youth standing at the end of the counter. He was putting my shopping in his bag.

'Put that back now,' I growled and grabbed a tight hold of his jumper. He looked at me. He looked astonished and scared.

'Put it back now,' I insisted. 'Or I'll rip your head off and shove it up your arse.'

'Excuse me,' said the checkout operator, 'but he's not a thief. He's our bag packer.'

It was a little embarrassing to say the least, but I gave him a two-pound tip for helping me to pack my bags and shook his hand firmly before I left.

Later that day, whilst one of Anne's friends had taken Gary out in his pushchair, and I was waiting for Anne to return home from work, I went for a run. When I returned, I did 30 minutes of circuit training in my garage and finished with a workout on my newly acquired punch-bag, which hung from the garage roof. I felt good as I trained and thought of people I didn't like as I gritted my teeth and repeatedly punched the bag hard.

'Excuse me, mate,' a voice called out, interrupting my concentration.

I turned around and saw it was the postman, who was stood smiling at me. He held a brown parcel in his hand.

'Hello, mate. Is that for me?'

He nodded his head and asked me to sign for it, which I did after removing my bag mitts (boxing gloves used for bag work). I took the parcel and went inside the house to open it. It was fairly heavy and I looked at the black postmark that was stamped on it. It read Northern Ireland. Butterflies ran through my stomach and I immediately thought I had been sent an explosive device from across the water. I paused for a moment and contemplated calling the police to report it. Then I thought about the embarrassment if I'd got it wrong, so I took the parcel into the kitchen and placed it on top of a wooden table. I climbed under the table and reached up for the parcel with my hands. If it explodes, I thought, it'll just get my hands. I cautiously pulled the brown wrapping-paper from it. I could feel the surface of a cardboard box and carefully opened it and felt inside. I could feel two cold bottles of liquid and what felt like lots of strands of soft string or straw. I took hold of one of the bottles and slowly lowered it down towards me. I used my other hand to feel for any trailing wires. There were none and the bottle came into sight.

You bloody dickhead, I thought, as I saw the label of a bottle of red wine. I shuffled out from under the table and looked inside the box, where I saw another bottle, this one of white wine. I smiled to myself and gave out a big sigh of relief. There was a small card in the box, which said many thanks for your services on our contract in Germany. It was sent by the agency that had employed me as a contractor on behalf of the oil company. I felt a bit silly now, but breathed a second sigh of relief anyway.

At the end of the night we put Gary into his cot and retired to bed for the evening. Anne fell asleep within minutes and I lay awake thinking about the events of the day. A small bang from outside grabbed my attention. I got up and looked through the bedroom window to see what it was. Two youths were laughing and joking on the other side of the road as they walked along and I watched them as they disappeared down an alley. Then all was quiet outside; nothing moved or stirred. I looked down at our car and noticed that the driver's door was slightly ajar. She hasn't locked the car door properly, I thought. I'll go and do it. I was only dressed in my boxer shorts but wasn't too worried about the neighbours or anybody else seeing me because it was late and there was very little chance that there would be anybody about. I walked downstairs and opened the front door. I could see the car a few feet away and suddenly noticed that someone was sat inside it behind the steering wheel. He was wearing a mask across his face and looked to be fumbling with my steering lock.

'BASTARD!' I shouted and looked around the area at the bottom of the stairs for some shoes. There were none there, so I turned towards the open doorway and looked back at the thief. He saw me and quickly jumped out of the car to face me. He was very tall and was dressed in a black coat and trousers. A black balaclava covered his face. He stood there with his fists clenched.

'FUCKING BASTARD!' I screamed, my voice roaring with anger.

I ran hard at him and he turned quickly and started sprinting off down the street. My fitness proved an easy match for his long strides and I tucked in behind him. I thought about rugby-tackling him, but knew that it would probably result in both of us falling to the ground and all the skin being ripped off my legs and body. I stayed just behind him. I could hear him puffing and panting for breath. I spoke to him quietly as we moved along.

'I'm right with you and when we stop I'm going to kick the shit out of you, you thieving bastard,' I said to him.

He didn't reply. I thought he couldn't draw enough breath to do this even if he'd wanted to. I knew he was afraid; I could sense it. We turned down a dark pathway that was dimly lit and the thief came to an abrupt halt. He turned around to face me and pulled off the balaclava.

I stopped too and grinned at him. He was a fairly young man who I would guess was aged around 16. He had a skinhead and thick bushy eyebrows. We were stood just a few feet apart and I watched him as he reached inside his jacket for something. I moved closer towards him.

'I've got you now, you thieving bastard, and I'm going to kick the shit out of you,' I snarled.

He pulled something from inside his jacket, which turned out to be a long chisel. He stood in a fighting stance and pointed it towards me.

'If you come any closer, I'm going to stick this in you,' he warned, nodding his head to assure me he meant what he said.

I went to pull the belt from my waist to fight him with, but realised I was only wearing my boxer shorts. I knelt down slowly to pick up some stones to throw at him, but could only feel blades of damp grass between my fingers. I slowly stood up and faced him. He was shaking and appeared to be more afraid of me than I was of him. For a moment I went to take the chisel from him. I knew how to do this because I'd learned unarmed combat in the Marines and knew the techniques used against knife attacks. Suddenly, for the first time in my life, I hesitated and a mental picture of Anne and my little baby boy shot through my mind. If I get this wrong, I'm dead, I thought. I've got too much to lose now. Instead I looked at the youth, who was moving a little closer now and was shaking. I knew this was a dangerous time for me. I needed to control the situation. I felt that if I turned away, he would stick it in me for sure. He was too close for me to make a wrong move.

'OK, mate, you've got the upper hand. Go on, beat it,' I told him, pointing down the dark path.

He looked surprised and at the same time confused, so I repeated my words. 'Go on, you can go. Beat it.'

He still did nothing and continued to stand looking at me. He was unsure of what to do.

'RUN NOW!' I yelled at him.

He seemed to suddenly realise that he could make a clean getaway and he turned and ran hard and fast into the distance. I watched him until he disappeared out of sight. Then I jogged back to our house, where I saw Anne standing on the doorstep.

'I heard you shouting at someone and watched you give chase down the street,' she said. 'I've telephoned the police.'

I nodded my head and went inside to put some trousers and a top on. A few minutes later two policemen knocked on the front door. They'd arrived on foot and had approached from the same dark pathway that the thief had used to make his getaway.

I invited the two men inside the house and asked them to sit down so that I could give them details of the incident. Initially they seemed more interested in the contents of my house than they were with me and sat staring at our furniture. I cleared my throat and got their attention to describe the height and build of the thief.

'That's a very good description,' one of them said. 'Do you know him or have you got something against him?' he asked. 'We came down that path and we never saw anybody.'

'What the hell is that supposed to mean?' I replied. I was flabbergasted at what he was insinuating. 'I'm an ex-Marine. I served in the Royal Marines Police. I know how to describe someone. And he did run down that path, about ten minutes before you arrived.'

The two policemen looked at each other and nodded as if to agree with my statement. One of them started looking around the room again at my furniture. It was quality furniture, but I'd worked damned hard for it.

'So what do you do for a living?' he asked.

I looked at him with disgust. I stood up and pointed at the door. 'Get out of my house now,' I insisted. 'Go on, get out now.'

The policeman stood up and walked outside. The other one stayed seated and took my statement. He told me that I had been very accurate with my description and that he thought he knew who it was. He asked me if I would be willing to attend an identity parade the following morning and I gladly agreed. Then he left and both policemen disappeared back down the dimly lit pathway.

I sat for a while and drank a couple of cool beers. I felt angry towards the thief but the request to attend an identity parade reminded me of one I'd attended several years before. When the Marines served in Norway, they occasionally had run-ins with the local Norwegian folk. Sometimes an assault took place that often led to a Norwegian losing a tooth or two and presenting the assailant with a hefty dental bill for one or two thousand pounds if they were caught and prosecuted. This particular parade consisted of three hundred Marines, and we all stood in four ranks whilst a Norwegian started to walk the long rows between us. However, on this occasion the Marine who had committed the assault was black, and he was the only black man in the whole unit. Instead of waiting for the Norwegian to pick him out, he just stuck his hand in the air and shouted, 'It's a fair cop, mate.' It was the biggest identity parade I had ever seen and also the funniest. The black guy was a very popular man amongst us, whom most of us respected, so we all contributed towards paying his dental bill and subsequent fine.

Six weeks later one of the two policemen returned to our house. Thankfully it wasn't the one whom I found to be irritating and rude. I invited him inside and he showed me a number of mug shots inside several photograph albums. I looked at them and felt really disappointed at how long it had taken the police to get back to me. I thought several of the pictures looked like the thief but couldn't be sure. The policeman told me that they had got a thumbprint off my steering wheel, but said it wasn't enough because he needed at least two fingerprints. This confused me and disappointed me further, but I just shrugged my shoulders and thanked him anyway.

I spent the next few weeks turning the events over and over in my mind. Maybe I should have gone for the chisel, I thought. Then I would change my mind and decide that I'd made the right decision, that the graveyard was full of heroes.

I drank heavily as usual on a weekend. Usually this would be three or four bottles of wine on both Friday and Saturday nights. To try to cut down I would buy two bottles and tell myself to take my time. I would drink these in a couple of hours and nip out to the off-licence to buy some more. On a couple of occasions when I did this, I saw a number of youths walking the streets. On two separate occasions I thought the thief who had tried to steal my car was among them. However, on both occasions I was wrong.

I mentioned the whole incident to a friend of mine, who told me that a youth fitting this description often caused a lot of problems for his wife, who worked in a local off-licence. When I asked her about this, she showed me some video footage of a youth causing mayhem in her shop. I recognised him straight away. It was definitely the same guy. The following Saturday I was looking for my newspaper at one of the local shops. I could hear a bit of a commotion going on next to a parked car. I looked over and saw a few youths arguing with an elderly man. I recognised one of them as the youth who'd tried to steal my car and threatened me with a chisel. It was like showing a red rag to a bull and I rapidly ran towards him. I knew that he may have been carrying a knife, so I was taking no chances. I approached him from his blind side and dragged him down to the ground by his now longer hair. He squealed loudly and his two friends ran off. I held him down and put my foot on his throat. I looked at him and made him choke. Suddenly a crowd of people surrounded me. They were shouting at me to leave him alone. An old woman stepped forward.

'Why don't you leave him alone?' she pleaded. 'He's done nothing wrong to you.'

I looked at the crowd and then at her. 'Look, this guy tried to steal my car and pulled a knife on me a couple of months ago,' I explained. 'It was on the front page of the newspaper. Did any of you read it?'

The crowd of people started to look at each other and nod. I saw the old woman nodding too. Then she stepped closer and whacked the youth with her handbag. The crowd started to applaud and I removed my foot from the youth's throat. After all there were too many credible witnesses now.

'You've got the upper hand again,' I said. 'Go on, beat it. We'll meet again.'

He ran off into the distance. Unfortunately we never did meet again. The same youth stole another car from our estate and this time he was confronted by an elderly gentleman. He drove off in the car to make his escape and sadly ran the gentleman down and killed him. Some time later I read in the local newspaper that he was sentenced to several years in prison and later again that he had hung himself inside his prison cell.

CHAPTER TEN

OUT OF CONDITION

It was just another night. I'd been out of work for nine months and our savings were almost all gone. I sat alone in the back garden feeling dismayed. It was raining and I was getting soaking wet but I really didn't care. Anne knew I was out in the rain, but she knew it was best just to leave me alone. I sat drinking a bottle of red wine and staring up at the twinkling stars. I need to get a job, I thought. I need to support my family. Then I thought about Nigel, my ex-SAS friend whom I'd met in Germany. I wondered how he'd coped with his move into civvy street. He was a lot older than I was, but he certainly seemed in control of his life.

Suddenly I heard the back door open and I saw Anne standing there looking at me. She's going to tell me that I'm stupid for sitting in the rain, I thought.

'Steve, there's someone on the telephone for you called Nigel,' she said.

I jumped up and drank the remaining wine from my glass. 'Nigel!' I exclaimed. 'Great, I was just thinking about him.'

'Hello, Nigel, mate,' I said, feeling overjoyed that he had called me. 'It's funny but I was just sat wondering how you were keeping.'

'I'm not very well, Steve. I've put a lot of weight on over the past few months and I feel like shit. I heard Darris had put you out of work.'

'Yes he did. He's a fucking arsehole.'

'Yes, I know he is. I did warn you about that.'

'How's their new company doing? Have they generated much business?'

'Believe it or not the company has folded. The bold Darris wanted more shares than everybody else and eventually they all went their separate ways.'

'Oh, that's the best news I've had in nine months,' I said, beaming with pleasure.

'Are you working?' Nigel asked.

'Am I bollocks. I'm sick as a parrot and have nearly spent all my savings.'

'Do you want a job with me in Germany?'

'Nigel, I'd love to have a job working with you.'

'Have you got any industry-related qualifications?'

'Funny you should say that, Nigel, but yes I have. I've been studying a lot whilst I've been out of work. Do you want me to work on the computer?'

'No, I want you to help me to lose weight and to get fit again. I can employ you as a piping inspector, but really I want you to work at getting me back into shape.'

'Fine by me, Nigel, as long as the cash is good.'

'The cash is good, Steve. I'll get a contract sent out to you in the post and you can fly out here next week.'

'Fabulous, mate,' I said, excited. 'I'll look forward to working with you.'

It was an unusual request, but I was more than happy to accept the offer of work, whatever shape or form it might come in. The following week I flew to Düsseldorf in Germany and picked up a hire car at the airport for a long drive to a place called Siegan.

I got a shock when I met up with Nigel. He was indeed overweight. His fat belly hung over his trousers and his facial cheeks looked all bloated. I also noticed that his eyes were bloodshot and discoloured.

'Bloody hell, Nigel, you look like shit.'

'Yes, I know. It was my 50th birthday last week but I feel a lot older. I really need your help, Steve,' he said, with a look of desperation on his face.

'No problem, mate. I'll get you back into shape,' I assured him.

The steel mill we were working at was a huge complex and our project was to track the production of steel pipes called cans. These were purpose-made as oil-rig platform legs and were a lot thicker and heavier than the pipes I had seen in other pipe mills.

I wasted very little time planning Nigel's fitness routine and signed us both up as members of a local gym. I started him off on light weights with lots of repetitions and fast walks on a running machine. He was a bit embarrassed at first because other people were lifting a lot more weight than he was, but I assured him that was just a male pride thing and that it actually took more determination to lift light weights in front of other people than big ones. I also insisted that we only socialised on a weekend. It was a long-term habit of mine and something I'd always done as a Marine when I wasn't on duty.

After a couple of weeks Nigel started to respond well to my training so I introduced some short runs along the peaceful country roads. This brought back some good memories of speed marches from my basic training. The difference was that we ran a lot faster then and carried a weapon and fighting order. Nigel puffed and panted and coughed and wheezed during the runs, but I respected his determination and will-power because he never gave up. The gym work, runs and the diet I got him to stick to started helping him to reduce his weight. After six weeks his face was no longer bloated and his fat sagging belly had reduced considerably in size. Even his eyes looked better and his complexion started to shine. Sometimes during our runs he insisted on wearing his SAS beret when he ran. Nobody was around to see him and he said it made him run faster and lifted his pride. Nigel had been a Paratrooper before he joined the SAS and sometimes he wore his maroon beret instead. Occasionally we joked about which fighting soldiers were the best. He said it was the SAS and the Paras and I said it was the Marines. Realistically we knew they were a similar type of troop, but we enjoyed the banter.

Nigel continued to make good progress with his fitness and I pushed him a little further each week to keep the momentum going. After three months he was in excellent shape and actually looked about five years younger than he was. His confidence grew with his agility and he said he felt fearless. Personally I was quite pleased too, as my bank balance was looking rosy and I'd always enjoyed physical training.

Socially we frequented a couple of the local bars and Nigel introduced me to a few of the local Germans who were friends of his. They spoke excellent English and always seemed enthralled when we talked about our past experiences in the armed forces and the many street fights we had been involved in. One of the Germans was called Klaus. He was a tall stocky man with brown curly hair and a moustache. For some reason he kept showing me that he carried a handgun, which puzzled me at first. Then Nigel explained that he did this because he was frightened of me. He'd said that I made him feel uneasy and that he was convinced I'd been hired as Nigel's personal bodyguard. I just laughed at this. My experience had taught me that people in civvy street who carried weapons carried them because they were afraid of at least one person who didn't.

One night we were sat in a bar having a beer with Klaus and a few English people who also lived locally. One of them asked Nigel and me if we had some sort of philosophy about street fighting. Nigel grinned broadly and answered with his reputed quick wit.

'He who turns and runs away lives to fight another day,' he grinned and all the attention moved to me as they waited for my comments.

'He who stays and stands his ground gets his fucking head knocked round.'

We all burst into laughter. There was a moral there somewhere but I don't know if our present company were capable of working it out.

Shortly afterwards I heard and saw Nigel arguing with a middle-aged man who was standing next to him at the bar. He raised his fist at Nigel, who reacted promptly with a forceful head-butt and followed up with a couple of punches. The man went down like a tonne of bricks and Nigel later said that he didn't get on with this guy and felt that he was fit enough now to take the world on.

During the last week of our contract we had to visit another pipe mill at a different location. Nigel told me that Darris was working there so I was keen to go and meet up with him. When we arrived, we went into Darris's office to chat with him. I wasn't sure how I would be greeted or what I would say or do to him when I saw him. First he saw Nigel and shook his hand. Then he saw me. He smiled at me and held his hand out to shake mine.

'Hello, Steve.'

I declined the handshake and looked deep into his eyes. I felt angry towards him – not just for using me to teach him about the computer tracking systems or for pushing me out of my last job, but for ensuring that I stayed out of work for such a long time.

'WHY?' I snarled at him and saw him start to tremble. 'WHY?' I repeated as Nigel left the room to leave us alone together.

'I'm sorry, Steve. I am really sorry. It wasn't just me who kept you out of work. It was Ian as well. He had you blacklisted because of your violent behaviour in France.'

I really felt like pulverising Darris, but I knew that this would mean longer spells out of work for me. Instead I told him what I thought of him and watched him tremble as I did so. Later, on the journey back to Siegan, Nigel told me I should have beaten the shit out of him, but I felt content with the amount of fear I had instilled in him.

At the end of the contract I was offered another job with a different team in Morocco. Nigel stayed behind in Germany. He was in great shape. He even left his wife and shacked up with a girl who was literally half his age. Lucky git, I thought.

CHAPTER ELEVEN

MOROCCO

Before I went to my next job I proposed to Anne and was delighted when she agreed to marry me. We chose just to slip off to a local registry office to get married because we'd lived together for four years by then and because Anne didn't like being the centre of attention.

The day after our wedding it was back to reality and I set off for my new job in Morocco. Turbulence made the aeroplane shudder as we headed for Malaga in Spain. This made me nervous. For some reason I've always felt nervous when I've travelled in aeroplanes, but the strange thing is that during my service days I travelled in a lot of helicopters and this never seemed to bother me.

After we landed in Malaga I caught another small charter plane, which flew across the Strait of Gibraltar to Melilla. This was a small town in Morocco that belonged to Spain. It was a similar sovereignty occupation to the British owning Gibraltar, which sits inside the Spanish borders.

A guy called Archie met me at the airport. He was around 40 years old with short dark hair. He came from London and had a strong cockney accent. Archie was driving an open-top jeep. I slung my suitcase in the back and we headed for the Spanish and Moroccan border. The border was about 200 yards long and ran between two walls. There was a sentry post at both ends as well as armed guards. As we passed through the Moroccan side I saw two guards beating up one of the locals. Archie told me that it was a common sight around here and that the poorer they were, the worse they were treated by the police.

When we arrived at our hotel in a town called Nador, I was introduced to the rest of the team. They seemed like a fairly decent crowd and all came from the north-east of England. I recognised one of them. He was called Larry and I had met him previously when I was working with Nigel. The hotel was a dump. The rooms were clean but gloomy, and there was no air conditioning so it was stiflingly hot and sticky. Unfortunately there were no pubs within the local vicinity.

'We've got a mountain of beer,' said Larry.

'That's fine by me,' I smiled. 'If you've got lots of beer and the right kind of people with you, you can have a good laugh anywhere. Even in this shithole.'

Everybody laughed. I guess they were acknowledging that we either made our own entertainment or we didn't have any.

Our place of work was a pipe-coatings plant. It was situated near Nador's port. The location was ideal for the purpose of the plant. Huge ships delivered hundreds of steel pipes, which were loaded onto long wagons that transported them to the coatings plant. The coatings plant covered the steel in a protective sheath, which helped to prolong the life of the pipes by preventing them from corroding.

I had dual tasks to perform for my job. I had to coordinate the unloading of the pipes from the ships to the coating plant and to enter the pipe details into a pipe-tracking system to ensure traceability. Archie was aware of my computer-programming skills and expressed a keenness for me to enhance the ability of the tracking system, which I did.

The coatings plant was situated in the middle of a huge complex that was enclosed by high fences. The local townsfolk manned it, supervised by members of our team. Their wages were a pittance: they were only paid twenty pence an hour. This might seem bad but the choice was twenty pence an hour or earning nothing at all. This was a far cry from the luxury of unemployment benefits that the unemployed received back in the UK. Every day there was a queue of people outside the gates of the plant. They turned up hoping to get selected for a job, even if it was only for one or two days' work. One day I saw one of them skip the queue and climb over the fence. He casually walked into the coatings plant and pleaded with one of the foremen to give him a job. My eyes widened as I saw two of the Moroccan workers set about him and proceed to beat him to a pulp. He lay on the floor covered in blood and I hurried to the foreman's office to tell him to phone the police. For some reason he bluntly refused to make the call and walked out of the office. I picked the telephone up and called them myself. Several minutes later they arrived on the site and I showed them where the assaulted man was. To my surprise and horror they too beat the injured man and clapped a pair of handcuffs on him before taking him away. I later heard that they locked him up for six weeks for causing a disturbance. Rough justice, I would say.

My English colleagues treated the locals like idiots, but I chose to treat them as I would expect to be treated myself. They weren't idiots at all. Some of them had a degree but just acted stupid because my colleagues insulted their intelligence. I learnt a very important lesson about these colleagues. They were very well paid but felt that they should have been getting paid more for the job we were doing. They sat complaining to me about this and I suggested that we should all confront Archie because he was a director of the inspection company. Everybody agreed so we went to see him.

'What's the problem?' Archie asked curiously as we entered his office.

'The lads and I aren't happy with the amount of money we're being paid,' I said, taking it upon myself to be the spokesman.

Archie frowned and scratched his head. 'But Steve, these guys have been here for over three months now and they've never told me that they're not happy with the amount of cash they're being paid.'

'Well, they certainly aren't happy now,' I replied, looking towards my colleagues. 'Are you, lads?'

To my annoyance they all declined to back up my statement and also to answer my question. Instead they all put their heads down.

'Are you, lads?' I repeated, but still I got no response. Suddenly it dawned on me that they'd baited me with the information and were letting me front the issue instead of them. Unfortunately none of them had the bollocks to back me up.

'Can I have a word with you in private?' Archie asked. I nodded and my colleagues quietly left the room.

'They haven't got the courage to back you up, Steve.'

'Yes, I know. Are you going to sack me now?'

'No. I'm going to give you the pay rise you asked for, but please don't say anything to them.'

'Fine by me,' I smiled, feeling confused but happy with what had transpired.

A week later I became flavour of the month again with my work colleagues. Larry, myself and a guy called Ben were travelling back to Nador in a hire car. It was about eleven o'clock in the morning and we'd been to another pipe-coating plant in a different part of the country. We were about 50 miles away from our destination when the car engine suddenly stopped.

'Oh shit,' said Ben, who was sat behind the steering wheel with a look of dismay on his face. 'The bloody car has broken down.'

We free-wheeled for about half a mile until the vehicle came to a halt. The three of us stepped outside into the blistering heat. We opened the bonnet and tried to work out between us why the engine had stopped. We had plenty of petrol so it obviously wasn't that.

'The car battery is knackered,' said Ben. 'I'm absolutely positive that's what the problem is.'

'Shit. We're 50 miles from civilisation in either direction. What are we going to do?' said Larry in despair.

'We have two choices,' I told them. 'We either walk the 50 miles or we stay put and wait for the daily bus that runs this route at nine o'clock each morning.'

'I don't think I could possibly walk 50 miles,' Ben answered.

'Me neither,' added Larry.

'That's that settled,' I said. 'We'll wait here for the bus.'

'What if it doesn't run tomorrow?' Ben asked.

'We'll cross that bridge if and when we come to it,' I replied.

We sat in the car and played games with a pack of cards during most of the afternoon. The heat was blistering and the inside of the car felt like a sauna and soon became too hot to occupy. To keep ourselves cool we collected some brushwood and a few dead tree branches that were scattered around the area. My two friends followed the instructions I gave them and assisted me in erecting an overhead shelter to keep us all in the shade. Whilst we did this, I noticed several sets of rabbit droppings, which gave me an idea of what we could use for food. I also found some clumps of nettles, which I collected to make some tea with.

I looked for some wire or string to make some rabbit snares but unfortunately we didn't have any in the car. What we did have was a load of long bungees, so I used these instead. I draped them over the branches of several trees to make loose nooses, and used bowed branches as the triggers, or noose-tightening mechanisms. Larry and Ben laughed at this. They didn't believe for a second that they would work.

When it started to get dark, we collected more brushwood and made a fire. Larry was a smoker and had plenty of matches to complete the fire-lighting task. Suddenly we heard a series of noises coming from the area where I had laid my rabbit snares. We went over to investigate and all burst into laughter as we saw three rabbits being catapulted back and forth as they tried to escape from my bungees.

To kill and skin the rabbits I used a knife from a small toolkit that belonged to one of my colleagues. He also had a large screwdriver with a long shaft that I pushed through the rabbits to make a spit. Lastly I pulled the full windscreen-washer bottle from the car and poured it into a metal mug we had along with the nettles to make nettle tea.

It was fun sitting under the stars living off the land that night. It was something I hadn't done since I'd served in the Marines, but the good thing was I knew what to do and how to do it. My two friends were more than pleased.

The night was still fairly warm, but we maintained a big fire to fend off wild animals and to use the light from the flames to play cards by. When we were tired, we got back into the car and went to sleep.

At 9.30 the next morning we all sat at the side of the road playing more card games. Ben kept checking his watch. Then I heard him cheering and jumping up and down as the bus approached us. We waved at the driver, who pulled over and let us climb aboard. As we sat down, I looked at Ben, who had a beaming smile on his face.

'Ye of little faith,' I grinned and he shook my hand.

We spent the next four weeks working for twelve hours a day and seven days a week. It was all work and no play or more accurately all work and no alcohol because there was nowhere to play. Eventually Archie decided that it was time to give us a break and told us that we could have a day off. There was nowhere to go, but we had an excellent stockpile of beer back at our hotel. I reiterated my statement of it's not where you are it's who you're with that counts socially, and Ben and Larry said they were more than happy to spend a full day drinking vast amounts of our beer with me.

Larry had the biggest room so we agreed to meet there around lunchtime. He also had a small vibes box (stereo) and plenty of music to play on it. Initially we spent a lot of time cracking jokes and then I got round to my experiences in the Marines. I enjoyed talking about this with most people I met. It gave me a sense of belonging. Even though I'd been out of the Marines for nearly four years by this time, I still missed it. It wasn't the discipline or the lifestyle so much; it was my fellow Marines. They were what being a Marine was all about.

By ten o'clock that night we were all well under the influence of alcohol and still thoroughly enjoying ourselves. We'd turned up the volume on our vibes box and were listening to some heavy rock music. This was much to the dismay of the hotel porter who had asked us several times to turn it down.

BANG BANG BANG, went a loud knock on the door.

'Just ignore it,' said Larry. 'It'll be that stupid porter again.'

Suddenly the door fell off its hinges under an immense blow from the other side. We all stopped talking and turned our attention to seeing who had done this. We saw that it was a Scotsman we knew called Andy. He looked angry and was standing in the doorway with the hotel porter and one of the senior Moroccan managers from the coatings plant.

'Turn that fucking music off now,' he demanded.

'Hey, don't be like that,' I replied. 'Come in and have a few beers with us.'

'I don't want your fucking beer,' he snapped. 'Turn that music off now.'

'What are you acting like this for?' Larry asked. 'And why have you kicked our door in?'

'Just turn that music off now,' he snarled and slapped Larry hard across the face.

The blow took Larry by surprise and totally knocked him off balance and onto the floor. At the same time his beer glass flew out of his hand and smashed against the wall. Then I saw Andy turn his attention to me, but I quickly anticipated an imminent attack and jumped up and hit him hard under the chin. His head went upwards and he fell back against the wooden railing at the top of the stairs. I ran at him and followed up with a powerful right-hand punch, which knocked his head through the railing and stunned him for a while. I turned and grabbed the Moroccan manager by the scruff of his neck, just as I saw the hotel porter running down the stairs.

'Please don't hit me,' the manager pleaded in poor English. 'It wasn't me who broke your door down.'

I saw Andy get back on his feet and released my grip on the Moroccan. He was right: I had no argument with him. Instead I ran down the stairs after Andy. When I got to the bottom, I saw him stood with three strange men who were dressed in uniform. It was fairly obvious that they were policemen. The hotel porter started shouting something in Arabic and the policemen surged towards me with big truncheons in their hands. They hit me hard several times but I chose not to retaliate. I knew that it would only make matters worse so I just took the beating they gave me. The truncheon blows just felt like hard thuds because my body was numb with alcohol. Eventually they realised that I wasn't looking to resist an arrest and they handcuffed my hands behind my back. A few minutes later they bundled me into the back of a van and drove me down to the police station. By the time we got there I felt very drunk and was finding it hard to stay awake. One of the policemen threw a bucket of cold water over me before two of them dragged me out of the van by my hair.

'You English pig,' one of them said. 'We're going to beat you again.'

The police station was small inside and had a front desk with several prison cells behind it. It was very similar to the guardrooms I had been used to in the Marines. Two of the policemen sat me down and were pulling my head about by my hair. Suddenly the third policeman reappeared and started shouting at them in Arabic. I don't know what he said but they stopped hurting me and both of them walked into an adjoining office and closed the door. I assumed the third man was more senior than they were and had ordered them to leave me alone.

'Are you OK?' he asked in fairly good English. 'We're not going to charge you with anything because nobody wants to press charges against you. I am also pleased you did not resist arrest.'

I nodded my head, feeling relieved. After all it was no fun getting the shit beaten out of me with my hands cuffed behind my back. The policeman removed my handcuffs and put me in one of the cells for the night. It was small inside, but I was only interested in getting into bed and going to sleep. The next morning I awoke early and looked up at the small window that allowed sunlight to shine into my cell. For a moment I felt like I was back in the Marines because the cell was exactly the same as the one I had spent two nights in during my court martial. Then I heard someone shouting in Arabic, which reminded me of where I was and the incident that had taken place the night before. My clothes were stained with blood and my head ached from the hangover I was suffering. A loud clanging noise startled me and I looked towards the cell door, where I saw one of the two policemen who had beaten me the night before. He gave me my wallet, my passport and a flight ticket to the UK.

'Go, Englishman. Go back to England now,' he shouted and punched me hard in the face.

The blow hurt, but I managed to absorb it. I quickly walked out of the cell and then left the building. The policeman followed me and pointed to a taxi that was parked on the other side of the road. I hurried towards it and climbed inside. The driver nodded his head when I sat down and drove off before I could mention that I wanted to be taken to the Spanish border. Several minutes later we arrived at the border and the driver informed me that Archie had already paid the fare. There was no sign of my suitcase, but I wasn't bothered because truthfully I just wanted to get out of the country.

Next I had to get past the Moroccan border police, who were stood in a small office where I would have to show my passport. When I got there, I saw two of them standing in the office with handguns fastened in holsters hanging from their hips. I recognised one of them as being the second of the two men who had beaten me the night before. He smiled when he saw me and vigorously snatched my passport out of my hand. He gritted his teeth and rubbed his truncheon under my bloodstained chin.

'Maybe we keep you here, Englishman,' he grinned. 'Maybe we put you in jail for a long time.'

I didn't reply. Instead I took a brief look towards the Spanish side of the border, which was a couple of hundred yards away. I could see a lone Spanish sentry stood there smoking a cigarette. The two policemen were stood looking at my passport photograph and one of them spat on it. They started talking in Arabic so I had no idea what they were planning. I could hear and see a big clock ticking on the wall behind them. Fuck this, I thought. When that second pointer lands on 12, I'm out of here.

One of the policemen spat on my passport photograph again. The two of them were standing right next to each other. Just as the second pointer on the clock landed on 12, I lunged forward and grabbed my passport. At the same time my body collided with the two men and they fell back against the wall. I turned and started running in zigzags towards Melilla and the Spanish border. A number of shots from their handguns fell around my feet but thankfully stopped as I neared the Spanish sentry on the other side. He stood shaking his head as he puffed on his cigarette and looked at my passport.

'Crazy Englishman. You are crazy.'

'Sometimes I am,' I grinned as he stamped one of the pages. 'Sometimes I am.'

CHAPTER TWELVE

THAILAND

I flew from Melilla to Malaga, and from there straight back to the UK. I had to abandon my luggage in Nador, but there was nothing much of value in it. I had to abandon my job, too, of course, but there wasn't too much bad feeling about this, and I got paid for what I did. I later heard that the coatings-plant owner was disappointed that I wasn't allowed to go back to work for him because the incident had nothing to do with him or his job.

Back in the UK I spent several months out of work and once again watched our savings dwindle. I was getting really fed up with losing jobs in this way but couldn't help resorting to violence every time somebody showed me aggression. I guess I was literally still a man of action rather than words. During this time I applied anywhere and everywhere for another job. I learned that it was better to send my resumé to an employment agency rather than a company, so I did this in bulk and literally posted hundreds of them through the Royal Mail.

I attended a couple of interviews. One was for a sales rep position but I felt disheartened when a young snotty-nosed 20 year old interviewed two of us at a time and spent most of the interview telling us how good he was. Next I went for an interview as a security guard at some local businessman's factory. When I arrived, I was met by him and a former Paratrooper who said he was keen to work with me. The Para seemed like a decent guy but I thought the businessman was an arsehole. Consequently I told him to shove the job up his arse.

Anne was waiting for me in the car outside. When I climbed into the car, she smiled at me.

'Did you get the job, Steve?'

'No. It wasn't right for me,' I sighed, pulling my jacket and tie off and throwing them onto the back seat.

As we made the journey home, I felt somewhat dismayed. We'd both worked very hard for the house we were living in, but unfortunately we literally had no money left to make the next mortgage payment. In fact our savings were a grand total of twenty-five pounds. I looked at Anne and breathed in deeply to prepare myself for what I was about to say to her.

'Anne, I'm sorry but we're going to have to sell the house. I just haven't got the money to support us,' I sighed deeply, feeling that I had let her down.

Anne turned her head slightly and looked at me. Then she looked back at the road and indicated before slowing down and pulling into a lay-by.

'I'm sorry, Anne,' I cried, with tears streaming down my face. 'I'm so sorry.'

Anne smiled and cuddled me. 'Don't worry about the house. It doesn't matter where we live as long as we're together. Sell the house; it's fine by me.'

I looked at her. She was a great woman, a great mother to my son and a great wife to me. I knew I was very lucky to have her, but I also knew that I needed to get a job somewhere soon.

We put the house up for sale and I spent the next few months working hard on my fitness. I met a guy at a local gym who worked in Angola. I told him I was an ex-Marine and he said that he knew some other ex-Marines who worked as mercenaries near his place of work. I saw him a month later and he told me that they knew me and were very keen to employ me to work with them. I made contact with one of them, who was called Ginge Barratt. I knew him well from my years in the Royal Marines. I also knew he was a guy whom I could depend on. Ginge told me to work hard at my fitness and said that he would be in touch in a few weeks' time. I did as he said and really stepped up my training routine. I saw the guy who worked in Angola again and he said that Ginge was overjoyed that I'd agreed to work with him and that he would call me at 3 p.m. the next Friday. When the day arrived, I went to the gym in the morning and worked out as usual. On the way back I saw a friend of mine leaning against his car, which had broken down, and I agreed to tow it home. Unfortunately this made me later than I had planned and Anne received the telephone call instead of me. When I walked through the door, I could sense her displeasure.

'You told me you were waiting for a phone call for a job, Steve,' she said in a calm voice.

'Yes. Has someone called for me?' I asked, knowing they had.

Tears started to stream down her face. She looked very sad indeed and held Gary in her arms, who was crying too.

'Steve, I've watched you fighting in your sleep. I've watched you drink yourself unconscious. I've seen you brawling in the street and sitting in the back garden in the rain, crying. I know you're unhappy because you can't get a job.'

'Anne, I need this job. I need it to support us. I won't get sacked from this job, Anne. I'm a Marine, Anne. I can't stop being a Marine. I'll be working with other Marines who understand me.'

'No, Steve. You're an ex-Marine now. You need to get the Marines out of your head.'

'But I can't, Anne. It's what I do. It's what I really am.'

'No, Steve,' she said in a cold calm voice. 'I'm not going to watch you go back to what you were when I first met you. I'm not; we're not,' she said, looking at our little boy. 'You have to think of us now. It's either the mercenaries or us. You can't have both.'

I didn't answer. I just walked out of the house and headed for a local pub. I drank a couple of beers and thought about my friend Ginge and the other guys I knew who were working with him. Then I thought about Anne and our son Gary. She's right, I thought. I have them to think of now. I want to go but I can't.

On the way home I thought about Ginge. I remembered when we were on a field patrol in Northern Ireland. We were sat in an observation post for two days watching the activity of a suspected terrorist in a farmhouse. Ginge nudged me.

'Steve, something doesn't feel right,' he said with a serious look on his face. 'I've got a gut feeling that something is wrong here.'

I looked at him and I looked all around. It was broad daylight and I could hear the sound of birds whistling and the wind gently blowing the long reeds of grass that surrounded us.

'Ginge, give your head a good shake, mate. There's nothing wrong.'

'No, Steve. It doesn't feel right. I want to move our position now.'

He looked very serious. He was a very good and experienced Marine and I fully respected him. I knew he felt strongly about this so I agreed to move. We quickly pinpointed another suitable location that we could see the farmhouse from and moved cautiously through the undergrowth of the grass reeds. About half an hour later we were in a new hide and began observing the farmhouse through our binos (binoculars) once again.

'Are you happy now, Ginge?' I asked with a sense of sarcasm.

'Yes, this feels better,' he smiled, just before we heard two successive loud explosions in the distance.

We looked around and saw that the position we had occupied earlier had been attacked by two mortar bombs.

'Fuck this, Steve,' frowned Ginge. 'We've been compromised. Let's get the hell out of here.'

I nodded my head. He was right. It was time to disappear.

All the way back from my local pub I walked with my hands in my pockets, dejected. I felt sad about the decision I had to make. My pride wanted me to go to Angola with Ginge and my heart wanted me to stay at home with my wife and child. By the time I got home I knew there was no choice really. I had a family to think of now. I had to move on with my life and to leave the soldiering behind.

When I walked through the door, I heard the telephone ring.

It was somebody from one of the employment agencies that I had sent my resumé to. They wanted me to go to work in Thailand and they wanted me to go the very next day. I accepted the offer and assured Anne it wasn't a ploy to bluff my way into Angola.

The next day I was on the aeroplane bound for Thailand. It was a long flight of about 13 hours, but eventually we landed in Bangkok. I found the climate to be hot and humid when I arrived and was surprised at the amount of beggars that lined the streets outside the airport. A taxi driver who displayed my name on a piece of card met me. He shook my hand and bowed. It was customary in this part of the world and was a courteous way of saying hello. We drove from Bangkok to Ayuthaya, which was Thailand's old capital city before Bangkok. Once there I went straight to the site I was working at and introduced myself to my new boss. He was called Dave and was a middle-aged Australian with black hair and a beard. Shortly after this I was driven to my hotel in a van along with several local Thai people. We arrived outside the hotel, which was called The Hotel Krungsri River, and I collected my suitcase from the driver. The hotel was very posh and fit for a king, I thought, but I was flabbergasted when I saw that the Thai workers were given some long tin sheets and told to make their own accommodation a few yards away under a nearby flyover.

I wasted very little time settling into my job and spent most of the time working on my own. I had to write and maintain a database tracking system that tracked all the pipes and related activities for laying an oil pipeline. To keep my physical fitness up to scratch I joined a local gymnasium. It was nothing special but it had all the equipment I needed and cost a full ten pence a session, which was a fantastic bargain by anyone's standards. Occasionally I went out on an evening for a few beers with an Englishman called Ronnie. He was in his late 50s and worked on a different part of the project to me.

At one point I developed a painful stomach bug and Ronnie laughed whilst he watched me trying to demonstrate that I had a problem with the toilet to a local chemist, so that he could give me some medication to help cure me. It appeared that most people initially suffered this fate and you could tell who the new guys were by the wet patch that showed in the seat of their trousers.

One night around Christmas (which is not really celebrated in Thailand) Ronnie took me to a bar that had a Thai boxing ring in the middle of it. We sat down and drank a few beers whilst we watched a couple of bouts that were taking place between the locals. At the end of the bouts a Thai spokesman stood up and spoke into a speaker. He spoke in Thai first and then in English. He said that the ring was open to challenges from anybody who was willing to take on his fighters. I sipped on my beer and thought about my days as a boxer in the mid-'80s. Generally I had been a good boxer and felt that I could still be a bit tasty now. I had done a bit of kick-boxing too, in the past, but I knew the Thais were infamous for using their knees and elbows. No one chose to step forward from the crowd to take up the challenge until the spokesman said that there was a prize of a hundred pounds for the winner. This made my mind up for me. I was still very sharp and fit and, most of all, I needed the money.

I stepped forward and raised my hand into the air. 'I'll have some of that,' I shouted.

'Are you crazy?' gasped Ronnie. 'These guys are professionals. They'll pulverise you.'

'No they won't,' I smiled.

'But you've drank about four pints of beer.'

'Don't worry about it, Ronnie. Beer is like petrol to me. The more I drink, the more energy I've got.'

Ronnie shook his head. 'You're crazy, Steve.'

'I know. People keep reminding me of that.'

The spokesman kitted me out with some shorts, boots and a vest. He also offered me some head protection but I declined to use it: an uncushioned head could come in handy.

My first fight was against a small Thai boxer. He was a lot shorter than me and very skinny. When we started fighting, he hit me about eight times before I hit him with a few combinations of my own. He was fast but he packed very little power in his blows and I made short work of him, knocking him out in the second round.

'Bloody hell,' exclaimed Ronnie with a shocked look on his face. 'You're a bit tasty with your fists, Steve.'

'I know, mate. Pass me my pint,' I asked him.

I removed my gloves and drank a full pint of beer. I was very thirsty and downed it in one go, just as the spokesman announced that there was another challenger.

I nodded my head to accept the challenge and saw a European guy step forward. He was about the same age and build as me and he had a skinhead. At first I thought he was English but then I saw a French flag on his vest and guessed by his many tattoos that he was a former French Legionnaire. The spokesman announced the guy as The Legionnaire and asked me what my name was. I was a bit surprised at this because he hadn't done so for my first fight.

'They call me Green Death,' I told him. This was a nickname that the Navy sometimes used when they were describing someone who had crossed the Marines and had consequently felt their wrath.

DING DING went the bell and we both met in the middle and banged our gloves together. The Frenchman looked deep into my eyes with a wicked grin on his face. He had a few scars and he smiled to expose a couple of missing teeth.

'I fight to win, English,' he grinned. 'I was a Legionnaire.'

I nodded and looked him in the eyes. His missing teeth made me think that he hadn't always been the victor in his fights. I bet he had a drawer full of runner-up medals. As far as boxing went, we were pretty well matched but the Frenchman was a lot better than me with his feet, knees and elbows. I exchanged combinations of punches with him but he gave me a lot of punishment with his knees and feet. The blows just felt like dull thuds because of the amount of beer I had consumed. At the end of the first round I retired to my corner, where I found Ronnie sat with a sponge and a bucket of water. He slapped the wet sponge on my head and squeezed it so that the water ran down my face. Then he dried it off with a towel.

'How did you end up in my corner?' I panted.

'I volunteered. I've been told that this French guy is pretty hot around here. He's come to fight a Thai champion called Wishad, but the Thai has been delayed until tomorrow so he wants to use you as practice.

'Cheeky bastard,' I snarled. 'Have you got a drink for me? I'm absolutely parched.'

'Yes. I've got some water.'

'Sod the water, mate. I want a drink of beer and quick because the bell will go any second.'

Ronnie quickly passed me a bottle of beer and I swilled half of it down before the bell rang for the second round. I passed the bottle back to Ronnie and he pushed a gumshield into my mouth. I had no idea where he got it from but it made me feel a lot more confident.

The Frenchman came out fighting and started throwing everything at me. He hit me with flurries of punches, kicks and blows from his elbows. I just kept my cool and used my boxing skills to block a lot of what he threw at me. I hit him low with a roundhouse kick and he lost his balance and fell onto the floor. Normally a referee would stand between you in a boxing ring, but there was no referee and the rules here were different. I stood back and let him get up, just as the bell rang to signal the end of the round.

This time Ronnie slapped the wet sponge on my head with one hand and pulled my gumshield out with the other. It was as if he'd been doing it for years. Next he grabbed a bottle of beer and pushed it into my mouth.

'You should've hit him when he went down, Steve. That's what they do here.'

I shrugged my shoulders. I knew this was a more lawless type of boxing, but I didn't realise there were no rules at all. Maybe that's why this guy has no teeth, I thought. Ronnie pushed my gumshield back into my mouth and the bell rang again.

DING DING.

This was the third and final round. I felt exhausted and

drained from the heat and humidity and walked out slowly to meet my opponent once more in the middle of the ring.

'LEGIONNAIRE, LEGIONNAIRE, LEGIONNAIRE,' chanted the crowd that had gathered. They obviously knew him.

'Come on, Green Death,' shouted Ronnie, trying to give me some support.

We met in the middle and banged gloves once more to signal the third and final round. The Frenchman looked at me. His eyes were full of hate and he looked like he wanted to kill me.

'You should have finished it, Englishman. I fight to win,' he snarled.

'So do I,' I snapped back at him. 'Come on. Come on!' I growled as I started to get angry.

The Frenchman came at me with a kick and then followed it up with a couple of punches. I managed to block them and could hear him panting and fighting hard to suck in some air, the same as I was.

I threw two good successive punches at him which both connected with the side of his face, causing a wound to open from a cut on his eyebrow. He looked up and stepped back for a moment. Then he lunged at me and kicked me hard in the bollocks. A pain shot though my lower abdomen and my head dropped down a little. He saw his opportunity and followed up with a hard upper-cut, which hit me in the mouth. One of my lips burst and blood dripped from my mouth. Thankfully the gumshield that Ronnie had given me earlier cushioned the blow.

I looked up and saw the Frenchman pause for a moment. He was using some valuable seconds to breathe in some air. I knew what to do and instantly lunged at him with my forehead, which connected heavily with the end of his nose. This was why I'd rejected the headgear. I felt his nose crack under the blow and head-butted him again in the same spot. The blow was deadly and he fell backwards onto the canvass. Blood oozed out of both of his nostrils and he rolled around holding his face with his hands. I waited for a few moments and used the time to breathe in some air. I looked around for someone to count him out, but that rule didn't apply either. Instead the Frenchman looked towards the spokesman, who was stood outside the ring, and shook his head. The spokesman nodded to acknowledge the Frenchman's defeat and I heard the bell ring. The crowd went wild and were shouting loudly, 'GREEN DEATH, GREEN DEATH, GREEN DEATH, GREEN DEATH.'

Ronnie passed me a bottle of water, which I threw onto the floor and grabbed the bottle of beer from his other hand. I drank it and could taste the blood that was still dripping from my mouth.

'That was some nut you stuck on him, Steve. Have you used that much in your past?'

'What do you think?' I panted and climbed out of the ring.

After the fight I took a shower, which was available on the premises, and got changed back into my clothes. My body ached all over and I felt exhausted. I sat at a table with Ronnie and the spokesman gave me two hundred pounds prize money for my two fights. He said he had been impressed with my performance and that I could earn five times that if I fought Wishad. I thought about it for a bit and then agreed to return in two weeks' time. Next I saw the Frenchman coming towards me. His nose was badly swollen and he had two black eyes. He held one hand behind his back and the other out to shake my hand. I felt wary about the hand behind his back and readied myself to retaliate if he held something to attack me with. He smiled at me, exposing his missing teeth once more, and produced something that he was holding behind his back. Thankfully and to my relief it was a bottle of champagne.

'You fight to win, Green Death. You fight to win,' he said and gave me a friendly hug and a pat on the back. 'Good luck,' he gestured before he turned and walked away.

The next morning I awoke later than normal and limped into work. My body ached all over from the injuries I had sustained as well as from all the alcohol I had consumed.

'You look like shit, Steve,' Dave grimaced.

'Yes. I fell over last night. I had too much to drink.'

'Yes, of course you did, Green Death. Now go back to your hotel and get some sleep.'

I nodded my head and limped back to my hotel room, where I slept through till the next day. A couple of days later I was feeling a lot better and decided to go back to the boxing bar to watch Wishad. I thought this would be a good idea, given that I was booked to fight against him in just over a week's time. When I got there, I remained in the background and watched the spokesman as he introduced Wishad to the crowd as a champion. I looked on as my future opponent stepped into the ring. He was about the same height and build as the Frenchman but was a lot more muscular. I watched him as he fought three opponents that night. His kickboxing skills were phenomenal and he easily defeated each of them within two rounds. One of them suffered a broken jaw and the other two broken ribs. I felt nervous, but still intended to take him on for the chance to win one thousand pounds prize money.

The next night was New Year's Eve, so I went into town at Ronnie's request to celebrate with him. We found a bar called Knock on Wood. It resembled a cowboy saloon and had a band who were dressed up as Mexicans playing country and western music. We spent most of the evening there and were eventually joined by one of the local Thai employees, who was called Joe. Joe was a biker and frequently took part in motorbike races with the neighbouring villagers.

Ronnie and I drank like there was no tomorrow and were heavily intoxicated by the time midnight struck. Suddenly everybody started to cheer and to wish each other a happy new year. Ronnie grabbed me and wrapped his arms around me. At first I thought he was trying to give me a hug, but then I realised he was so drunk that his legs were giving way and he was using me to hold himself up.

'Happy new year, Steve,' he slurred heavily, just as a load of confetti was released from containers in the ceiling and party poppers were going off everywhere.

'Happy new year, mate,' I replied with a lesser slur and slowly lowered him down into a wooden chair.

'Good year to you, Steve,' smiled Joe as he put his hands together and bowed his head.

I also put my hands together and bowed. My beer glass was empty so I staggered over to the bar to order another round. When I got there, I stood next to one of the local Thai townsfolk, who was also waiting to buy a round of beer. He was a short guy with black curly hair. He smiled at me. I returned the warm smile and patted him lightly on the back of his head with the palm of my hand.

Suddenly he started screaming something at me in a loud and angry voice. I didn't know what he was shouting or why he was doing this. I felt completely confused and thought hard about what had happened during our brief meeting. I watched him as he pointed at his head and the reason for his anger dawned on me. Ronnie had once told me that you should never touch anybody's head here because they believe that the sacred spiritual life-force is in there and that to touch it is a great insult.

I looked around and saw three other Thai men coming towards me. They each held a machete in their hands and had their eyes firmly focused on me. My heart felt as if it had stopped and fear shot through the whole of my body. It was time for fight or flight, and flight seemed like the best option to me. I bolted out through the swing doors that marked the entrance to the bar. They banged hard against the walls as I pushed them open. Outside it was dark and the streets were littered with people. I saw a man sat on a motorbike. He was one of the local taxi drivers who used their bikes as taxis. I ran towards him and jumped onto the bike behind him. I put the bike into gear, let out the clutch and pulled the rider's hand back hard on the accelerator. The rider was startled as we started to speed off, but I held on tight to him and the bike. I could hear other motorbikes roaring behind me. It was my assailants. Unfortunately the bike I was on had a very small engine and only travelled about 20 miles an hour. It made a loud spluttering noise as we sped down a long dark alley. My assailants rode scrambling bikes and caught up with us within a few minutes. The rider I was hanging onto pulled hard on the brakes and the bike came to an abrupt halt.

The way ahead was a dead end and I saw that there was

nowhere to run. The only way out was past the three men who had climbed off their bikes and were walking towards me with their machetes held in the air. To say I was frightened would have been an understatement. I felt petrified and actually accepted the fact that I was going to die. Then I heard another motorbike engine that was accelerating fast towards us. It screeched to a halt just behind the three men, who started shouting at the driver in their own language. The mystery rider's face came into view and I saw that it was my friend Joe. All three of the men were screaming at him and pointing at me with their weapons. One of them started to run towards me. He was screaming something in Thai and was preparing to swing his machete at me. Suddenly a shot from a pistol filled the air and everybody stopped still. The man who had been running towards me started shouting at Joe and Joe fired another round close to his feet. Then he walked forward, shouting at the men and pointing the gun at them.

I don't know what he said because I couldn't speak their language, but I watched with relief as my three assailants got back onto their bikes and rode back down the long alley and out of sight. I sighed with a great sense of relief.

'Thanks, Joe.'

He nodded his head and told me to get on the back of his bike. I did what he said and he gave me a lift back to my hotel. Thankfully the hotel had night guards so I knew I would be safe once I'd got inside.

Joe's motorbike came to a halt opposite the building and he shook my hand.

'Steve, you must leave Thailand very soon. Those men are bad people. They will kill you for sure if they see you again.'

I nodded my head to assure him that I fully understood what he was saying to me and I walked past the security guard and back inside the safe walls of my hotel. Once inside my room I picked up the telephone and called Anne at home in England.

It was very late where I was but the time difference meant that it was six hours earlier in the UK.

'Hello, Anne. I'm in trouble,' I said in a desperate voice.

'Oh no, Steve. What have you done now?'

'I've upset the local Thai people. They're going to cut me to pieces with machetes. They're going to kill me.'

I was very drunk and the room started to spin. I shifted my position on my bed and fell backwards and onto the floor. Suddenly everything went black and I fell into a state of unconsciousness.

The next day I awoke around 9 a.m. and looked up at the ceiling. My back ached because I had slept on the floor, so I stood up and walked around my room. Well, I'm still in one piece, I thought, but I need to get my act together and get out of here today.

I saw the telephone receiver was off the hook so I replaced it before I stepped into the shower to get washed and to try to sober myself up. Later that day I picked up the telephone and called Dave to explain the situation to him. I told him that I needed to collect my wages and go home. However, this wasn't that straightforward because the agency I was employed through, which was called Vectorine, had not paid up. I felt very disappointed because they owed me around five thousand pounds.

'There is another idea,' said Dave.

'What's that?' I asked desperately.

'I can send you to the other site at the other end of the pipeline. It's a long way from here. You will get paid by a different agency.'

'Well, the answer is yes, Dave. I have no choice.'

Thirty minutes later a company car came to collect me and drove me to a place called Siracha, where I checked into another hotel. Later I was driven to the works site in Chonburi by one of the pipeline drivers and was introduced to the management team, who were all Australians. These people turned out to be some of the most professional people I had met since leaving the Marines nearly five years before. They worked hard, they drank hard and they always maintained a good sense of humour. I seemed to fit in with them like a hand into a glove.

One evening after I'd finished working out in the hotel gym I took a shower and went into a coffee bar to get something to eat. It was cool inside and a Thai female singer dressed in traditional Thai dress provided some light entertainment. The atmosphere inside was relaxed. A waiter came over to serve me with a drink. He looked at the Royal Marines T-shirt I was wearing and stared at my bulging biceps.

'You same same Lambo,' he nodded.

I knew he was referring to Rambo, starring Sylvester Stallone, which was about a former American Green Beret.

'Well, I suppose to you, my friend, I am a bit like Rambo. I'm a former Royal Marine Commando.'

'You Lambo,' he insisted, nodding his head.

The waiter said his name was Wood and told me that he was a queer. He continued to stare at my biceps and insisted on pouring my beer all the time. I found this amusing because he filled my glass up to the top every time it was nearly empty.

'You can look but don't touch,' I told him. 'If you touch, I kill you,' I laughed.

Another thing I found funny was that every time I went to the toilet to take a leak a well-dressed Thai gentleman placed a warm towel over the back of my neck and started massaging the backs of my shoulders and the backs of my legs. At first I felt offended but then realised that it was his way of making a living, so I started pointing at my back for a massage every time I relieved myself. The only downfall with this was that sometimes it tickled and caused me to shudder and to urinate onto my shoes.

After a few nights in the coffee bar Wood became more familiar with me and understood that I would kick the shit out of him if he touched me.

'English Steve, Lambo,' he smiled.

'What do you want, Wood?'

'How you say English gleeting?'

He was asking how he would greet someone in English. I saw this as an ideal opportunity to take the piss and jumped at the opportunity.

'You say good evening, sir. I am hung like a donkey,' I told him.

An hour later the team of Australians entered the bar. They saw me and came over to sit with me.

'Hello, Steve, mate. Is this where you hang out?' one of them said.

I smiled and nodded my head, just as Wood came rushing over to greet them.

'Good evening, sirs. I hung like a honkey,' he smiled.

The Aussies burst into hysterical laugher and were literally slapping their sides and holding their ribs. Even funnier was the fact that Wood had pronounced the word donkey as honkey.

Wood didn't look very impressed at all and scurried off out of sight. Later the Aussies left and bid me goodnight. I drank a few more beers and decided to go back to my hotel room to get some sleep. Then Wood came towards me. He was crying and had tears streaming down his cheeks.

'What's the matter, Wood?' I asked him.

'I not hung like a honkey,' he answered, holding his hands up to express the size of a donkey's penis.

'Don't worry, mate,' I smiled at him. 'Who knows, you might be one day when you grow a little.'

He grinned and bowed towards me to show me that he still respected me. I bowed back towards him before I left the bar for the evening.

The next day at work I joked with the Australians as usual and then had a serious discussion with them to agree how they wanted me to adjust the tracking database to enable it to produce the progress reports they needed. Afterwards I stepped out of their office and walked towards mine. On the way I saw a motorbike rider dressed in black leathers stop his bike a few yards in front of me and get off his bike. He was wearing a helmet with its dark sunscreen visor pulled down, hiding his face. This was unusual. Most people here never even wore helmets because it wasn't against the law. He walked towards me, stopped a few paces away and reached inside his jacket. I stared at him as he produced a sawn-off shotgun and pointed it in my direction. They've found me, I thought. It's one of the bikers from Ayuthaya. The gun went off and there was a loud bang. I heard something fall behind me and turned around to look. A Thai worker was on his knees, holding his stomach. He had blood gushing like a fountain from a gaping wound in his abdomen. I turned and looked back at the biker, who had put his gun away and was casually walking back to his bike. I breathed a deep sigh of relief as I watched him look back as he sped off and out of sight. The injured man was now lying face down in a pool of blood. I knelt down and felt for a pulse in his neck, but unfortunately he didn't have one. For a few moments I thought he had taken a bullet instead of me, but I learnt from the Australians that he was the cousin of another Thai worker who owed the local mafia some money. Apparently, I was told, the mafia start to kill the relations of people who owe them money to convince the debtor to pay up. A great way to get rid of relations you don't like, I thought.

A week later my contract came to an end and I was on the aeroplane heading home. I felt relieved that I had got out in one piece and nodded my head when I thought about my potential fight with Wishad. Yes, I thought, if the locals hadn't killed me, I'm pretty sure he would have!

When the aeroplane landed in the UK, Anne and my son Gary, who to my delight was now walking without aid towards me, met me at the airport. I hugged them both and was overjoyed to be reunited with them.

A few days later I sat stewing on the fact that the Vectorine agency still owed me a lot of money. I'd been told by other people who had been working for them in Thailand that I wouldn't get paid and that I should take out a lawsuit against them. I discussed this with my brother Martin and he told me that the pen is mightier than the sword. That might have been true, but at that time I couldn't afford the cost of a good solicitor to use one.

Instead I made a spontaneous decision whilst walking past the Vectorine office in Gateshead with my wife, who was pushing Gary's buggy. I stopped and paused for a moment as I stared at the Vectorine sign, which hung above their office doorway.

'What have we stopped for?' asked Anne with a puzzled look on her face.

'That's the agency that owes me five grand. I'm going inside to get my money. Wait here and leave quickly if you see any cars with blue flashing lights on the roof.'

Anne sighed and looked at me seriously. 'Steve, let's just go home.'

'No. I want my money. I earned it and I want it,' I insisted.

Then I walked up to Vectorine's door and pulled it open. Once inside I went up some stairs and along a corridor to a room labelled Reception. A young lady who was dressed in a smart cream suit greeted me.

'Hello, sir. Can I help you?' she smiled.

'Hi, my name is Steven. I'm looking for the managing director.'

'Are you looking for work, sir?'

'No. I'm looking for the managing director.'

'Oh, I am sorry, sir, but he's in a meeting discussing business with some gentlemen over there in one of our meeting rooms,' she told me, pointing to a room on the opposite side of the corridor. 'He's going to be a while yet. Do you want to leave a message?' she continued.

'No thank you.'

'OK, sir,' she smiled again. 'Have a nice day.'

Then she walked into another room behind her. I turned around and looked at the meeting-room door. I could see several gentlemen who were dressed in suits talking to each other across a long table. I felt like walking away, but decided not to because I wanted my money. I opened the door and stepped inside.

'Excuse me, sir, can I help you?' a short skinny man with grey hair asked me.

'I'm looking for the Vectorine managing director.'

'That's me, sir. Can you make this quick? I'm busy having a meeting.'

'Yes, with me,' I snapped. 'I've just got back from Thailand and you owe me money. Five grand, to be exact.'

'Err, excuse me, gentlemen. I won't be a minute,' he said to the other men. 'There appears to be a misunderstanding here.'

He pointed to the door and we both walked outside and closed it. He wiped his forehead with a handkerchief and cleared his throat.

'Err, what's your name?' he stammered nervously.

'It's Steve Preece and you owe me five grand.'

'Look, if you leave your address with my receptionist, I'll ensure you get your money next week,' he said, trying to raise a smile.

'No way, mate. You either give me my money now or I'm going to smash your fucking head in and ransack your office.'

'Oh. I haven't got any money here. Will you take a cheque?'

'No I won't,' I snapped, showing my teeth. 'Give me my money now or I'll punch your teeth so hard that they'll come out of your arse and bite you,' I snapped again and grabbed hold of him by his tie and shook him.

'I've . . . I've only got a cheque book.'

'That's not a problem. The bank is just around the corner. Let's go now,' I growled and dragged him out of the entrance door and into the street.

Several minutes later we were in the bank and the man drew five thousand pounds out of his account and gave it to me. I walked outside with him and back towards his office. I looked around for Anne but she was nowhere to be seen. The managing director looked at me and raised his hand to offer a handshake. I grabbed it and squeezed it tight.

'AARRGGHH,' he squealed.

'The pen may be mightier than the sword, but the sword is sharper than the pen,' I snarled at him. He looked puzzled at my words and ran in through the office door and locked it shut behind him.

I never worked for Vectorine again and some time later I heard that it had gone into liquidation. Apparently there were several lawsuits filed against it by other former employees whom they owed money to. I think I was the only one who actually got paid!

CHAPTER THIRTEEN

BUSINESS PROPOSITION

Sweat dripped down my face as I pounded away on a running machine at the local gym. I'd been out of work for several months again and my savings were starting to dwindle. I was fed up and desperately needed to get back into work. I'd been out of the Marines for nearly five years now, but I continued to work hard to maintain a high level of physical fitness. After my workout I got in my car and drove home.

As I opened the door, I heard the telephone ring and answered it. It was a guy called Lee who was an old piping inspector and also a dab hand with writing computer tracking systems. He was one of the partners who had previously set up a limited company with Darris and then folded it because Darris couldn't be trusted. Lee was in his late 50s and was still keen to make a success of supplying computer tracking systems to the oil industry. To my delight he made me an offer to set up a limited company with him and to be his partner. Obviously I jumped at the chance and accepted his proposal.

Following this we attended a course at a local college and learned the ins and outs of starting up in business. The course instructors also acted as consultants and offered their services at a cost to our limited company to help us to obtain start-up funds. One of them was a black guy called Neville. He told us that he needed to fly from Newcastle to London to visit a Japanese bank to discuss acquiring a loan for our company. He said that he would be back in a few days and would charge us a consultancy fee of five hundred pounds. Lee and I sat together discussing our business plan.

'Steve, please pay attention. You're not listening to what I'm saying to you,' he said seriously, nudging me with his hand.

'Sorry, Lee. I just can't seem to get my head around Neville needing to fly to London to discuss the possibility of getting a loan for us. Why can't he just apply over the telephone?'

'What are you insinuating, Steve? Are you trying to accuse Neville of ripping us off?'

'I'm not sure, but Neville said he was going to spend a few days at home in Africa after he had visited the Japanese bank on our behalf. It sounds like he's using us to pay for the first leg of his journey.'

'No, Steve, don't be silly. He's a professional consultant.'

'He's a professional con man,' I snapped.

Following our conversation I obtained the telephone number for the Japanese bank and gave them a call. The bank confirmed my suspicions and said that they had never heard of Neville.

When he returned from his trip, he told us he had been unable to convince the bank to loan us some money, but would still have to charge us for his consultancy. He handed us an invoice for five hundred pounds, at which point I informed him of my telephone conversation with the bank. He glared at me for a few long moments and then looked at his watch. He said nothing and quietly left the room. We waited for a while for him to return, but he didn't, so we left.

We were annoyed on our way out, but I suggested to Lee that we could obtain the necessary funding by selling the story to the newspapers. Lee disagreed, so we still needed to seek a bank that would loan us some money to get started. We succeeded in booking a bank interview, but we didn't end up borrowing any money because Lee told me he wanted 51 per cent of the shares and wanted to be the senior partner. He said he still thought about the way Darris had let him down the last time he'd formed a limited company and that he wanted to be sure it never happened again. I felt very disappointed at his lack of trust in me and told him that we were either equal partners or not partners at all. After a long discussion he agreed that any partnership we'd go on to make would be on equal terms.

In the weeks that followed we both worked hard on writing new computer tracking systems and put together a brochure to advertise them to the oil companies. The Australian oil company I had previously worked for in Thailand expressed great interest in our enhanced systems and offered us a one-hundred-thousand-pound support contract on a forthcoming pipeline project. We were thrilled to bits and Lee said that he would write up a contract with the company and would agree start dates.

Four weeks passed and I still hadn't heard anything from Lee. I telephoned him and he said he hadn't agreed the contract yet but would do it very soon. A week later I called him again and found that he still hadn't done it so I called the Australians myself. The manager expressed great disappointment that he hadn't heard from Lee as previously agreed and said that the project had to start without a tracking system. He concluded that he would be happy to deal directly with me, without Lee, but I declined his offer because I didn't want to let Lee down.

Consequently, my savings were running out once again and I vigorously searched for another job. Eventually, I got offered a six-week contract working as a mechanical inspector in an oil refinery in the south of England. I jumped at the chance and was put in touch with two other inspectors who would be working on the same contract. The two of them agreed to hire a car to use for transport to get down to the refinery. A couple of days later I packed my bag and said goodbye to Anne and Gary before making my way to an agreed location where my two work colleagues would pick me up in the car. It was a cold wintery morning and sleet fell all around. My body shivered as it fought to keep me warm until eventually the hire car arrived. The journey south was a long one and we talked about the feast-and-famine lifestyle we experienced as contractors. It was late when we arrived and another contractor met us at the refinery gates. He knew one of the guys I had travelled with and informed us that the agreed hourly wage had been cut by two thirds. My two friends were angered by the news and said that they were going straight back home. Unfortunately I had very little money left in the bank to support my family with and had no choice but to stay.

The contractor who was driving the car looked at me. 'Are you staying, Steve?'

I nodded my head. 'Yes.'

'Well we're not. Give me twenty pounds towards the cost of the hire car and we'll be on our way.'

'I've only got twenty pounds to live on, mate. Can I post it to you after I get paid?'

'No, you can't. I haven't got much money either.'

I sighed deeply and handed over my twenty-pound note. A few minutes later I watched the car accelerate in the opposite direction and out of sight. I walked into the refinery and explained who I was to the security guards who let me enter the grounds.

The job wasn't scheduled to start until the following day so I looked for an open shed to sleep in for the night. There were lots of sheds inside the complex, but all were locked. I looked around an open field with small trees in it and plastic bin liners blowing around it. I collected the bags and some dead wood and built myself a small shelter out of them, which was basically just a wooden frame with the bags tied around it. When I'd finished, I climbed inside to try to keep warm. The shelter actually offered me good protection from the cold blustery wind.

Suddenly I heard the noise of a vehicle outside and poked my head through a gap in the plastic bags to see who it was. The headlights from the vehicle dazzled me, and then I heard someone climb out of the vehicle and walk towards me. Shit, I thought, it's the security guards. They're going to throw me off the site.

'Excuse me,' said a middle-aged man who approached. 'The security guards said you'd know the whereabouts of the new mechanical inspectors.'

I climbed out of my shelter and stood up. 'Three of them have gone home because the pay has been cut. I'm the only one left,' I said with a shiver.

'Oh,' he grunted, looking around the open field. 'What on earth are you doing inside that thing?'

'I'm using it as a shelter. I have no money because I had to give my last twenty pounds to the guy who hired the car to get us down here.'

'Bloody hell, mate,' he exclaimed. 'It's freezing out here. Are you really going to spend the night inside there?'

'Yes,' I nodded.

'Who told you that they've cut the pay?'

'One of the inspectors who left as we arrived.'

'Come on, mate,' said the man, pointing to his van. 'Get in and let's get this sorted out.'

About an hour later I found out that this man was a fairly senior manager within the company and he spoke to the subcontracting company who were carrying out this piece of work for him. He insisted that they pay me the agreed rate and give me an advance. My fortune got even better as he booked me into a nearby hotel and loaned me the van he was driving for the duration of the contract.

A few days later a lot more contractors joined me and I moved out of the hotel and into some holiday chalets in a place called Canvey Island. The company that owned them let them out to contractors from the refinery during the winter months only.

In the evenings I worked out in a gym that I had joined and went into a local pub for a few beers. One night in the pub I was sat amongst a group of men who were watching a football match on the television. The teams playing were Newcastle United and Crystal Palace. A player from Newcastle scored a goal and I jumped up and cheered.

'Get in,' I shouted, as I thrust my hand into the air.

The group of men I was sat amongst didn't move and began to stare at me. One of them had short blond hair and a prominent square chin. He stood up and walked towards me. He had a serious look on his face and his fists were clenched.

'Are you a Newcastle fan?' he asked, staring into my eyes.

'Yes, I am.'

'Who the fuck said you can come in here and sit with us?'

'I did,' I answered calmly.

'Do you know who I am?' he asked, and a couple of his mates started giggling behind him.

'I don't care who you are, mate,' I assured him.

'Fucking deck him, John,' interrupted one of his friends. 'He's a fucking northerner.'

He swung his fist hard towards me and it connected with the side of my head. I grabbed his arm and swung a hard head-butt into his face, which caused him to fall back amongst his friends. My aggression intensified and I started to scream at the group with my fists clenched.

'COME ON THEN IF YOU WANT TO FIGHT ME. FUCKING COME ON!'

I moved towards the crowd, which quickly dispersed. My aggression seemed to frighten the hell out of them and they ran for the doors. The man I had just head-butted got up holding his face with both hands. He stood looking at me and seemed unsure what to do.

I walked up to him. 'Like I said, mate. I don't care who you are.'

He looked startled and ran out through the exit like the others. Just as he left, a barman came over and gave me a pint of beer.

'Here you are, mate. This is for you,' he smiled.

'What for?' I asked curiously.

'For walloping that arsehole with the blond hair. He's the local hard man, but I think he more than met his match today.'

I nodded my head and gratefully accepted the pint of beer offered to me by the barman. I sat down to watch the remainder of the football match and was pleased to see that Newcastle won the game 3–2.

At the end of my contract I gave the company I was working for one of our tracking-system brochures and gave them a demonstration of how it worked. The demonstration impressed them so much that they verbally agreed a support contract worth fifty thousand pounds. I felt great when I drove home and went straight round to Lee's house to tell him the good news. He was pleased too and said that he would put the agreement in writing and send it to the company's director.

I felt sceptical about this because of the last fiasco, but had to agree with him because I had to go to Denmark for a few weeks on another short-term contract. When I returned from this, I played back a message on my telephone-answering machine. It was from the director of the company I had worked for previously. His message was to give him a call. When I spoke to him, he informed me that Lee had doubled the costs I had agreed with them, so he no longer wished to do business with us. I racked my brains wondering what Lee had been playing at. Either he was trying to make up for losing the previous contract in Thailand, or he was just being greedy. Whichever it was, though, he'd messed up again, so I resigned from the limited company we formed and Lee and I went our separate ways.

CHAPTER FOURTEEN

THE SCAM

Money soon became an issue again as I spent yet another long spell out of work. This time the reason was that the steel industry had fallen into decline. I spent my days working out in the local gymnasium. Money might have been in short supply but my keenness for physical exercise wasn't. I tended to watch videos about the Marines before I went training because it put me in the right frame of mind and boosted my determination to work hard. Additionally I always took a portable stereo with me and played loud music that reminded me of my days as a Marine in the 1980s.

Gary was starting to grow now and was comfortably running and playing around the garden. I watched him as he laughed to himself and ran round the side of the house. I heard him chuckle and followed him to see what he was up to. Suddenly my mouth dropped open and fear shot through my body as I clearly saw him standing a few feet away holding a razor blade in his hand. He opened his mouth and brought the blade towards it.

'NO!' I yelled at him and rushed forward with my hands outstretched. I grabbed his arm just as the razor blade touched his lips and thankfully he remained unharmed. I stood looking at the blade as Gary trundled off to play in another part of the garden. I wondered how it could have possibly ended up here. We lived in a quiet close where it was highly unlikely that someone would walk up to the house and throw a single razor blade down the side of it. A scraping noise distracted my thoughts. I looked up above the garden fence and saw the nine-year-old boy who lived next door peering over the roof of his father's shed.

'Did you throw this over the fence?' I asked him, holding the razor blade up with my fingers.

He stood up on top of the shed roof and shrugged his shoulders. I noticed he had a silly grin on his face and remembered that Anne once said she'd told him off for pointing a spud gun over the fence and firing it in Gary's direction.

'Well, did you do this?' I repeated my question.

He shrugged his shoulders again and climbed down off the shed roof onto the dustbin that was near the fence. The kid looked down at the bin and then at me before shrugging his shoulders again. Because of his body language I felt fairly certain that he had pulled the razor blade out of the bin and thrown it over the fence. I also noticed that there were blonde hairs on the blade and knew that his mother had blonde hair. I felt angry: very angry. This stupid kid could have killed my son.

'Go and get your father now,' I yelled at him, pointing towards the back door of his house. 'Go on,' I insisted and he turned and ran into the house.

A minute later the kid came back outside again and his father, who was called Matthew, followed close behind him. Matthew was a tall skinny man in his mid-30s. He had black curly hair and a long protruding nose. He hardly ever spoke to me unless he couldn't avoid it.

'What are you shouting at my lad for? He said you've accused him of throwing something over your fence,' he said in a not-really-interested tone of voice.

'It's quite serious actually, Matthew. Your son has thrown a razor blade over my fence and my little boy picked it up and nearly put it in his mouth.'

To my surprise Matthew started to grin. 'How do you know it was him? It could have been anybody,' he commented, standing with his hands on his hips.

'It has to be him,' I replied seriously. 'Nobody would walk into a quiet cul-de-sac, walk up to my house and throw a single razor blade over the wall, would they? Anyway, it's got blonde hairs on it and your wife has blonde hair.'

He grinned again. 'Actually she uses an electric razor to shave her legs with.'

'You're not taking this bloody serious are you?' I snapped, feeling annoyed at his cocky attitude. 'This could have cost my son his life.'

'No need to get shirty,' he smirked, staring directly into my eyes.

His negative remarks and attitude enraged me and I leaned over the fence and grabbed a tight hold of his hair. I grabbed his clothing with my other hand and dragged him hard and fast over the top of the garden fence. The movement caused his head to bang against the wall of my house and I scraped his face up and down it a couple of times.

'That's what I call shirty, Matthew,' I yelled at him. 'That's what I call shirty.'

After this I pushed him back over his side of the fence and shouted at him again.

'If you or your family ever come anywhere near my son again, I'm going to pulverise you.'

Matthew didn't reply and didn't hang around any longer. Instead he ran back into his house and slammed the door shut behind him. Gary ran into my legs and I picked him up and hugged him.

'Steve,' shouted Anne. 'Where are you?'

'I'm here, Anne,' I smiled. 'I've just been talking to Matthew next door.'

'There's a phone call for you. I think it's a man who wants to offer you a job.'

I picked up the telephone receiver and spoke to a man called Henry Schultz, who was calling from a private employment agency in Holland called OilTrack. He told me that there was a big contract coming up in Thailand, which involved the building of oil platforms for an oil company who were based in Guam. He said that there would be around 30 people hired for the job and that they would consist of welders, pipe fitters and labourers. He went on to say that he wanted to hire me to write and maintain a computer tracking system that could be used to track the materials that would be needed and used to put the structure together. He finished by saying that a local guy called Benjamin would be responsible for putting the team together and would be in touch shortly with the details of the contract.

I felt overjoyed at the news and told Anne. She was pleased that I would be working and earning again, but a little sad that I would have to spend a lot of time away from home once again.

A few days later I received a telephone call from Benjamin, who told me that the pay would be based on paying each of us one thousand pounds a week on a four-weeks-on and two-weeks-off rota. They would also pay us five hundred pounds a week as a retainer when we were on our two weeks off. The pay sounded too good to be true, but it was vaguely similar to that of other contracts I had worked on in the past. Then came the bombshell: Benjamin said that the company who were employing OilTrack to supply the labour force for the job insisted that all employees should pay a seven-thousand-pound goodwill bond. This was to ensure that the employees behaved themselves during the course of the contract and would not overindulge in excessive drinking. It was also to guarantee that employees would commit themselves to working on the contract for at least six months. After this time the monies would be returned in full.

This made a lot of the skilled workers, including Benjamin and myself, very suspicious as to whether or not the whole thing was a scam to con us out of a lot of money. The contract sounded too good to be true, but goodwill bonds were not uncommon in that part of the world. A few days later Henry Schultz flew into the UK and arranged a meeting with us all. At the meeting he assured us that he'd also thought it was a scam when he was initially asked to obtain this bond from us, but also said that he had flown to the oil company's office in Thailand where he met with two of their directors to discuss the requirements of the contract. He assured us that he was more than satisfied when he left the oil company and had agreed to pay a five-hundred-thousand-pound goodwill bond for his company to remain the sole supplier of resources. This made our seven-thousand-pound individual goodwill bonds seem like peanuts.

After the meeting Henry said he would be in touch with us all very soon to provide us with more details of the contract and that he would arrange our flights to Bangkok. The majority of us were out of work at the time as the steel industry had gone through a quiet period over the past few months. We wanted to believe the contract was legitimate but remained sceptical pending further information.

Benjamin was a fairly easy-going type of guy with a good sense of humour. He had a balding head and wore glasses. We arranged to meet up a couple of times for a few beers and we became good friends. We repeatedly discussed the pros and cons of the contract and the possibility of it turning out to be a scam. After one of our debates we decided to make a few enquires and checked out the legitimacy of Henry Schultz and his OilTrack agency in Holland. The outcome of this was that the agency was legitimate.

'Oh well, I guess that makes me feel a lot better,' said Benjamin as he sipped his pint of beer.

'Hhhmmm,' I replied, still feeling sceptical. 'What it could also mean is that OilTrack are being scammed too, and for a lot more money than we are.'

'Yes, half a million quid,' laughed Benjamin. 'It makes seven grand seem like nothing at all.'

'Maybe it does, mate, but seven grand is a lot of cash when you're not working and have to borrow it.'

Benjamin stopped laughing and adopted a more serious expression. 'Yeah, you're right, Steve. We'll have to borrow the money to pay the bond.'

About an hour later we were both in the bank giving our details to separate bank clerks to apply for a seven-thousand-pound loan each. I felt nervous when I did this as I had never had to borrow money before and had always survived my spells out of work by living off the money I had managed to save.

A week later Henry Schultz, who had previously sent us a contract to sign, contacted us. He sounded quite excited about the whole thing and said it was too great an opportunity to miss. He also gave us travelling instructions and said that we were to meet up with the rest of the team at Newcastle Airport to firstly fly to Holland and then to catch a connecting flight to Bangkok in Thailand.

When we arrived at the airport, we met up with the rest of the team. There were around 15 of us flying from Newcastle and another group of a similar size were to fly from Liverpool. We all shook hands and introduced ourselves to each other before we boarded the aeroplane for the first leg of our long journey. During the flight everybody talked about the job and the possibility of it turning out to be a scam. Ben was having none of it and informed everybody that he had checked out OilTrack and that he was more than satisfied that the contract was legitimate.

This made a lot of the men feel more comfortable than they previously had, but I still felt uncertain, especially when I found out that two of the guys had funded all the flight tickets for the first flight to Holland out of their own money and had been told that the second flight tickets were waiting for us on arrival and that they would be reimbursed when we arrived in Thailand.

We arrived in Holland about one and a half hours later and made haste to catch our connecting flight to Bangkok. I sat up straight from the soft material of my comfortable seat and looked around the inside of the aeroplane. It was a huge passenger carrier with three sections of seating separated by two long walkways. I hope this job is legitimate, I thought. I really need the money to support Anne and Gary.

'Can I have a large brandy and Coke and can I have the same for my friend here?' a man sitting next to me asked the Oriental air-hostess who was serving in-flight drinks.

I smiled and looked at him. He was a big guy with broad shoulders and blond wavy hair. He was dressed in a brown leather jacket and was aged around 40.

'Hi,' he grinned, holding out his hand. 'I'm Geoff. I'm one of the welders.'

'I'm Steve,' I replied, shaking his hand and taking the drink from the air-hostess at the same time. 'I'm responsible for programming the computer tracking system.'

'That sounds difficult to me, Steve.'

'No,' I grinned, 'not really. Computers are like welders; you have to punch information into both of them.'

We both burst into laughter and drank our drink in one, just as I saw another air-hostess approaching us on the opposite walkway. She was serving drinks too.

'Excuse me, can I have a large brandy and Coke and can I have the same for my friend here?' I requested, pointing towards Geoff.

The air-hostess served us our drinks and we continued to repeat the request. I felt amazed that they just kept pouring the drinks until eventually they got so fed up with our little game that they gave us a large bottle of brandy each and a large bottle of Coke. Consequently my newly found friend and I drank heavily together and enjoyed the remainder of the flight.

On arrival in Bangkok we were plastered and fought hard to control our staggering walks as we got off the aeroplane. To our amusement we noticed that a lot of the other guys were in a similar state, much to the annoyance of a very sober Henry Schultz. Nevertheless, we climbed into an awaiting bus and were driven to a large hotel in the heart of Bangkok. Once there we were told go to our rooms and rest until the next morning when we would get the opportunity to meet our employers. This was music to our ears, as most of us were either heavily jetlagged or indeed heavily drunk.

The next morning I awoke around 7.30 a.m. and went downstairs for breakfast. I was the first of the group to rise but was soon joined by the majority of the men. Henry Schultz appeared at 9 a.m. and said that he was going to the oil company's office to meet with the two directors and would be back in a couple of hours. He told us to sit tight and to wait for further instructions.

When he returned, he seemed excited and asked us all to congregate in a private meeting room he had booked inside the hotel. He did this so that he could talk to us all in private. The room was stacked with chairs and Henry took his position at the front and stood facing us. We sat silently and listened carefully for what he had to say.

'Right, gents, I've spoken with the directors of the oil company and have a lot more information to pass on to you. The speculation about the project being a scam is complete bullshit and I can assure you it is 100 per cent legitimate. So I want you all to know that I don't want any bad apples spoiling things here and all the rumour-mongers can either shut up or leave now.'

We all remained silent and listened as he continued to tell us about the contract.

'I can now inform you that the details about the project have been kept quiet because the project has been sanctioned on behalf of the American government. We are to form a team that will build a number of oil-rig platforms for the American Department of Defence.'

'What about the seven-grand bond?' somebody asked. 'Why do we have to pay that?'

'The reason for this is to ensure that you all behave yourselves whilst working on the contract. The last thing the American government wants is bad publicity. Remember, loose lips sink ships.'

At that point a dapper Thai gentleman entered the room. He was dressed in a three-piece suit and had a camera slung over his shoulder. He was also carrying a notepad and had a tape measure dangling from his hand.

'This gentleman is the tailor from the oil company,' said Henry. 'He needs to take your measurements for your safety helmets, overalls and footwear. He also needs to take your photographs for your security passes. Please be gentle with him and don't get offended when he's using his tape measure on your inside legs,' he laughed and left the room.

He had also announced that Benjamin was to be the team leader and had asked him to coordinate the collection of details for the tailor. After this we were told that we would have to wait for a couple of days whilst our kit was being delivered and also to allow time for our security passes and clearances to be organised.

The oil company was paying for everything in the hotel for us so we all headed for the bar where we sat and drank together. Morale was high for the first time since we'd all met, but there was still a variety of rumours about the contract going around and some were still not convinced that it wasn't a scam. I personally was optimistic.

My previous knowledge of Thailand came in useful and I headed to one of the local clothes shops, where I made a deal with a local tailor. He agreed to give me a two-piece cashmere suit and a blazer for twenty pounds instead of two hundred and to give me a free shirt for every client I brought into his shop who spent more than fifty pounds. I told most of the team about the low prices in the clothes shop and a lot of them asked me to show them where it was. Obviously I was only too pleased to oblige. I also asked Benjamin if he was interested but he just smiled and said he wasn't. At the end of the day I went back to the shop to collect my free shirts. When I arrived, I realised why Benjamin had said he wasn't interested earlier. He had made a similar deal with the tailor and was collecting his free shirts too.

A couple of days later we assembled in the meeting room again and were met by Henry Schultz, who supplied us with our safety helmets, overalls, boots and ID cards. This gave some of us a feel-good factor until Henry told us that we needed to register our bonds with him. Three or four people said they were happy to pay and did so on the spot. The rest of us were still unsure and declined to hand over any money at this point. Henry seemed very disappointed with this and said he would hold further discussions with the two directors.

'I've got an idea,' I whispered to Benjamin. 'When I was in the UK, I heard that one of my former Marine colleagues was posted to the British embassy in Bangkok. Let's go there and ask him if he can check out this oil company for us.'

'Yes, good idea,' agreed Ben, and we headed for the embassy.

On the way I thought about my former Marine colleague. We'd been good friends during our careers and I was his best man when he got married in Plymouth in 1987. When we got to the British embassy, we found that it was encircled by a huge 12-ft wall and had large steel gates that led to the entrance. There was a small gatehouse in front of the gates, which was manned by an armed Thai police officer. I told him that I had a friend who worked at the embassy and asked if I could see him. Regrettably he refused my request and also refused Ben's request to speak to the British consulate. We stood arguing for a while until he put his hand on the gun that hung in a holster from his waist and started shouting at us in poor English to go away.

Back at the hotel we tried telephoning the embassy, but this also proved to be a waste of time because we had a problem trying to get somebody on the phone who could speak English.

Another day passed and Henry Schultz called yet another meeting. However, at this meeting he invited and introduced the two directors. One of them was called Des Freeman. He was an Australian and was in his mid-50s. He was tall and thin with short dark hair that was shaved around the back and sides. The other was called Glyn Walton. He was an American and was also in his 50s. He was short and chubby with light brown skin and black hair.

Des was the spokesman for the oil company. He reiterated what Henry had told us previously about the job being part of an American defence project. He said that we needed to hand our bond money over so that he could arrange our next flight to an island in the Philippines where we would wait until they arranged our flights to Guam.

A couple more people handed over their money in cash, which Glyn put into a briefcase and gave them a written receipt for. They might have been convinced by this but half of us still weren't willing to part with our cash yet. Des seemed to become a little agitated at our refusal to pay our bond and said that he would organise a final meeting with the owner of the oil company, who was called Sheik Abdullah Fallud.

Two hours later Henry received a telephone call from Des, who invited us round to another hotel where Glyn and himself were staying. When we arrived, our prospective employers greeted us and sat us down to wait for their boss to arrive. The area we were seated in overlooked the entrance and gave us a view through some large plate-glass windows. Suddenly we heard a commotion outside and looked on as we saw a long black estate car with small flags on the front pulling up outside the entrance. The commotion was coming from the local people outside, who seemed to instantly recognise the car and started to bow. Then the driver got out and opened the door for the Sheik, who was dressed in robes. He walked slowly towards the hotel door with two bodyguards standing by his side. The locals stayed on their knees, bowing to him.

'They recognise his royal robes,' said Glyn. 'He is part of a royal family in the Middle East.'

One of the Sheik's bodyguards opened the hotel door and the Sheik walked in. As he entered, the hotel staff, who were busily working in the reception area, stopped what they were doing and politely bowed in the Sheik's direction. He waved his hand at them and they smiled and carried on working.

The Sheik had dark skin, a round chubby face and a short beard. He sat down opposite us and the two directors. A hotel maid appeared with a tray of coffee and biscuits and served him some refreshments. Meanwhile his bodyguards stood alert behind him with their arms folded. We all sat in intrigued silence whilst the Sheik held a brief discussion with the two oil company men. We couldn't clearly hear what he was saying, but we looked on as he stood up and shook the two men's hands. After this, we saw his bodyguards scanning the reception area and doorway. One of them nodded at the Sheik and he calmly walked out through the open door. We looked through the window and saw more passers-by bowing when they saw him, as the estate-car doors banged shut and they drove off out of sight.

The whole group of workers sat in awe of his visit and waited patiently for the two directors to tell us what the Sheik had said. Des ordered some coffee for everyone and stood up from his seat.

'OK, gentlemen, that was our boss. He has told us that the project will go ahead as scheduled and has asked us to book the flights to Manila for you. He is not too worried about the seven-thousand-pound bond but we personally insist that you place this as a goodwill gesture.'

Several more of the men, including Benjamin, stood up and walked over to Glyn with envelopes in their hands containing their bond money. Glyn pulled a briefcase out from under the table he was sitting at and opened it. One at a time the men queued up and paid their bond money. I felt butterflies churning around in my stomach. I wanted to believe it was legitimate but I still had some reservations. There was no concrete proof that it wasn't a set-up.

I joined the queue and watched as each of the men received a receipt for their monies. Soon it was my turn. I kept my envelope inside my jacket and looked Glyn in the eyes.

'What type of welding process are they using to make the legs that support these oil platforms?' I asked him. 'Is it ERW pipes?'

I knew that ERW (electrical-resistance-welded) pipes were not used for supporting the great weight of oil platforms.

Glyn looked hot and bothered and sweat was dripping down his cheeks. He looked at the bundles of money in his briefcase and then looked at me.

'Yes, it is,' he smiled.

'Are you sure?' I asked politely.

'Not really. I'm responsible for the manpower on this job, not the engineering processes. All will become clear when you arrive in Guam,' he assured me.

'That's fine,' I said amiably. 'I do have a small problem, though. My bond money hasn't been transferred yet. Can I pay you when we arrive in Manila?'

He looked startled and turned to Des, who was listening to our conversation. Des stood up and asked for everyone's attention. Everybody stopped what they were doing and looked in our direction.

'This gentleman here has not received his bond money yet and cannot pay it until he arrives in Manila. We can accept his goodwill that he will pay once he arrives in Manila or we can have him struck from the contract and sent home.'

I gulped at his words and felt like reaching inside my coat and handing over my money. I had too much to lose if my suspicions proved correct, though, so I sat tight for the time being.

'You guys have paid your money. It's up to you,' said Des.

For a few moments there was total silence, and then some of them started nodding their heads to say yes, it's OK. Following this Des told me that he would collect my money when we arrived in Manila and said that I should thank the guys for their support. He selected one of the team, a guy called Sam, to stay behind with him and Glyn whilst the rest of us were given our flight tickets to Manila and told to check out of the hotel immediately.

Henry Schultz shook hands with the two directors and we all returned back to our hotel to collect our belongings. The mood amongst the team was more positive now and I felt a little guilty about pretending that I didn't have my bond money yet. Henry informed us that our employers had paid our hotel bills and he gathered us together prior to boarding the flight to Manila.

'Right, lads, they're not shy with the drinks on this flight, so I want you to take it easy. You've paid your bond money now, so don't do anything silly and lose it.'

Everybody nodded to acknowledge what he said and we all boarded the aeroplane. Henry was right about the drinks being plentiful, and we all totally ignored what he said and drank plenty. The funny thing was so did he and his speech about behaving ourselves was worthless because he got very drunk during the flight and threatened to beat up one of the workers.

When we arrived in Manila and walked out of the airport, I saw people begging everywhere. The poverty was bad in Thailand but this seemed a lot worse. Police cars were rushing around everywhere and bomb scares were being announced over the airport intercom system. There were reports of three unexploded devices in the airport so we quickly hired a number of taxis and headed for the Imperial Hotel, which had been booked for us.

The Imperial was without doubt very luxurious. The rooms were far better than those in the Thai hotel and the food was first-class. I called Anne.

'Hello, Anne. I'm in Manila. Everything looks OK and I guess I was wrong about the scam.'

'OK, Steve, but I'll be glad when you come home because there's something I want to tell you.'

'What's that?' I asked curiously.

'You're going to be a father again!'

My face lit up with pride. I felt good inside. I was going to be a father again and would be able to make enough money from this contract to support my family for years to come.

'That's great news, Anne. Everything seems to have fallen into place. I'll call you in a few days. I love you.'

'I love you too, Steve,' she replied, and she put the receiver down.

The lifestyle in Manila was fairly relaxed. The beer was cheap and the sunshine was plentiful. One of the things I found amusing was that a small bottle of whiskey cost fifty pence and some headache pills to help you get over your hangover cost one pound fifty. Something more amusing was that a guard stood watching us with a pump-action shotgun whilst the shopkeeper served us.

The bad side of Manila was clearly its poverty. It was heartbreaking to see children begging on the streets for food when we were sat in the lap of luxury. There were a couple of occasions when Benjamin broke down in tears about it and had to leave the room. You could give the children your money, but there was never enough to go around. You just had to accept it and get on with life.

After a couple of days here we began to get bored and asked Henry Schultz when he thought we would receive our instructions for the flight to Guam. He was uncertain, but said that he had been holding daily conference calls with the two directors.

A group of us were sat in the lounge reading newspapers when we heard Henry shouting at someone. We looked up and saw Sam, the guy whom the directors had chosen to stay behind with them in Thailand.

'What are you doing here?' Henry snapped in an angry tone

of voice, looking towards the hotel entrance lounge where Sam stood. 'What the hell are you doing here?'

'I've been told to fly here and bring you this,' he answered, holding out a brown package that was sealed with Sellotape.

'What's this? What the hell is this?' Henry screamed. He was making the rest of us feel very uneasy.

'Calm down, man,' replied Sam. 'It's our flight tickets to Guam.'

Henry didn't answer. Instead he ripped the Sellotape from the package and tore it open. A bundle of flight tickets dropped out of the parcel and onto the floor.

'I told you they're our flight tickets, Henry.'

'No, NOOOOOOO,' Henry bellowed. 'These are flight tickets all right, but they're not for Guam, they're for the fucking UK.'

We all heard what he said and watched him as he dropped to his knees and sobbed into his hands. Everybody started to look at each other with total disbelief on their faces. Henry got off his knees and made a telephone call to the oil company office. The line was dead and he smashed the receiver hard against the wall.

I felt a heavy dread in my stomach and saw that everybody was feeling a great disappointment as they tried to come to terms with the bad news. Some of the other men broke down too, and I headed for a telephone to inform Anne.

'It's a scam, Anne. It's a bloody scam,' I told her.

'Just come home, Steve. At least you're still in one piece.'

'OK. I'm going to catch the next flight out of here,' I replied and put the receiver down.

We all collected our passports from reception and argued about the cost of the bill. The hotel manager refused to give some of the men their passports back because they couldn't pay. I didn't know the men personally but paid the manager the five hundred pounds he was asking for. After this it was like the retreat from Stalingrad and was literally a case of every man for himself.

Benjamin and I got into a taxi together and headed for the airport. The roads were jammed and our progress was slow. We saw riots in the streets and scuffles amongst angry crowds.

'It looks rough out there,' said Benjamin.

'Yes,' answered the taxi driver. 'What we need is a revolution.'

'Would you mind driving a little faster?' I quipped, and Benjamin sniggered.

Everyone eventually arrived at the airport and we boarded a flight to Bangkok. This time nobody took advantage of the complimentary drinks and everybody sat in silence during the majority of the flight. Even though we now believed it had been a scam, deep down we all wanted to believe we were wrong.

When we arrived in Bangkok, we headed back to the hotel where the directors had been staying but found that they had checked out the day before. Henry Schultz was more distraught than anybody else. His stake of half a million pounds was far greater than the money other people had lost.

Next Henry eagerly headed for the oil company offices he had previously visited. We followed close behind and found him down on his knees once again inside an empty and derelict building. By this time we didn't need any more assurances that we'd been had and we headed for the airport to make the long journey home. Not everybody followed us. Some said they wanted to stay behind to try to find the two directors. Benjamin and myself didn't hang around and were soon flying towards the UK. During the flight we fell back on our humour and joked about the scam. We both laughed continuously and claimed that we'd seen through it all along.

When I eventually arrived at the airport close to my home town, I was met by Anne and my son, Gary. I felt down and disillusioned. My dreams of wealth for my family were shattered and the pain of reality struck home. I desperately needed a job now. I had mouths to feed and money was shorter than ever.

A few days later I managed to make contact with Henry Schultz's secretary in Holland. She told me it had been a terrible deceptive scam and that Henry had lost everything he had in the whole world. She went on to say that Henry had caught up with the two con men in another part of Thailand and had shot them dead with a pistol. Apparently he had been arrested for this and had been thrown into an infamous Thai prison. She concluded that she too was out of work now and that OilTrack would be dissolved in a short space of time.

A while later I wrote to a government office to complain about the fact that the job had initially been advertised in the local jobcentre. They told me there was nothing they could do about this because the Dutch Employment Agency that placed the advert was legitimate. I replied saying that one day I would write a book about this and received another letter from them offering me their sympathy and wishing me good luck with the book.

CHAPTER FIFTEEN

THE SEARCH FOR SAM

In 1995, after another long spell out of work, I was offered a job in Sheffield as a computer programmer for the Employment Service. I was responsible for writing a database that was to be used to test the feasibility of privatising parts of their service.

The money I was being paid was fabulous at twenty-five pounds per hour so I jumped at the chance. This was more per hour than I got paid per day as a Royal Marine five years earlier. It made me laugh when I thought about the time when I paraded in front of my commanding officer and gave him my reasons for wanting to leave the Marines. One of the reasons was that I thought the pay was crap. His words to me were, 'How much do you think you are worth, Preece?'

And my answer was, 'A lot more than this, sir. We all are.'

My pay at that time was £24.95 per day before tax, national insurance and food and accommodation were taken out. Now I truly was earning a lot more, and it felt like one hell of an achievement.

After work I spent one or two hours in a fitness gym I had stumbled across and joined. This was a good habit of mine. Everywhere I went I searched for a gymnasium and used it to work hard at maintaining a high level of physical fitness.

My accommodation was a room in a local B&B. The room was clean and tidy and had a portable television and coffee-making facilities. A few other guys who worked for a different company also stayed there. Unfortunately we had to share the same bathroom on a morning and these men left their facial hairs all over the sink and quite often sat on the toilet smoking for ten or fifteen minutes. Both of these things were taboo in the Marines, because personal hygiene was maintained at all times. You always cleaned the sink after you used it and you never smoked where people washed. Another disgusting habit one of them had was smoking at the breakfast table. This was also something I didn't like and was unused to in my previous career.

The main culprit was called Jodper. He was a tall scruffy-looking building contractor, with multicoloured spiky hair. He was aged around 30 and had a spotty complexion and yellow teeth. I think the colour of his teeth were probably down to his smoking habit because he always seemed to have a cigarette in his mouth when I saw him. The builders often went out drinking on an evening and always came back late. I always heard them return because Jodper had a bad habit of either banging on people's doors when he walked past them or singing out loud to himself.

'Hurry up, mate,' I asked quietly one morning as I tried the locked bathroom door. 'You've been in there for ages.'

'You'll have to wait, mate,' Jodper replied. 'I'm busy.'

Fifteen minutes later I tried the door again. Maybe somebody else has gone in there, I thought.

'Will you be long in there?' I asked, tapping on the door.

'I've already told you once, mate,' said Jodper. 'I'm busy, so piss off.'

I waited in my room a while longer and eventually heard him flush the toilet and open the door. I brushed past him in the corridor and he gave me a serious look. The bathroom was clouded with cigarette smoke and the toilet seat had splashes of crap on it. I opened the window to let in some air and looked down at the sink, which I saw was full of his facial hair and samples of human saliva. The dirty bastard, I thought, as I proceeded to clean it with some tissue paper. This Jodper is a filthy pig.

Later I sat at one of the tables in the breakfast room and sipped my coffee. I saw Jodper and his colleagues sitting opposite me on another table. He looked at me with a silly grin on his face and giggled like a child with his friends. As he got up to leave, he purposely looked at me again and blew me a kiss with his lips. This made my blood boil but I managed to stay calm and ignored him. He was similarly annoying in the mornings of the following weeks until I started to rise earlier than him and get into the bathroom before he did. He wasn't too pleased about this so he started to urinate on the toilet floor and spit in the sink in the evenings when he returned from the pub. I could hear him doing this and often lost sleep because I was fighting hard to control my temper. I could have taken the easy way out and moved to another B&B somewhere else, but I didn't want to be beaten by this fool, so I stayed.

Whilst I was in Sheffield, I thought about a former Marine colleague of mine called Sam Olsen. Back in 1989 when I was still a Marine, I went into town to meet Sam. He'd left the Marines a year earlier and worked as a mercenary in Africa. He once came back to Plymouth to see me and pushed a role of fifty-pound notes into my hand. Although it was a lot of money and most people would have snapped his hand off, I insisted he took it back because our friendship was far greater than anything money could buy. Prior to the night I got involved in the incident that led to my court martial, I was waiting to meet Sam but he never showed. He had told me when we arranged this meeting that he had a very dangerous mission to complete in Angola and if he never made it to our meeting, he was dead. Some of the funny memories that stuck in my mind about him were the time when he set fire to the training shoes I was wearing when I was lying on my bed after a night out on the town, the time he bit a military policeman's dog in Norway, the time he drank a full bottle of Southern Comfort aboard ship then removed all his clothing and put his wet fingers in a power socket and grabbed hold of me, and the time we were on patrol and were lying in a lie-up point (LUP) when a badger startled him as it ran over his back in the dark. I was never sure who got the biggest shock, Sam or the badger.

I initially went to the town hall to check the electoral roll. There were a few families with the surname Olsen recorded but there were no Sams among them. Maybe he's never voted, I thought. Next I scanned the telephone books and found literally hundreds of people with the name Olsen. There was only one thing for it: I had to telephone all of them who had the first initial of S. After a while I began to feel that I was wasting my time, then suddenly my luck appeared to change.

'Hello, my name is Steven Preece. I'm looking for an ex-Marine called Sam Olsen,' I said, holding on to a faint glimmer of hope.

'Yes, I'm Sam Olsen,' a voice replied.

At that moment I felt elated. Could it really be him?

'Are you an ex-Marine?'

'Yes, I am.'

'Did you serve at 42 Commando and the Commando Logistic Regiment in the mid-'80s?'

'Yes, I did. Who is this?' he asked curiously.

'Sam, it's Steve Preece. I've been searching for you for years.'

'I don't know anybody called Steve Preece. Are you sure you've got the right person?'

'Sam, it's me. I'm your buddy. Stop taking the piss.'

'I'm not taking the piss, mate. There's another guy called Sam Olsen who served in the Marines. I've heard of him, but I've never met him.'

'Shit,' I sighed, with a great feeling of disappointment. 'I thought your voice sounded different.'

'I have heard of the Sam Olsen you're talking about, Steve, but not for a number of years now. I'm really sorry, mate, but I'm afraid I'm not the Sam Olsen you are looking for.'

'OK, mate. Sorry to have bothered you.'

'That's OK, Steve. Good luck, mate,' he said kindly and put the receiver down.

I never gave up my search for Sam until I'd exhausted all possible avenues, but unfortunately I drew a blank with this.

Back at the B&B I continued to put up with the antics of Jodper until eventually I decided I'd had enough.

'Hurry up, mate,' I said politely as I tapped on the locked bathroom door.

'I'm busy; piss off,' Jodper replied.

I'd managed to get into the bathroom before Jodper for some weeks now but on this occasion he'd got up earlier than normal because he hadn't been out on the town the night before.

'Come on, mate. I'm getting fed up with this,' I replied, getting riled by his continued efforts to annoy me.

'Fuck off, wanker,' he shouted, as he opened the door slightly. 'Fucking fuck off.'

I saw his face peer out through the small opening he'd created. I raised my foot and kicked the door hard. The force knocked him back and away from it. He fell over the toilet as the door slammed hard against the wall. I ran in behind him, very angry and fully intending to vent my months of frustration on him. Consequently I quickly grabbed him by his greasy hair, before thrusting his head down the diarrhoea-stained toilet and flushing it.

'Arrgh. Fucking get off!' he screamed.

I ignored his words and held his head there longer. As I did this, I looked into the sink, where I saw his facial hair and the saliva he'd left behind. This intensified my anger and I lifted him up and slammed him hard against the wall with one hand pulling on his hair and the other pushing against his throat.

I looked at the fear in his face. He looked like he'd got the message I was trying to relay to him.

'If you leave these toilets in a shit state again, I'm going to beat the shit out of you,' I snapped.

Jodper looked at me and nodded his head. I released my grip on his hair and throat and momentarily stared at him before slamming a hard punch into his gut. He groaned and held onto his stomach as I walked out of the B&B. I'd decided not to wash there that morning and instead I took my wash-bag to work and used the bathroom there. At the end of the day I went to the gym as usual and worked out. I didn't work too hard that evening as I intended to keep some energy in case of repercussions from Jodper and his friends. To my surprise and delight I found that

Jodper and the rest of the builders had left the accommodation and had moved on elsewhere. The landlady told me they had not paid the bill for the last two days of their stay but she really didn't mind because she was fed up with cleaning up after them. To thank me she gave me free breakfasts for the remainder of my stay. At the end of the job I received an offer to work for a building company as a computer systems analyst in Liverpool, which I obviously accepted to keep my earnings coming in.

CHAPTER SIXTEEN

LIVERPOOL – HEAD INJURY

'Excuse me, mate,' I shouted to a middle-aged gentleman through my open car window.

The man stopped walking and looked at me.

'Can you tell me where Kirkby industrial estate is please?'

He didn't answer and just looked at my tie before turning and disappearing down an alleyway between some houses. I held my tie in my hands and paused for a moment. He must have thought I was a police officer or CID or something.

I looked around at the long rows of terraced houses on both sides of the quiet street. There were a couple of people walking about so I decided to get out of the car and ask someone for directions. As I stepped out of the car and looked around again, I saw a couple of people appearing at the doors of their houses and looking out at me. Then other house doors started to open and more people did the same. Even the few people who were walking along the street stood still and looked in my direction. This made me feel uneasy and unwelcome so I quickly retreated to my car and drove off.

Eventually I arrived at Kirkby industrial estate and found the building company I was looking for. It had a sign next to its huge black entrance gates with the words K.U. Erectors Limited inscribed on it. I went inside and introduced myself to my boss, who was called Peter Baker. Peter was in his late 30s with brown curly hair and glasses. He seemed like a pleasant fellow and he introduced me to two other computer systems analysts whom I was assigned to work with. One of them was called Ryan, who was about 28 with long shoulder-length hair and glasses. The other was called Paul and was about four years younger than Ryan. He had a red chubby face and short black hair that was combed across his forehead.

My two new colleagues were not very receptive towards me working with them. This was apparently because I was employed in a more senior position than they were and because I was hired on a contract basis, which meant I got paid a lot more money than they did.

My duties were to write and maintain databases that were used to track materials used for building gas emission systems within the oil and gas industry. I was based in Liverpool but frequently travelled to a number of sites where the company had live projects to make enhancements to their databases. Additionally we had modem access and could dial into any site network from whichever office we were in. I generally chose to visit the sites myself because my two colleagues created an atmosphere between us. They usually fell silent when I entered the room and started talking again once I left. This was a difficult situation for me to be in because I needed to get on with them and I also needed to stay in work.

On one occasion I had to drive down to a location in South Wales because a senior project manager said his printer wasn't working. The distance was over 200 miles and when I got there I couldn't find anything wrong with the printer. The manager was adamant that the printer was faulty so I switched it off, tied a knot in the power cable, gave him a load of bullshit about electromagnetic interference and switched it back on again. He tested it and said it seemed to be working fine so I made the long return journey back to Liverpool. A few weeks later he visited the company office and came to see me. He said he thought my work was commendable and gave me a case of wine, for which I was very grateful.

My accommodation was a room in a small hotel that was situated in the heart of Liverpool's city centre. The rooms were spacious and clean but the furniture and bedding were old and shabby. An elderly gentleman owned the hotel. He had short grey hair and was called Roddy. I saw him each morning when I rose early for breakfast. His manners were impeccable and he always smiled and bid me good morning.

I spent the evenings studying a computer-networking course. This was because I was told that 99 per cent of businesses would be using networks by the year 2000. I also wanted to enhance my knowledge in this field to ensure that I didn't suffer any more long periods out of work. Ryan and Paul were also doing this course but they were fortunate enough to get the company to pay for it and were able to attend courses during work time. I unfortunately did not have this privilege as a contractor and had to use my own money and time for this.

My two colleagues attended the courses but chose not to sit the six required exams to gain the networking qualifications. I, however, did the opposite and worked hard to pass them. This seemed to enrage my colleagues, who seemed jealous that I'd achieved the qualification and they hadn't. Consequently the silent treatment got worse, but by this time I had got used to it.

'Hi, Steve,' Roddy waved at me as I walked in through the hotel door. 'Are you still studying?'

'No, Roddy. I've just managed to pass my final exam. I'm going to concentrate on my physical fitness more now.'

'Sounds good, Steve. I was like you when I was a lad. I served in the Army for seven years.'

'I was in the Marines for about the same amount of time,' I told him and we shook hands.

'I served in Korea in the late 1950s and early '60s. I have some great memories, young man,' he smiled.

'Yes, me too, Roddy. I enjoyed being a Marine, but I found it hard to adapt to civvy street when I left.'

'Yeah, me too, Steve. It takes a long time to get used to being a civilian.'

'I know. It also takes a long time to get used to the back-stabbing shithouses you have to work with, too.'

Roddy smiled but didn't answer. He knew the type of person

I meant. This reminded me of watching *Jaws* when I was a kid. It frightened the life out of me. I told my father I was frightened of sharks after watching it and he told me it wasn't the sharks in the sea I needed to worry about. I didn't know what he meant back then, but I'd certainly worked with enough of them over the past five years to understand by now.

'Will you join me for a drink in the bar, Steve? You must have the time now that your studying has finished.'

I knew the hotel had a bar but I'd never ventured into it before. Usually I spent my nights training in a local gymnasium or studying, although I had mainly just been studying recently, at the expense of my fitness.

'Next week or the week after would suit me, Roddy, because my wife is very close to giving birth to our second child and I want to be there for the birth if I can make it.'

'OK, young man,' he smiled. 'I understand.'

That weekend, in July 1996, I went home and Anne went into labour. We rushed into the hospital and I had the great pleasure of watching my second son being born. Anne held him tightly in her arms as we agreed to call him Kieran. She smiled at me. She looked drained but happy.

'Is this one of the greatest moments in your life, Steve?'

Her words reminded me of the birth of our first son, Gary, when she'd asked me the same question.

'Yes,' I replied, with a warm smile on my face. 'This is one of the best moments in my life. Along with the birth of our first son and our marriage and . . .'

'Don't tell me, Steve, I know: passing out of your basic training as a Royal Marine and getting your Green Beret.'

'I never said that, Anne. You did.'

'No, but you were thinking it. I know you were.'

Early the next morning I drove back to Liverpool. I felt excited about the addition to our family and wanted to tell everybody I saw at work. As expected, Ryan and Paul weren't the least bit interested and just nodded their heads and pulled a face when I told them. They don't understand, I thought. They haven't got children of their own yet.

Roddy, however, was the total opposite. He was keener than ever to invite me into his bar for a few beers when I told him the good news. This time I accepted his kind invitation and joined him as his sole guest. The inside of the bar was warm and cosy. The walls were covered with pictures of Liverpool and Everton footballers and managers from years gone by. The famous Bill Shankly had signed one of them; this was one of Roddy's favourites. The room was full of tables and chairs and the toilets were situated at the far end.

Roddy stood behind the bar and poured me a beer. I sat at the bar and waited for him to pour one for himself. He stood looking at me.

'Are you going to drink your beer, Steve, or just stand there looking at it?'

'What about you? I'll wait until you've poured yours before I drink mine,' I smiled at him, but he just looked at me with a serious expression on his face. For a moment I felt unsure of what he was doing.

'What's the matter, Roddy? Is there something you want to tell me?'

'I've recently received some bad news, my friend. I've got terminal cancer.'

'I am sorry to hear that,' I sighed.

'Yes, it's bad news, Steve, but I guess we've all got to die some time.'

'That's true. I guess I will drink that beer now.'

Roddy shook my hand and smiled. 'There is something else I want to ask you, Steve.'

'What's that, mate?'

He placed a litre bottle of blue label vodka on the bar and licked his lips. He stared at it for a moment before switching his attention back to me.

'I want to get drunk one more time before I die, Steve, and I want to get drunk with you.'

I rubbed my hand across the bristles on my chin. I didn't normally drink to excess during the working week; I usually saved that for the weekends at home. The circumstances were different, though, and this influenced my decision to grant Roddy his request.

'OK, mate, let's do it. Let's get drunk,' I smirked and twisted the top off the bottle.

Roddy's face lit up. He was overjoyed that I had agreed to do this with him. He leaned down behind the bar and grabbed two half-pint glasses and placed them on the bar. Next he poured vodka into them until they were half-full and he topped them up with orange juice and added some ice.

'Cheers, Steve,' he chirped up and we tapped our glasses together.

During the evening we laughed and joked about the antics we got up to during our service days and Roddy showed me some photographs of himself and some of his fellow squaddies when they served in Korea in the late 1950s.

'Where's the toilet, please?' I asked politely.

'It's over there,' he answered, pointing to a door at the far end of the room. 'Be careful on the tiled floor though, Steve. It's very slippy.'

'OK, mate. No problem,' I said and pushed the toilet door open.

Inside I saw the tiled floor he was talking about. It was wet in places and my feet slipped slightly as I walked across to the urinals. After I had finished I washed my hands and treaded carefully across the tiled floor again. Roddy was right, it was slippy: very slippy.

Back at the bar Roddy was busy filling up our glasses again. He was singing to himself. 'Pack up your troubles in your old kit bag and smile, smile, smile.'

I knew the song and smiled at him. It briefly reminded me of the day I set off to join the Marines early in 1983. I sang this song in the early hours of the morning on the way to the train station.

I looked at Roddy and watched him drink his half-glass of vodka and orange in one go. He gargled the last mouthful and laughed out loud. I laughed too and did the same with my drink. Roddy topped our glasses up again and showed me all the memorabilia photographs of former and present Liverpool footballers that were scattered around the walls of the room. He had many treasured memories and told me all about them. He was a really pleasant fellow and I enjoyed his company.

Around eleven o'clock we drank the final drops of the bottle of vodka and sat slumped together leaning against the bar. Roddy offered to pour more drinks, but I knew I was very drunk and still had to get up for work in the morning.

'No thanks, Roddy, mate. I've had enough,' I slurred. 'I'm going to the gents and then I'm going to bed.'

'OK, Steve,' he slurred back. 'Be careful in there. The floor's slippy,' he repeated.

I waved my hand in the air to acknowledge his warning and staggered towards the toilet door. It creaked open as I walked inside. Suddenly my feet slipped from under me and I lost control of my balance. I fell backwards in what seemed like slow motion. Then I felt a hard crack on the back of my head and a blinding pain shot through my head and ears. I groaned and held my head with my hands. I felt something wet on them and looked at my palms. They were covered in blood.

I rolled onto my front and pushed myself up off the floor. I stood looking into one of a row of mirrors that were fixed to the wall. I could see my reflection and saw blood pouring steadily out of both of my ears. I could feel myself losing consciousness and my eyes started to close. Oh no, I thought. Oh no. Then I saw my reflection in the mirror falling backwards and out of view. I felt another hard thwack on the back of my head and a loud ringing noise sounded out in the air around me. Then all was silent as I slipped into a state of unconsciousness.

I could hear a faint bleeping noise in the distance. It started to get louder so I opened my eyes to see where it was coming from. I stared up at a ceiling that was covered in rows of fluorescent lights. I don't recognise this place, I thought. The bleeping noise started to intensify so I turned my head slowly to the left. My head ached all over and I felt as if I was being held down on the bed. The bleeping continued and my eyes focused on some red flashing lights. It was some sort of machine next to my bed. I urgently needed to know where I was. Somebody moved next to me. I turned my head upwards to see who it was and saw a woman dressed in blue. She was calling something out to me, but I couldn't hear her clearly. Her appearance was blurred and I struggled to see her face clearly. I could hear a ringing noise in my ears and put my hands over them. They were sore, even to touch.

'Steven, Steven, are you awake, Steven?' the lady in blue asked.

I struggled to answer her question. My lips moved but my voice remained silent.

'Steve, you're in hospital. You've had a serious accident.'

Her voice and the bleeping noise became distant once more. My eyelids were heavy and started to close. I fought against it, but could not keep them open. Then all was quiet. The bleeping noise started again. I opened my eyes quickly and saw a nurse standing over me. I groaned because my head ached and I felt a tightness in my diaphragm.

'Are you awake, Steve?' asked the nurse. 'You're in hospital.'

'What happened?' I asked.

'You slipped on a tiled floor in the gents toilet at your hotel. The doctor will be around to see you soon.'

I just nodded because I'd experienced violent pains in my head when I'd spoken. She went away and I waited patiently for the doctor to arrive.

'Steven,' a man's voice called out.

I looked up and saw a man dressed in a white coat, who I assumed was the doctor. He was studying a clipboard that he was holding in his hands. I could hear a bleeping noise again and turned my head to see what it was. The noise was coming from a machine next to my bed. I also realised that I was connected to it with wires attached to my chest, as well as having blood and water drips in the back of my hands.

My vision and thoughts started clearing up and I sat up in bed. 'What am I doing here?' I asked the doctor. 'What's happened?'

'You've had a serious injury, Steven. You've fractured your skull and broken several bones in your ears.'

'Fractured,' I answered.

'Yes, fractured. You've also got lots of old fractures in your skull. Where did these come from?' he asked.

'I need to go to work,' I told him. 'I need to go to work now.'

'But you've got broken bones in your ears and your skull is fractured.'

'I don't give a shit,' I snarled. 'I've got a mortgage and a wife and children to support. If I stay here, my mortgage will be fractured. Where are my clothes?'

'No. You're not well; you must stay here,' he pleaded.

'Bollocks. Get me my clothes now,' I insisted and ripped the cables off my chest and the tubes from my veins. 'Get them now,' I shouted at him.

He had a horrified look on his face and instructed a nurse to get my clothes and to let me sign myself out. When my clothes were given to me, they were covered in bloodstains. I didn't question this; I just put them on and walked towards the door. I winced from the pains in my head. Bloody vodka, I thought.

Outside I caught a taxi and travelled to work. It was a cold fresh morning and I was pleased because I was arriving on schedule. On site, I made myself a cup of tea and went into the office I shared with Ryan and Paul. I saw them sat working at their computers.

'Morning, you miserable pair of bastards,' I snapped.

They looked at me and looked back at their computers. Ryan got up from his seat and left the room. A few minutes later he returned with our boss, Peter.

'Steve, can I have a word please?' Peter asked.

'Yes, of course,' I replied amiably. 'What's the matter?"

'You look like shit, Steve. The back of your head is covered in blood and there's blood all over your clothes.'

'Oh yes, I had a drink last night and fell over in my hotel. My head is aching and there's a ringing noise in my ears. I'm OK, though.'

'Look, Steve, it's Friday. Go home early and go and see a doctor. You really don't look very well,' he said with a concerned frown on his face.

My head ached. I felt dizzy and sick. 'OK, Peter. I'll go home now.'

Peter nodded his head and left the room. I looked at Paul and Ryan, who put their heads down and looked at their computer screens. Then I stood up and left the room to make the journey home. I could hear them laughing behind me as I walked down the corridor and out into the car park. I got into my car and made the three-hour drive home.

When I walked through the front door of our house, Anne smiled at me. I just stared at her. She said something but I couldn't hear it because it sounded muffled.

'What's happened? You look terrible,' she said with a tearful look in her eyes.

'Yes, I know. Everybody keeps telling me that. I'm going to get a shower and go to bed.'

After this I showered and climbed into bed. My head ached badly and the ringing noise in my ears annoyed me. I slept heavily and awoke just a few times during the days and nights that followed when Anne brought me something to eat and drink. Then I heard Anne talking to me.

'Steve, it's Monday morning. You've been in bed for nearly three days. I'm really worried about you.'

'What day is it?' I asked.

'It's Monday, Steve. It's only five o'clock in the morning.'

'Monday!' I exclaimed.

'Yes, Monday,' she replied.

'Time for work. I've got to go to work, Anne,' I insisted and quickly got ready and packed my clothes for the week into a suitcase.

'No, Steve. Please don't go; you're not very well.'

'I'm OK, Anne,' I assured her. 'I'll see you next week.'

I left the room and went downstairs. I opened the front door and locked it behind me before I climbed into my car. Then there was darkness and everything was quiet. In the distance I could hear the wailing of sirens. I hope my house isn't on fire, I thought.

Suddenly I was moving, but I couldn't feel my feet touching

the floor. I saw a blue light flashing like a light in a discothèque. Then it was dark and I could hear voices in the distance. Then they were whispers. Then they were gone.

The next day I awoke in a hospital ward. It was full of people who wore Green Berets. They were Marines. I recognised them all. There was a wooden coffin on a bed next to me. The person in the coffin wasn't wearing a beret. He was bald. He sat up and looked at me. My heart pounded heavily. It was my dad. He seemed really happy and he smiled at me.

'Do you want a cup of coffee, Dad?' I asked him.

He smiled at me again. He seemed very happy. He shook his head and his coffin suddenly disappeared. I saw him lying on his side, where he continued to smile at me. Then he too disappeared.

I felt disappointed when he went. I remembered his funeral, which took place when I was still in the Marines. My mother had suffered a serious head injury in a road traffic accident in 1989 and I had made a decision not to let her see him in his coffin. My reasons for this were that they had separated some time before and that he had frequently inflicted violence on her during their marriage. I wanted to make sure she didn't see his dead body because I felt she might express her anger towards him. I also made the decision at that time to have his body cremated because I didn't want her clawing at the grave wondering where he had gone when she came to her senses. He'd never really been the father to me or my brothers that I'd wanted and consequently I too chose not to see his body lying in the coffin. At the time he died, my mother was convalescing and I was waiting for my court martial. We had severe problems, but we were still alive and had to face them. He was dead, and nothing could be done about that. I stuck to my decision. Deep down I hated my dad, but when he died it hurt me immensely. He was my father and that was the top and bottom of it.

That was why I'd been so pleased to see him in the hospital: he was my dad and irreplaceable. The last time I'd seen him was in a dream on the last night of my court martial. He told me I would be found not guilty and, against all the odds, this later turned out to be true when the verdict was announced in my favour. When he vanished and I saw an empty bed beside me, I thought about the times I'd sat with him in some of the local pubs at home. He was very proud of me. He used to tell his friends that I was in the quiet regiment. They'd ask him what he meant and he'd say I was a Royal Marine: one of the toughest and most professional forces in the world. The funny thing about this statement was that the Marines didn't really have regiments like the Army do: they had units, which were an equivalent. However, the exception to this was the Commando Logistic Regiment, where I served for two years. The regiment's predominant role was to provide logistical support and supplies to the frontline commando units.

I looked around the ward at all the Marines that I knew. Some of them fiddled with their Green Berets to put them straight on their heads and to make sure their insignia badges were directly above their left eye. For the first time in five years I felt comfortable. I was suddenly back amongst the Marines. The feeling was great and I wanted to get out of bed to tell Anne how good I felt. I walked to the end of the ward and picked up the receiver of a payphone. I pushed some money into the slot and dialled my home number. My mind felt blank and I had no idea what I was going to say.

'Hello. Who's speaking, please?' asked Anne in her usual soft voice.

'Hi. It's me, Steve,' I laughed. 'I'm back now. I'm back where I belong.'

'Steve, are you OK? I'm worried about you,' she cried.

'Anne, I'm back with the lads. My dad has even been to visit me. I'm a Marine again, Anne. I'm a Marine.'

'Steve,' she cried. 'You're in hospital. You're not very well. You're not back in the Marines.'

'I am, Anne. My friends are with me now. I love the Marines. I don't love you or the kids any more. I love the Marines. I want you to divorce me, Anne. I'm going back where I belong.'

I heard Anne crying, but she seemed so distant. I felt like I was standing in Stonehouse Barracks in Plymouth once again and that I had dreamt about getting married and having children.

'Steven, please,' she pleaded, as she sobbed heavily.

'I can't give you my love, Anne. I want a divorce. I'm a Marine again now,' I said harshly.

'Steven, please don't say this. You aren't very well. You're not a Marine any more,' she cried.

'I am. I'm a bootneck. My friends are here with me now. Goodbye, Anne,' I snapped and put the phone down.

After this I walked back into the ward and sat on my bed. I could feel my Beret on my head and for the first time in years I felt 10-ft tall. Apart from Anne I hadn't bothered making friends with anyone over the past five years. But it was different now. My friends in the Marines surrounded me. All of a sudden I felt very tired and drifted off into a deep sleep.

When I awoke, I had no sensation in one half of my face. Sadly the Marines had gone and I felt alone. A nurse came to collect me and took me to see a doctor, who carried out some tests on some parts of my face. He told me that one side of my face had frozen and that it would only ease off with time. He also mentioned that some bones in my ears were broken and that the ringing noise in my ears was a result of this and referred to the condition as tinnitus. He went on to say that I wasn't back in the Marines like I thought and that the other patients weren't Marines either. He said I must have been hallucinating because I had fractured my skull and had suffered minor brain damage. I sighed deeply. He's wrong, I thought. He's the one who's hallucinating.

A week later I was discharged from the hospital and allowed to return home, where I remained in bed for another week. For some strange reason or other I kept thinking about my violent past and the many fights I'd been involved in over the years. I also kept dreaming about my court martial over and over again and had several dreams that I'd rejoined the Marines. Anne had to wake me up on several different occasions because I was shouting and fighting in my sleep. She told me that I was even sounding aggressive when I was awake, as if I was angry all the time. This anger disappeared from my tone of voice over the next few months, but not, regrettably, from my behaviour.

After another week I was beginning to feel restless. I was back on my feet again and had got my gym work on track and my fitness levels up. I managed to convince Anne that I was well enough to return to work. She wasn't too pleased about it but supported me because I was adamant it was what I wanted. In all honesty I wasn't fully myself again yet, but I needed just to get on with things. I'd been taught as a Marine not to give in when the odds were stacked against me, so I set off back to Liverpool.

'Hello, Steve,' Peter grinned with a look of delight on his face. 'It's good to have you back. Are you OK now? You look a lot better than you did the last time I saw you.'

'Yes, it's good to be back,' I replied, and shook his hand. I tried to smile but the left side of my face was still frozen.

'What's the matter with your face?'

'My face has frozen. It'll free off with time.'

I went into the dining hall to get some breakfast. I saw Paul and Ryan sitting at a table together. It was still quite early and they were the only people in the room. I got some food from the hotplate area and sat down with them.

'What are you doing back?' murmured Ryan.

'Yeah. We thought you wouldn't bother coming back,' Paul added with a nasty tone in his voice.

I didn't answer and looked down to concentrate on my breakfast. I cut a piece of egg from my plate and pushed it towards my mouth. Only half of my mouth opened because of the temporary paralysis and egg yoke dripped down my chin and onto my shirt and tie as I struggled to push it inside.

Ryan and Paul rolled around laughing hysterically. Ryan even spat out the mouthful of coffee he was drinking at the time. I looked at them both as they continued to laugh. I had put up with their resentment towards me for nearly a year now without retaliating. This time my anger dramatically erupted. I grabbed hold of Ryan by his tie with one hand and dragged him over the table towards me. I grabbed Paul by the throat with the other. I ran hard at the wall and furiously slammed them both into it. The table, chairs, plates and cutlery clattered around on the floor beneath us.

'I've put up with your shit for a year now and have fucking had enough,' I stammered, with a half-open mouth and saliva dripping uncontrollably down my cheek.

'If you piss me off again, I'm going to beat the hell out of both of you. OK?'

They both gazed at me with wide-open eyes and a distinct look of fear on their faces. They looked at each other and then at me again and nodded their heads. I released my grip on them and allowed them to leave the room whilst I picked up the table and chairs and cleaned the mess off the floor. I really wanted to vent my anger on them but knew that getting sacked from my job would have been inevitable if I'd done so. We spent the remainder of the day working in our office together. There was the usual silence, but this time there were no sarcastic gestures or whispering coming from them.

After work that day I drove back to the hotel outside the Liverpool football ground where I was staying when I had suffered my accident. I was looking forward to telling Roddy I was well again. When I got back to the hotel, I saw a notice on the reception door, which said, 'CLOSED DUE TO FAMILY BEREAVEMENT'. I felt a sudden dread in my stomach and rang the doorbell. A middle-aged woman answered a few minutes later.

'I'm sorry. We're closed,' she said, pointing to the notice on the door.

'Err, my name is Steven. I was staying here a few weeks ago.'

'Are you the one who had the accident in the toilets?' she asked.

'Unfortunately yes, but I'm OK now. Apart from this,' I added, pointing to the side of my face that was frozen. 'Where's Roddy?'

'I'm afraid he passed away a week ago,' she sighed deeply with tears in her eyes. 'I heard about your accident. He was really worried about you.'

'I'm sorry to hear the bad news. I had a lot of respect for him,' I said and turned and walked away.

Roddy's death was very sad news, but I felt pleased that I'd fulfilled his wish to get drunk with him before he died.

A few months later we decided to move house. My finances had improved dramatically and I wanted a house with two garages for both my wife's car and my own. That situation with the car thief had given me a scare, and I wanted to eliminate the chances of it ever happening again, especially to my wife.

We'd spent the weekend packing boxes and were waiting for a removal van to turn up to move our furniture. I was busy checking that the upstairs cupboards were empty when I heard somebody outside trying to start their car. I could hear the engine whining but it was failing to start. I walked over to the window and looked outside to see who it was.

My next-door neighbour Matthew was standing with his head buried under the bonnet of his car. I hadn't seen or spoken to him for over two years now: not since I had dragged him over the fence when Gary nearly swallowed a razor blade. I wasn't one for holding grudges so I decided to go and give him some help as a gesture of goodwill before I moved house.

'Are you having problems there, Matthew?' I asked politely.

Matthew looked out from under the bonnet and gazed at me with a fearful look on his face. He went to speak but words did not come out of his mouth. Instead his body started to shake. Bloody hell, I thought. I must have scared the shit out of him when we had our disagreement.

The removal van we were waiting for suddenly turned the corner into our street so I immediately moved my attentions to that and helped them to pack up our furniture. I never saw Matthew again, but heard that he celebrated wildly shortly after our departure.

Back at work I was as busy as ever and was asked to make a visit to a power station in north Wales to write some reports in the company database to produce statistical information. I did this in a short space of time and tested it to make sure it was working. The reports were very important and were to be used by the quantity surveyors to work out the cost of materials on this twelve-million-pound project. Once I was satisfied I returned to the head office in Liverpool. When I arrived, I was met by Peter, who seemed annoyed by something.

'What's the matter, Peter?' I asked curiously.

'I need you to go back to north Wales and check the report you wrote. It's imperative that you get it right, Steven. Those statistics have to be correct. The project manager is going nuts about this.'

I felt puzzled because I had checked that the report ran OK before I left. Maybe I've missed something, I thought, and got back into my car. Back at the power station I sat with a disgruntled project manager and checked the configuration of the report. It looked very different from the way I'd left it earlier. I modified it once again and sat with the manager whilst he ran it. Before I left this time, I made sure he was happy with everything.

Back at my hotel that evening I sat awake in bed wondering about the report. Perhaps I'd missed something or had had another hallucination. My thoughts drifted to my children. I don't want them to be like me, I thought. I want them to be more passive than I am and I want them to be able to resolve issues without resorting to violence. But what if they wanted to be like me? No, I couldn't allow that. I didn't want to influence them in that way. Then I drifted off into a deep sleep and dreamt about the Marines once more. I saw both of my sons standing in a crowd with me. They had grown up and were wearing Green Berets and were dressed as Marines. Kieran said he wanted to fight me and Gary said he wanted to fight Kieran.

'NOOOOO!' I shouted. 'NOOOOOOOO!'

There was a knock on the door. 'Mr Preece, are you OK?' a woman's voice called out.

I opened my eyes. Oh, thank God, I thought, it was a bad dream. It was another bloody dream.

'Are you OK, Mr Preece?' the lady called out again.

'Yes, sorry. I was having a bad dream.'

The next morning I sat eating my breakfast and thought deeply about my dream the night before. I concluded that I didn't want to influence my sons to join the Marines or the armed forces in any capacity. They wouldn't necessarily turn out like me if they did – after all I had been a loose cannon – but the possibility of it happening was bad enough.

Back at the office that morning I received a phone call from the project manager from the site in north Wales. He was furious and said that the report I had written had stopped working again. This annoyed me and I was beginning to suspect foul play. I wondered if Paul and Ryan were messing with it. I travelled to the site and reconfigured it. However, because of my suspicions that someone was tampering with it, I added a task to the programme that made a copy of the database each evening and compressed it into a single file. Once this was complete it would automatically copy the file into a hidden folder on the network that only I would know about.

Back at the Liverpool office I sat working on another database. I watched Paul and Ryan configuring databases at other remote sites across a modem line. If they were fiddling with the north Wales site database, then this was how they were doing it.

A few days later Peter asked to have a quiet word with me about the issues with the database reports. He told me that they were not running correctly again and that the continuing problem was costing the company a hell of a lot of money. He also said that the project manager and the board of directors wanted me to explain the reasons for the poor administration of the reports and would be reviewing my position with the company in the boardroom the next day.

That night I stayed back at work later than usual. Paul and Ryan both bid me goodnight and smiled at me as they left. This was strange, because they usually just left without saying anything to me. After they had gone, I went into the boardroom and set a computer up at the end of the long table that dominated the room. I connected a modem to it and dialled into the network at the north Wales site. Then I checked the database and saw that the report was not configured how I had left it. Next I checked my back-up files and decompressed the folders they were contained in. When a file is modified, it is stamped with certain details. These are the time, date and name of the person who was logged into the network carrying out work on the file. It came as no great surprise to me when I found that one of the copies had Ryan's name on it and another had Paul's name on it. I also had a copy that was taken shortly after I had carried out the initial configuration work and the report was still intact. Now I had all the ammunition I needed to prove my innocence, but I wanted to be professional about how I delivered the evidence. I knew very well that the following day was going to be a witch-hunting exercise to place the blame on me before they sacked me. With this in mind, and secretly having another job lined up for myself, I wrote out my resignation, with the intention of presenting it to them at the close of my defence.

'Morning, Steve,' said Ryan, looking pleased with himself.

'Morning, Steve,' said Paul when he arrived a few minutes later.

Again this was unusual, because they usually said nothing to me. For some strange reason they were both very friendly and talkative. It was more than obvious to me that their unusual behaviour was a result of their expectations of what would happen at the boardroom meeting that morning.

At 10 a.m. I made my way to the boardroom along with Ryan and Paul, who were still in good spirits and very talkative. Peter and two of the directors were already seated and were soon joined by the project manager from the north Wales site. Ryan and Paul sat with them whilst I stood alone at the opposite end of the table.

I felt nervous, but at the same time I buzzed with excitement. My two colleagues thought they knew my fate, but what they didn't know was what I had in store for them. Peter held a brief conversation with the directors and looked towards me.

'Steve, we are very worried about the maladministration of the north Wales site database. We are paying you a lot of money to maintain these databases and need to question your ability as well as the amount of money this company has lost as a direct result of the issues with the database reports. Can you give us a logical explanation of the cause of these problems?'

For a few moments there was complete silence and all eyes

were fixed on me. I could see Paul and Ryan smirking as everybody waited patiently for my answer.

'Yes, I can give you a logical explanation for the problems with the database.'

I switched the computer and modem on and dialled into the network at the north Wales site. Paul's and Ryan's smirks turned to frowns as they anxiously waited to see what I was going to show them.

I pointed to the computer screen. 'This, gentlemen, is the north Wales computer network. This is the database and these are the database files. You will notice that the files are stamped with the time and date they were modified as well as the name of the person who carried out the changes. These are copies of the database which were taken at the end of each evening. If we look at the times and dates, you will notice that they were modified after I had made my changes to the required reports. You will also notice that the name stamped on the file is not mine.'

I opened another copy of the database and showed them the name that was stamped on that one. I also showed them a copy that was taken after I had made my initial amendments. Next I opened a log file, which showed the times, dates and the names of people who had dialled into the network over the modem. The names on the files were Paul's and Ryan's, who were now sat with red flushed faces and their heads bowed down.

'If you want to question anybody about maladministration of the north Wales databases, I suggest you ask my two colleagues here,' I concluded, pointing to Paul and Ryan.

Everybody turned their attention towards them, but they both just shrugged their shoulders and didn't answer. Peter also looked very embarrassed.

I raised an envelope that I was holding into the air. 'This is my resignation. I'm leaving now and have got another job in Aberdeen to go to. You can ask these two pathetic arseholes to explain why your poxy database isn't working.'

I placed my resignation on the table in front of Peter and casually walked out of the room and closed the door behind me.

As I climbed into my car to make the journey home, I heard somebody call my name.

'Steve, Steve,' shouted the project manager from the north Wales site.

'That was unbelievable, mate. I am sorry for putting you on the spot today. I guess you've more than proved your point. Is there any way we can persuade you to stay here?'

'No thank you,' I replied, shaking his hand. 'I don't want to work with those two idiots any more. Anyway I've got another job to go to in Aberdeen.'

'OK, Steve. Good luck, mate.'

I smiled at him and sped off into the distance towards home.

CHAPTER SEVENTEEN

REUNION

The 30-ft ropes on the bottom field of the Royal Marines Commando Training Centre were blowing in the wind as we walked through the entrance gate for our planned reunion.

'That brings back some memories, Steve,' said Nosey, a former Marine colleague of mine.

Nosey was in his late 30s and came from Blackpool. We had served together during the mid-'80s and had kept in touch after we'd left the Marines. He had accompanied me on the train journey down from the north.

After being allowed to enter by the Marine gate sentry, we stood together looking around the assault course. A strange feeling came over me. Although it was 1997 and I had been out of the Marines for seven years now, I actually felt as if I had never left. I cast my mind back to basic training and thought about the many months of relentless physical training that we'd had to endure. I remembered the first time I donned a fighting order and rifle and tried to climb the 30-ft ropes. It was a culture shock, which we eventually managed to overcome when we mastered the rope-climbing techniques that we were taught. I smiled to myself when I looked across the assault course and pictured myself running round it and shouting out my surname when I got to the end as I panted heavily for breath. After this we had to do a fireman's carry. We had to run 200 metres in full fighting order carrying our own weapons as well as a colleague with his fighting order and his weapon. Next we looked at the water tank and the long ropes that spanned its length on the metal framework above. This was used to practise regains. You would pull yourself along the rope on your belly, with one leg dangling down and one foot hooked over the top of the rope to keep you stable. When you reached the middle, you had to hang down below the rope with your feet dangling towards the water and your arms outstretched. Then you had to swing yourself back and forth until you had enough momentum going to hook your foot back over the rope. The technique was to put your arm over the top, swing your hanging leg back and forth, then kick down with your foot and look up at the rope as the momentum pushed your body up and over it. Generally, if you got this wrong and failed to do the regain, you would drop into the tank of water. This was a major inconvenience because it meant all your kit and your weapon were soaking wet and you had to spend time cleaning them afterwards. It was also a body shock during the winter months because the water was often covered in ice. Before you were allowed to climb out of the water, you always had to shout out your name, rank and service number.

'Come on, Steve, stop reminiscing about basic training,' said Nosey. 'Let's go and see who else is here. We're supposed to meet up in the NAAFI.'

'Yes. I'm coming, mate,' I answered.

The NAAFI bar was full of familiar faces when we arrived and we started to shake hands with all of our former colleagues and friends. Some had put a little weight on, some had long hair, some were bald and some hadn't changed one bit. We ordered a couple of beers and sat down with the crowd to find out what everybody had been up to over the past seven years.

After about an hour or so it actually felt like we hadn't been apart for as long as we had, that it hadn't really been seven years since most of us had last seen each other. We joked a lot about the antics we used to get up to. The Marines who were still serving enjoyed talking about what was going on around the Marine corps and the former Marines were more interested in finding out how well each of us was doing financially in civvy street. The conversation suddenly became a competition of salaries and some of them tried to impress everyone with their earnings. Personally I was more content talking about our past service together and conversed about some of the tours abroad we had completed.

One of the men I was talking to was an old former regimental sergeant-major (RSM) called Gus Keegan. He was a prison officer now and was getting close to retirement age. We joked about a time when he once tasked me with incinerating some confidential information that came from the COMCEN (Communications Centre). That night there was free beer on in the NAAFI bar and I would have missed it if I'd used the proper incinerator as instructed. Instead I threw them into a nearby skip and tossed a flaming torch into it to burn them in bulk. What I didn't know at the time was that the skip was full of half-empty tins of paint. This resulted in excessive damage to the skip. The RSM tried to get me to admit I'd done this, but I had denied it at the time and knew he couldn't prove it.

I took this opportunity to confess to him and he just laughed. He said he knew it was me but also knew he couldn't prove it. He told me that he was pleased I had had enough sense to keep my mouth shut or else I would have got into a lot of trouble. I bought him a pint and we shook hands to laugh off the incident.

Later in the afternoon we were shown around the Tarzan course, which is a form of assault course made up of a death slide and a number of high-up rope obstacles. We were given a demonstration by some of the current-serving Marines. This also brought back some great memories.

When we went into the gymnasium, it reminded me of an exercise routine we used to do called Initial Military Fitness (IMF). It was an early form of aerobics that was put together years before aerobics became as popular as it is today. Another thing we had to do were sit-ups with straight legs. This often caused our lower backs to bleed and bloodstains to appear on the backs of our white shorts. Blood also used to drop onto our white plimsolls and was very difficult to cover with whitener. Later I heard that they had learned that straight-leg sit-ups were bad for you and they had moved onto doing them with bent knees. I believe they also changed the colour of the white shorts and plimsolls to black. Progress, I would say!

Lastly we visited the swimming-pool area. I laughed to myself when I saw the pool and remembered when the recruit troop I was part of had to jump off a high platform and swim a couple of lengths wearing full kit. There was a short guy called Billy Gibson. He jumped off the platform first. He hit the water with a huge splash and sunk down to the bottom. After a minute or so everybody realised he wasn't coming back to the surface and was being held down by the kit he was carrying. It was funny at the time, unless, of course, you were Billy.

'Hey, Preecey,' a familiar voice called out when we walked back into the bar.

My face lit up when I saw who it was. It was a guy called Shiner, who was once a big mate of mine. He was dressed very smartly in a three-piece suit.

'Shiner, how the hell are you? You look like you've just won the pools.'

'It's good to see you, Steve,' he said as he hugged me and patted me on the back. 'You're still looking very fit.'

'I am still very fit. I can still drink like a fish, too.'

'No big surprises there, then,' he laughed. 'Work hard, train hard and play hard. Some things never change, do they, Steve?'

'I guess not, Shiner. Let's drink some beer and chat about the old times.'

Shiner seemed overjoyed to see me again. We'd been very good friends during our careers and used to train in the gymnasium together. He'd often chosen not to go on the lash with me in those days. He said he thought I was a tough nut, but also unstable and unpredictable after a few beers.

We drank through the afternoon and listened to a few goodwill speeches. Later we were invited into the sergeants' mess to continue drinking into the night. There was a rule that you had to wear a jacket to be invited into the mess, but fortunately one of the currently serving sergeants loaned me one of his. By

10 p.m. I was feeling quite drunk. The present company were a great bunch of men and the atmosphere was friendly and sociable. Shiner and I stood leaning against the bar and continued with our conversation.

'Have you got any children, Steve?' asked Shiner.

'Yes, mate, I've got two very young boys,' I answered with a heavy slur.

'Are they going to take after you when they get older?'

'What do you mean?' I frowned. 'Do you mean are they going to be Marines?'

'No, Steve. Are they going to be hard and unforgiving to anyone who annoys them?'

Suddenly I burst into tears and fought hard to control my emotion. Tears streamed down my face and dripped onto the floor. Shiner looked surprised and pulled a handkerchief from one of his pockets and offered it to me.

'Here, Steve, use this. Are you OK? I wasn't expecting an outburst of emotion from that question. I just thought you would have laughed and said yes.'

'No, Shiner, I don't want them to be like me. I want them to be better than me. I've been too violent in the past; I know I have. It's not what I want for them.'

Shiner consoled me and passed me another beer. I told him about my search for Sam Olsen and my accident in Liverpool. I also told him that I still missed being a Marine and about the dreams I was experiencing in which my children wanted to fight me and each other.

'Come on, Steve. Cheer up, mate. You certainly seem a lot more in control of your life than you were the last time we met. You've done very well for yourself over the past seven years. I'm sure your children will be very proud of you when they grow up.'

Shiner's comforting words helped to cheer me up. He said he too missed the Marines from time to time but had moved on with his life. He told me that I needed to do the same.

A little later we all went back to the accommodation that had been provided for us in one of the recruits' tower blocks. I sat awake for a while staring at the ceiling. If I could have turned the clock back at that point, I would have done, but I realised that Shiner was right. I needed to move on with my life and put my career in the Marines behind me.

The next morning I was awoken by a rattling noise in the room I was sleeping in. I looked at my watch and saw that it was 6.30 a.m. Some of the other former Marines who were sharing my room were already awake. One of them was already up and out of bed and was rattling a padlock in one of the lockers.

I smiled to myself as it brought back another memory from when I was in basic training. A recruit in the next bed to me used to get up 30 minutes before everybody else and rattle the lock as he opened his locker. The result was that we were all awoken when he decided to get up and were robbed of a vital 30 minutes' sleep each day, which meant a lot when you were constantly on the move as a Marine recruit. A couple of us asked the guy to rise when the rest of us did, but he refused and said that he was a martial artist and would take no shit from any of us. One morning I got fed up with this behaviour and leaped out of bed at him. I grabbed hold of him and slammed his head hard against the locker door. He didn't retaliate like I thought he would and just walked away. From that day onwards he decided to rise when the rest of us did and ultimately we were all a lot happier than we were before.

After breakfast we all shook hands and went our separate ways. I didn't head straight for the train station like the others did; instead I walked around the establishment. I wanted one last look before I left. I looked at the new commando statue outside of the imprest (pay office) and the long rows of classrooms in the training wings. I walked across the parade square and remembered the words shouted out by the adjutant on the day I passed out of basic training. ROYAL MARINES, TO YOUR DUTIES, RIGHT WHEEL, QUICK MARCH. I smiled to myself and felt good inside and looked across at the Tarzan course. Then I walked through the gymnasium and looked at the sports hall and the swimming pool before sitting at the top of the embankment which overlooked the assault course. Basic training had been no easy ride, but by the end of it I was bursting with pride and was part of one of the best fighting forces in the world. It was a memory I wanted to cherish forever.

'Come on, Steve,' shouted Nosey as I made my way to the Lympstone Commando train station to catch the next train.

'I thought you had left, Nose. How come you're still here?'

'I've been waiting for you, mate. I want to sit with you on the train. You've been having one last look, haven't you?'

'Yes, I have. I still miss being a Marine. When I left the Marines, I wasn't spent. I had to leave, though, because I couldn't keep out of trouble and would probably have ended up in jail eventually.'

'Yes, I would agree with that, Steve. You were at times a bloody nutcase.'

'Hhhmm, maybe I was. But at least the Marines understood me.'

'Come on, Steve. Let's go home. We've done our time here,' said Nose, beckoning me to follow him.

I looked around and saw a train from Exmouth approaching the platform. I took a deep breath of fresh air and sighed heavily before slinging my backpack over my shoulder and climbing onto the train. Several hours later I had to change trains and say farewell to Nosey. We shook hands and patted each other on the back before wishing each other good luck.

'Keep in touch, Steve,' Nose shouted through an open window as his train pulled out of the station.

I nodded my head. He knew he had no worries about that because he was one of the few people I often rang late at night when I'd consumed a few beers.

'Hi, Steve,' Anne chirped as I entered the front door of our home. 'Did you enjoy your reunion?

'Yes, thank you, I did,' I called out.

Then I saw her sitting with Kieran, our baby, in her arms and I gave them both a big smile. I put my heavy bag down and looked around the room to see where my eldest son, Gary, was.

To my horror he was sat wearing my Green Beret. I frowned at him, dumbstruck, feeling that my greatest fear was starting to come true.

'I want to be like Daddy,' he said, happily waving his arms in the air.

'Take that off now,' I shouted in a firm and serious tone of voice. 'You're not going to be like me. I don't want you to be like me.'

I snatched the Beret from his head and he immediately burst into tears. He cried heavily and I felt the hurt he was feeling as I took it upstairs and threw it in the cupboard. Anne didn't say anything, because I had told her previously about my fears concerning the children.

That evening I felt quite depressed and decided to go out with a friend of mine for a few beers. My friend was called Gerry. He was a tall skinny man with short black hair and a stubbly complexion. Gerry wanted to socialise in our usual watering hole, the Black Swan, but I had other ideas. I insisted that we went to another venue called the Lamb's Head, because I had heard a school reunion was being held there by my former fellow pupils.

When we entered the pub, it was warm, cosy and busy, with soft music playing in the background from a wall-mounted jukebox. I vaguely recognised the faces of some of the people but wasn't sure because I hadn't seen them for over 17 years. Gerry and I sat together at an empty table and drank several beers. Gerry saw somebody whom he recognised and slipped away for a few minutes to talk to them. I sat alone and sipped my beer. I thought about my visit to the Commando Training Centre and how thoroughly I'd enjoyed the reunion with my former Marine colleagues. Then I thought about my conversation with Shiner and my fears about my children growing up to lead a life full of violence like I had. I felt dismayed about this and decided it would be best if I removed the many pictures and plaques that littered the walls of our home. At least my kids wouldn't see the Marines every time they got up in the morning or when they went to bed or to play in the majority of rooms in the house. Yes, this would reduce the chances of them wanting to join the armed forces, I thought. Truthfully this wasn't a reflection on the armed forces; it was a reflection on me.

I needed to visit the gents' so I drank the remainder of my beer and walked through the toilet door. I stood at a urinal and once again thought about my reunion. I felt content and smiled to myself.

'Who are you laughing at?' somebody asked me from the opposite end of the long urinal.

I turned my head to the left to see who it was and studied the familiar face of a man who was stood glaring at me. 'What did you say?' I asked him.

'I said, who are you laughing at?'

Suddenly I recognised the face from my school days. I also remembered that this was a guy who once took my dinner tickets off me when I first went to senior school. He was later expelled for one reason or another and I hadn't seen him again after that.

'Never mind who or what I'm laughing at; who the hell do you think you are?' I snapped.

'I'm Graham Spencer,' he snapped back. 'I said, I'm Graham Spencer.'

'Is that supposed to impress me?' I asked him. 'Are you meant to be someone who's dead tough and all that bollocks?'

Suddenly he thrust a head-butt onto my forehead and I felt a thud. The blow must have hit a hard part of my head because it didn't really hurt me. Graham stood back rubbing his head and looking at me in surprise.

'That wasn't much of a head-butt, Graham. Can you hear that train coming?' I asked him, whilst cupping my hand to my ear.

'What train?' he snapped.

I thrust my head hard into his face and he bounced off me like balsa wood, screaming in pain on his quick way to the floor.

'That fucking train,' I growled at him.

Graham stayed on the floor holding his face and staring at me. He made no effort whatsoever to get up.

'If you missed that train, you can catch the next one,' I said to him as I casually washed my hands before I left the room.

I sat back down with Gerry, who had just bought a fresh round of drinks. A few minutes later I saw Graham slip out of the gents' toilet and out of the pub through a nearby exit.

'You're looking a bit flustered there, Steve. Is everything OK?' Gerry asked.

'Yes, I'm OK,' I replied.

Then I saw another familiar face. It was a guy called Aaron whom I went to school with. The last time I saw him was when I was 17, just a few months before I joined the Marines. He used to hang around with one of the local hard men from a nearby village. He'd got him to beat me up one night because he didn't like me. I'd caught up with the so-called local hard man when I was a Marine and pulverised him. Now I intended to do the same to Aaron. I quickly got up and sat opposite him.

'Now then, Aaron, it's been a while since I saw you,' I said to him sarcastically.

His face dropped and he looked afraid. I thought about the good hiding he had arranged for me some years before and the times I had wondered if I'd ever catch up with him.

'Today, my friend, is pay day,' I grinned.

He looked terrified and started to cry. I quickly realised that he was far removed from the person I had known 17 years ago and I almost felt sorry for him.

'You don't know what I've been through,' he sobbed. 'My wife has left me and I can't have access to my three children.'

Then he burst into uncontrollable emotion and sobbed heavily into his arms, which were folded and resting on the table. I suddenly had a change of heart and drank the rest of my beer before heading home.

It was late when I got back and Anne and the children were in bed. I looked around the walls at the pictures of me when I served in the Marines and an oil painting of me wearing my Blues uniform when I passed out of basic training. I looked at another that hung in one of the children's rooms from my service in the Arctic and another of me in the field. There was also a large Royal Marines poster and several commando-unit plaques hanging on the walls in our spare bedroom, which I used as an office. I opened my wardrobe and pulled out a jumper and several T-shirts with Royal Marines logos on them and a blazer jacket with a Royal Marines badge on it. If I wanted my children to follow in my footsteps and run the risk that they turn out like me, then I was certainly going the right way about it. I realised that I was literally advertising the Royal Marines in practically every room in the house as well as on the clothes I was wearing. I paused for a moment and thought about the dreams I had been experiencing and the fears I had for my children. I didn't know it at the time but these fears had a lot to do with the accident I had suffered in Liverpool. A hospital psychiatrist explained this to me later.

I needed to get rid of this lot, and I needed to do it now. I tore every single picture off the walls and pushed them into a large plastic bag along with my T-shirts and my blazer and ties.

'What are you doing?' asked Anne. 'What's in the bin liner?'

'All my Marine photograph albums, pictures, plaques and clothing. I need to get rid of them,' I slurred.

'But Steve, you've always been so proud of them.'

'No. I need to get rid of them now,' I slurred again and pulled my portrait off the wall. I tried to push it inside the plastic bag, which was full to the brim, so I jumped up and down on it. The glass on my portrait smashed and Anne suddenly burst into tears.

'Steve, I know you don't want to do this. You still aren't very well. Please stop,' she cried.

I turned and looked at her. I didn't understand why she was crying. 'Don't worry, Anne. I know what I'm doing,' I told her and walked down the stairs with the bag slung over my shoulder and went out the door.

'Steve. Steve,' she shouted in a tearful voice. 'Steve, please come back home now.'

I ignored her pleas and carried on walking down towards the beach. It was about two miles away and I focused on getting there as quickly as possible. I was staggering slightly and I ran every so often when I caught my breath. About half an hour later I arrived at the beach and looked out onto the long pier. I walked its length and stood on the end watching the calm waters of the high tide gently splashing up and down the sides of the walls. I sat down and looked into the darkness at a distant light that flashed on and off from a beacon that bobbed up and down in the water.

I looked inside the plastic bag and pulled out some of my photographs and laid them down beside me. I took hold of my painted portrait and held it for a few moments. The broken glass from it caused cuts to my hands and blood dripped between my fingers. I ignored this and cast my thoughts back to the days of basic training. My passing-out parade may have been one of the best days in my life then, but now it wasn't. I cast the portrait into the sea and watched it float away on the tide. Next I pulled lots of pictures out of my photograph albums and looked at them briefly before casting them into the sea. My hands continued to bleed as I pulled out more photographs, looked at them and threw them away. I gazed down at the water again and felt as if my life was drifting away. For a brief moment I felt like following them into the depths of the cold sea. Then a mental picture of my wife and two children came into my head. They were so proud of me as a husband and a father. They often told me this. They loved me; I knew that. They were all that mattered now. I suddenly realised that even though my memorabilia was no longer important to me, it was once, so why throw it all away. I'm going home, I thought, and I'm taking the rest of my pictures with me.

I picked up the half-empty bag and began the long walk home. The night air was cool and fresh and I felt more alert. I thought again about my recent visit to Commando Training Centre in Lympstone, Devon, and the days when I walked tall as a Royal Marine. Suddenly I was glad I hadn't thrown everything away. They were my memories and now I wanted to hold onto them.

'What have you done, Steve?' asked Anne with a look of fear on her face.

'Don't worry, Anne, I'm OK. I've just had to make something clear in my mind. I think I've done this now.'

Following this I got myself cleaned up and put a couple of plasters on my hands. I took the remaining pictures and photographs from the plastic bag and placed them in a box. I secured the box with heavy masking tape and put it into the bottom of my wardrobe. At least they were there if I ever wanted to look at them.

'Goodnight, Anne,' I said as I climbed into bed next to her. 'I love you.'

'I love you too, Steve. Goodnight.'

CHAPTER EIGHTEEN

ABERDEEN

In January 1998 on a cold blustery winter morning I packed the boot of my car with my luggage and set off on the long journey north to start my new contract in Aberdeen. It was a long drive, but I had planned to do it just twice: once at the start of my contract and once at the end. I'd fly home at the weekends, as this would be much less stressful than driving. The wage I had negotiated for this job was three hundred pounds per day, so I was easily able to manage this.

It was snowing when I arrived and I tried hard to find a room in a guest house that was as close to work as possible. This wasn't easy because Aberdeen was full of oil companies and had a hefty population of contractors who were employed in similar circumstances to my own. Eventually I found a vacant room in a small guest house in a part of Aberdeen called Dyce. The room was small and poky, yet clean and tidy. The air inside was cold and the only form of heating was a very small radiator that was lukewarm to the touch. I didn't have to start work until the following day so I drove around for a while to check out the office I was going to work in and also to try to locate a gymnasium I could train in. The building I was employed in was four storeys high and was located next to the airport. Unfortunately I was unable to find a gymnasium so my fitness training would have to take a hit for a while. My room was so cold that evening that I had to unpack my tracksuit and wear it over my pyjamas to keep warm in bed. I also needed to keep my socks on and pulled the hood of my tracksuit top up over my head.

The next morning I rose early and quickly got shaved and showered before eating a hearty breakfast and going to work. The people in work were generally very polite and professional and a pleasure to work with. I wasted very little time in evaluating the work I needed to carry out, which was network-administration tasks and database maintenance. One of the first things I was asked to do was to break into a database that they had lost the password for. Fortunately I'd once seen this being done by another programmer when I worked for the employment agency in Sheffield but was unsure whether I could remember how to do it. My boss was an Asian gentleman called Nan and he told me that the database held valuable information about costs of materials used to maintain an offshore oil platform. Many had failed the task before me, but this just made me more determined to succeed. I spent the first few hours trying all sorts of tactics I'd learned over the years but met with no success. Then I searched my briefcase to see if I had made any notes when I'd watched the process in Sheffield. It turned out that I had written a few things down, and I tried hard to apply the instructions.

'YEEEEEEESSSSSSSSS!' I shouted out loud when I finally got the database user file to list the administrator password and I logged in.

Nan came running up the aisle of the huge open-plan office. All eyes seemed to be on me and the many faces that looked on were wearing happy smiles. Nan was very pleased and shook my hand before telling me that the database contained information about costs of materials worth three million pounds. I felt really pleased with myself that I had got off to such a good start in my new job and even more pleased when Nan told me that I would receive a one-thousand-pound bonus in my first pay packet.

After working for 14 days without a break I decided to fly home and spend a weekend with my family. As I passed through the airport lounge, I noticed a familiar face from the past smiling at me. I instantly recognised him as a former Royal Marines adjutant officer from one of the commando units I'd served in. I remembered that I once asked him what he thought of the Dutch Marines when we were in the field with them in Norway. His answer was that we should never underestimate anyone. We had a brief couple of words together and exchanged a firm handshake because the boarding announcement had been made for my flight. He seemed pleased that I was doing well for myself.

When I got home, I was delighted at seeing Anne and my two young sons again. I missed them immensely when I was away and longed to one day get a job closer to home. I sat on the sofa and placed Gary on one knee and Kieran on the other and hugged them. Suddenly a spot of light from an infrared beam came in through the window and danced around the three of us. Initially I thought it was an infrared sight from a sniper's weapon so I rapidly put my two children on the floor and crawled towards the window to look outside.

As I peeked through the net curtain, I saw two youths shining a light from an infrared pen into my window. One of them was tall with dark hair and the other was much shorter with brown hair. Initially I felt relieved that it wasn't from a weapon's sight, but I knew these things were banned in public because they were known to cause issues with people's eyesight. I felt angered that they were shining this thing into my window and even more annoyed that they could have caused damage to my children. I pushed the net curtain to one side and peered out.

'Piss off now,' I shouted at the youths, who laughed and ran off down the street.

The estate I lived on only had one way in and one way out so I guessed that they would return later. I quickly put my training shoes on and sat back down with my children. Sure enough my assumptions proved to be correct when the infrared beam started to dart around our living room once again.

Bastards, I thought. I'll bloody strangle those two. I hurried around to the back of my house and left through the back gate, which was out of sight of the street. I casually ran onto the pavement as if I was going for a jog. The youths had moved on so

I jogged around the corner, where I saw a large group of them standing together. I recognised the youth with the brown hair and I grabbed hold of him with both hands and threw him up and onto the bonnet of a car. He looked at me with startled eyes.

'It wasn't me, mate; it was him,' he said, nervously pointing to his friend.

'Excuse me, mate,' said another voice behind me.

I turned around and saw that more youths had joined the group. One of them was looking straight at me. He was a lot taller than I was and I suddenly felt like a fox in the middle of a pack of wolves. Consequently I made a quick decision to lash out at him if he moved any closer. He's the biggest, I thought. If I floor him, then the rest will probably disperse.

'What do you want?' I asked him as I readied myself to make my move.

'We're really sorry for what our friends did and we would like to apologise for our behaviour.'

Suddenly I was gobsmacked. His polite words of apology were the last thing I was expecting. I actually felt rather silly and smiled at him. As I did so, I released my grip on the youth I was holding over the car bonnet.

'Normally nobody says anything and they get away with it,' he continued. 'I can assure you that they won't bother you ever again.'

'That's OK,' I replied. 'I appreciate your apology. I'm just looking after the well-being of my children, who were sat with me when this guy shone the infrared pen into my living room.'

'Yes, we are sorry,' he repeated and I casually walked back home.

The flight back to Aberdeen only took a little over an hour or so. It was late and cold when I arrived back at the guest house and the window in my room had ice on the inside of it. I quickly put my pyjamas and tracksuit on and pulled my hood over my head. I felt very tired and, minutes later, I drifted off into a deep sleep. I dreamt that night that both of my sons grew up and joined the armed forces. One joined the Marines and wore a Green Beret and the other joined the Parachute Regiment and wore a maroon one. They stood facing each other dressed in combat uniforms. Both of them looked angry and started to fight with each other.

'Noooooooo!' I shouted. 'STOP NOW!'

'Mr Preece, are you OK?' a woman's voice shouted. 'Are you OK in there?'

'Uh? Oh, I'm dreaming,' I said. 'Thank God for that.'

'Are you OK, Mr Preece?' the landlady asked again as she tapped lightly on the door.

'Yes. I'm sorry. I was having a bad dream. Sorry,' I repeated.

'OK. Goodnight, Mr Preece.'

'Goodnight,' I replied.

The next morning I apologised to the landlady for my inadvertent actions and she politely told me that she had heard me shouting in my sleep on a number of occasions, but had only knocked on my door twice when I had shouted very loud. She suggested that I should see a doctor.

After breakfast I set off for work and arrived about ten minutes later. The large open-plan office was fully populated that day and everybody was busy working. As usual I picked up the telephone to call Anne and the children. My eldest son, Gary, answered, which amazed me because it was the first time he had ever done this.

'Hello, who's speaking please?' he more or less sang into the telephone.

'Hello, Son,' I said happily. 'Have you been a good boy?'

'Hiya, Daddy. I'm missing you. When are you coming home?'

Suddenly I heard two men laughing and looked up to see a guy called Brian who normally sat at the next desk to me. He had long brown hair that was tied up in a ponytail and was in his late 20s. Another guy about the same age as Brian sat next to him. They were both looking at me with big grins on their faces.

'Daddy? Hello, Daddy,' my son said on the telephone.

'What are you two laughing at?' I asked Brian and his colleague.

'You're talking into the telephone like some sort of paedophile,' laughed Brian.

'Daddy, are you still there?' asked Gary.

My temper was raging and was about to explode. 'I'll call you back in a few minutes, Son,' I said and put the receiver down.

I felt furious at the insult Brian had just thrown at me. My anger erupted like a volcano spitting lava and I ran at Brian and grabbed him by his ponytail with both hands.

'AAAARRRGGGHHH!' he screamed as I dragged him across the busy office. Everybody looked on in amazement.

'You bastard. I was talking to my son,' I growled as I stopped in front of an open window. For a moment I considered throwing him out but that would have meant certain death for him. He wasn't worth it so I just slammed his head down hard on the carpeted floor. I looked up and saw that dozens of people were stood looking at me. One of them was my boss, Nan.

'I'm bloody angry, Nan, and am going over to the office on the other side of the airport until I calm down. If you want to sack me, then do it; it's up to you.'

Nan didn't answer as I stomped off past all the onlookers and out of the office. I still felt furious as I climbed into my car and drove around the airfield to the other office. Once inside I called Anne and told her that I may be coming home shortly. Anne sounded a little disappointed because she had thought I had finally learned to curb my aggression. After I put the telephone receiver down it rang again and I answered it. This is it, I thought. I'm going to get the sack.

'Hello, Steve. It's Nan.'

'Hello, Nan. I am sorry, mate. I'll understand if you're going to sack me.'

'Sack you, Steve?' he gasped. 'I heard what he said to you. He's lucky you didn't sling him out of the window. Do you want me to reprimand him?'

'No. I think he got the message.'

'He certainly did,' laughed Nan. 'He's gone home sick because he said he doesn't feel very well.'

I didn't see Brian again in my final month in Aberdeen, but I successfully completed my contract and left with my professional reputation still intact.

CHAPTER NINETEEN

THE NUTHOUSE

After working away from home for eight years I finally managed to get a job closer to home as an IT project manager for the National Health Service. Anne and the children were delighted, and so was I, because we were fed up with being apart all the time. Also my head injury seemed to have finally cleared itself and the bad dreams I'd been having went away for good. All that remained was tinnitus in both ears, but after a while I learned to live with this.

'Morning, I'm Steven Preece,' I said to the receptionist at the hospital. 'I'm starting a new job here today and am looking for a gentleman called Warren Smith.'

'The IT director?' she replied, and I nodded my head.

Warren came out to meet me and we shook hands. He was a skinny-looking man of about 50 with brown curly hair. He explained the requirements of my job to me and began to show me around the hospital. The building was old and undergoing some repairs in certain areas. It also had long dimly lit corridors that were unusually quiet and eerie. They reminded me of the film *One Flew Over the Cuckoo's Nest*.

'What is this place?' I asked Warren. 'A bloody nuthouse?'

'Shush,' he replied with a grin on his face and a finger placed over his lips. 'Yes, it is. The organisation is a mental-health trust.'

We walked around several of the wards and Warren showed

me all the areas that held computers. A lot of these wards were secure rooms and were always kept under lock and key. As we walked through these areas, I felt nervous. The patients looked docile and stared at us with empty gazes. Some reached out to try to grab us as we walked past and some were shouting out loud. Their words weren't directed at us or anybody else; they seemed to be involuntary. It was if the lights were on but nobody was at home.

There was a final secure unit that Warren wanted to show me. For some reason or other he had saved this one till last. As we approached it, I saw that it was surrounded by 12-ft high fences that were monitored by CCTV cameras housed on top of high poles.

'This is where the real headcases live,' grinned Warren. 'A nurse got sacked here last week for putting a notice up on her wall that said, "You don't have to be mad to work here but it helps".'

I laughed nervously as Warren pressed a switch and it buzzed. A moment later I heard a click from the door and it swung open. We stepped inside into a glass-walled reception area. A nurse smiled at Warren through the glass and unlocked another door to let us in. She then gave us both a small personal alarm and told us to press it if we were attacked. Next, two other nurses came to escort us. They were dressed in black overalls with big thick leather belts around their waists that looked like a weightlifter's belt put on back to front. Both were heavily built and looked more like doormen from a nightclub than nurses employed in a hospital.

I felt even more nervous as we unlocked another door and walked down a long corridor with our escorts on either side of us. Firstly we passed a row of locked cell doors with thick reinforced windows in them. The patients' faces that peered through them looked bitter and twisted. Some of them banged hard on the cell doors and screamed out loudly and aggressively. The two nurses smiled at each other, whilst Warren and I exchanged glances and gulped. We were so nervous that we couldn't really pretend not to be.

We walked into an open ward that resembled a normal hospital ward. Patients sat up in bed and stared at us. They all looked alert and active, but uttered little, if any, words. One of them tried to grab my arm but the escorts acted quickly and pushed him away.

'Get off now,' shouted Warren as another put his hand on his shoulder.

Again the escorts acted quickly and pushed the man away. They told us that the patients thought we were doctors because of the way we were dressed and they were trying to grab our attention rather than inflict any injuries on us.

After we had finished our tour, we stepped outside and went somewhere quiet for a cup of coffee. I was relieved to leave the secure unit as my feeling of fear was immense and very uncomfortable. Warren sat grinning at me as we sipped our coffee.

'You'll have to go in there at least once or twice a week,' he grinned. 'You'll need to run reports from the computers in there.'

I nodded my head and let out a nervous laugh. 'This place reminds me of a joke I once heard.'

'What's that?' asked Warren.

'A man goes into a hospital to have his leg amputated. After the operation he is met by a doctor, who tells him he has some good news and some bad news for him. The patient is distraught and asks for the bad news first. The doctor tells him he has amputated the wrong leg and will have to remove the other one. The patient asks for the good news and the doctor tells him that the man in the next bed wants to buy his slippers.'

Warren howled with laughter. Our friendship grew from that day and we became good friends. I found the hospital a good place to work in apart from the twice-weekly visits to the secure unit.

A short while later I had to visit another hospital, but this time it was for personal reasons. At 4.30 one morning the telephone on the dressing table next to our bed started ringing. I opened my eyes and looked at the clock. The ringing woke Anne too and she looked unimpressed when she saw what time it was.

I picked up the receiver. 'This better be good,' I snapped to whoever it was who'd awoken us.

'Is that Steve?' a young lady asked.

'Yes. Who the hell is this and what do you want at this hour?'

'My name is Lizzy and I'm staying at your mother's house on a visit for a couple of days with my husband. We had a few drinks last night and I'm afraid your mother got up to go to the toilet in the middle of the night and has fallen down the stairs.'

'Oh no!' I said with alarm. 'Is she hurt badly?'

'Yes, she is. She's been taken into hospital and is in intensive care.'

'OK. I'll make my way to the hospital,' I said immediately and put the receiver down.

I felt a huge sadness and a heavy dread that her accident may turn out to be fatal. She had thankfully managed to recover from her severe road-traffic accident almost ten years previously, and I strongly hoped she had enough strength left to recover from this one.

First I went to visit my mother's house, because I knew that her partner Kevin was staying there as well as my brother Peter. When I arrived, I was quite shocked at the state they were in. Peter seemed to be heavily under the influence of alcohol and could hardly speak. Kevin, on the other hand, was sound asleep in bed and I was unable to wake him.

The only two people who seemed awake and strangely sober were the young girl and her much older husband. The young girl asked if she could accompany me to the hospital and I agreed to let her. When we arrived, we were shown to a waiting room, where I tried to collect as much information about the accident from the girl as possible. I found it strange that she kept changing the subject from my mother's accident to her own illness, which was some sort of cancer. I was also surprised when a doctor entered the room and told me that my mother was so intoxicated that they would have to wait until the alcohol had cleared before they could carry out their scans. My mother only ever drank one can of beer and I was puzzled at how she could have got into such a state.

Fifteen minutes later, while the young girl was in the toilet, my eldest brother, Martin, arrived. His deep expression of sadness said it all before he opened his mouth.

'Not again, Steve. Not again. Why does it have to be her?'

'I don't know, Martin. Something is not right here.'

'What do you mean?'

'Well, I've been to the house and found our Peter absolutely plastered. And Kevin is so drunk I was unable to wake him from his sleep in bed.'

'Kevin doesn't drink very much.'

'I know, and neither does our mother, but she currently has so much alcohol in her system that it will mask the results of the scans they want to carry out.'

'But she hardly drinks,' Martin frowned.

'I know, and this girl and her husband are totally sober. She's more concerned about her own illness than our mother.'

When the girl returned, Martin looked at her for some answers but she said nothing and remained silent. We both suspected something wasn't right, but couldn't quite put our finger on it.

A doctor came into the room and said we could go in to see her. Martin looked at me and slowly shook his head.

'I can't do it, Steve. It was bad enough the last time. I just can't face seeing her in a state.'

'Don't worry, Martin. I'll go,' I said and walked out of the waiting room and accompanied the doctor into an adjacent room.

The room was full of life-support machines and a group of nurses were stood around my mother's bed. Her face looked all battered and bruised and some sort of padded headguard cushioned her head. She was conscious but unable to speak. She looked at me with dark tearful eyes and my heart ached with sadness as I held her hand.

'We can beat this, Mum,' I said. 'We've done it before and we'll do it again.'

I turned and looked at the group of nurses. I was surprised to see a couple of them crying with their heads bowed. Maybe she's not going to make it, I thought. Maybe they already know this.

A nurse told me that my mother had suffered a fractured skull and consequently had minor brain damage. She also said that she had a collapsed lung and several broken ribs.

I frowned and held her hand. 'I love you, Mum. We can beat this,' I repeated as I fought hard to hold back the tears that were building up in my eyes.

I turned and slowly walked out of the room and back into the waiting room. When I got there, I saw Martin. He was sat holding his head in his hands.

'Are you OK, Martin?' I asked him as I placed my hand on his shoulder.

'Never mind me. What about our mum? Is she OK?'

'It's too early to tell but it doesn't look very good at the moment. Where's the girl gone?'

'She's gone back to our mum's house to pack her bags and go home.'

Later I gave Martin a lift to his place of work. On the way he expressed his concern for our mother to me.

'I don't think she's going to make it, Steve. We're going to have to accept that.'

'Martin,' I snapped. 'She's not dead yet, you know. So don't give up on her whilst she's still breathing air through her lungs.'

'OK, Steve, but it doesn't look too good.'

Next I drove back to my mum's house. Peter and Kevin were now in a better state. They were extremely concerned about our mum's health and I informed them of her current condition. The visitors had left and we talked about the events of the previous evening. When we commented on the intoxicated state that everybody except the visitors had got into, both Kevin and Peter seemed confused. They said that they had only drunk a few beers each and couldn't figure out why it had affected them so much. Slowly but surely it was becoming evident that their visitors may have spiked their drinks with some sort of drug. This would certainly explain why everybody was so intoxicated and why they were completely sober. I suspected that my theory was right, but unfortunately I had no way of proving it.

The next two weeks were crucial to my mother's recovery and

I visited the intensive-care ward twice a day on my way to and from work. She was mostly unconscious so I just held her hand and talked to her whilst she slept.

Back at home my children were due to be baptised, so we went to the church to meet the Father. When we arrived, he greeted us and told us he was a former Paratrooper. This cheered me up a lot and we discussed the perils and fun of military service. Later we prepared for the baptism and the Father stood before the font.

'Has anybody here seen *The Exorcist*?' he asked, and we all nodded our heads. 'Well, if these heads start spinning, I'm out of here.'

Everybody burst into laughter and the Father showed he had still maintained his forces sense of humour. After the service I took a few moments and said a prayer for my mother. It was the least I could do as I was becoming increasingly worried about the prospects of her ever regaining consciousness.

A few days later I felt as if my prayer had been answered because my mother finally pulled through. She was awake but was facing a long road to full recovery. I told her my suspicions that the couple had spiked her drinks and she seemed confused but not necessarily shocked. She told me it was a long story, but the girl blamed her for her parents splitting up some years before. Unfortunately the couple had now returned to where they lived in the north-west and neither Mum nor anyone else had any memory of what had happened in the house that night. I wanted to pay them a visit, but my brothers said they thought it was a bad idea because we couldn't prove anything. Consequently, we left it there. The most important thing was that my mother was well again.

'Hi, Steve,' said Peter as he walked through the intensive-care-ward door.

'Hello, Peter. She's looking good.'

'Yes, I know. I said a few prayers for her in the hospital chapel.'

I smiled at him and thought about the time in the mid-'80s when I had once beaten him up. I was told he had hit his girlfriend Rebecca, which reminded me of the unforgiving violence our father used to dish out to our mother when we were children. The thought that he was a woman-beater too made me see red, and I dragged him out of bed and attacked him. What I didn't know then was that Rebecca was as handy with her fists as he was, and she had hit him first.

'I know it's a long time ago now, Peter, but I want to apologise to you for beating you up. I really am sorry about that.'

'No problem, Steve. I forgive you.'

'Thanks, Peter. I appreciate it.'

At work in the mental hospital the following day I had to visit the secure unit. I'd done this many times now but it was still an ordeal. I signed in as normal and waited for an escort to arrive. After a while I started to get fed up with waiting and told the nurse that I felt confident enough to walk through the wards without one. The nurse agreed and gave me a personal alarm to carry. Moments later I passed through the secure door and made my way down the long dimly lit passage that led to the ward. I felt nervous as I passed the cells and nearly jumped out of my skin when a face appeared at the reinforced-glass window and the patient started banging hard on the door. A patient in the next cell repeated this action. My heart pounded heavily and I held on tight to my personal alarm as I passed the last cell. I looked at the window and saw no movement. Out of curiosity I stepped closer and peered through the glass. Suddenly someone grabbed my arm from behind.

'Arrgghh,' I gasped and turned around.

'You shouldn't come in here without one of us,' smiled an escort.

'Oh, thank God for that,' I panted. 'I thought one of this lot had got loose.'

She laughed at my comments and walked with me down to the office at the end of the ward. Afterwards I walked with my escort back to the entrance of the building. She was still laughing as I bid her goodbye, but I still felt nervous and startled. Outside it was dark, wet and windy. There was very little light to guide me as I hurriedly made my way through the poorly lit car park to get to my car. The hairs stood up on the back of my neck and I felt as if I was being followed. When I got to my car, I looked in the back seat, then in the boot and lastly underneath the vehicle. The last thing I wanted was for one of these people to escape and to want to come home with me. I quickly got into the car and started the engine. I still felt as if I was being watched and drove at speed out of the car park. Later, when I arrived home, Anne greeted me.

'Hello, Steve. Are you OK? You don't look very happy.'

'I'm fine. I just get a bit nervous when I have to visit the secure ward.'

That night we retired to bed early. I was exhausted and dozed off in seconds. For some reason or other I dreamt about the secure ward. I was alone and walking down the corridor again. I looked in through the window of the empty cell. All of a sudden someone grabbed me from behind and I turned and smiled, expecting to see my escort. Instead I saw one of the in-patients. He was tall and broad with scraggy black hair, thick eyebrows and dark bulging eyes. He was growling at me like an animal and saliva was dripping down his cheeks. I turned to run but my legs wouldn't move. The only thing I could feel was the in-patient holding on to me as he let out a hideous laugh.

'Steven! Steven!' shouted Anne. 'Steven, wake up.'

'Uh, oh, shit, it was a dream,' I sighed deeply, with sweat running down my forehead.

'Steve, you were running in your sleep.'

'You would have run if you saw what was chasing me,' I answered seriously.

'You weren't scared, were you, Steve?'

'Me? Scared? No way,' I grinned as I got up and went to the toilet.

When I returned, I had a quick look under the bed and climbed back under the covers.

CHAPTER TWENTY

THE BOYS ARE BACK IN TOWN

In the year 2000 I saw the Royal Marines working on a peacekeeping mission in Sierra Leone on the television. Even though I'd now been out of the Marines for ten years, I still wished I was out there with them. Just seeing the green-coloured berets on the television excited me and I consequently put a renewed sense of drive and determination into my fitness.

I changed my twice-weekly training sessions at a local fitness gym to five nights a week and put together a circuit-training programme. My goal was to return to the very high level of fitness I'd had as a Marine. I was taught as a Marine that to get results you should give 100 per cent effort for 45 minutes when you trained. To achieve this, and a little more, my circuit involved 20 minutes on a running machine, starting with a two-minute warm-up and then running as fast as I could for 18 minutes; 20 minutes on a cross-trainer machine, which was a similar motion to the cross-country skiing I did during arctic-warfare training, 15 minutes on a stepper machine and 15 minutes on a cycling machine. After I completed this, I worked with some weights and finished with a few sets of sit-ups and five minutes on a boxing bag.

For motivation I put together a tape of rock groups that were popular during the '80s and put it into my personal stereo. This included records from groups such as The Clash, U2, Simple

Minds, Thin Lizzy and Queen. I could relate the records to the places where I'd served with the Marines and somehow I managed to regain the Green Beret frame of mind for hard rigorous physical training.

I always started my circuits with three sets of pull-ups on an iron bar that was attached to the wall at the front of the fitness room. This always drew attention from the locals because there weren't many of them who could do this. They often asked me what I was training for, but I just told them I trained for enjoyment. I smiled to myself as I regularly saw the Royal Marines deployed to Sierra Leone on the TV in the gym and felt proud to have once been a part of them.

After a few weeks my excess pounds of body weight started to dissipate and my fitness levels started to soar. For the first time in several years I felt good inside. My mind continued to drift constantly back to the mid-'80s and to some of the many fond memories that I still had. It was easy to do this because the songs were linked in my mind to the various places I'd served in when they were in the charts.

For the first time in a lot of years I drastically reduced the amount of alcohol I consumed on a weekend. Instead of drinking three bottles of wine on both nights I reduced this to one. Occasionally I'd go back to drinking three, and this would get me absolutely plastered, but I still had the knack of being able to get up early the next day and perform well in the gymnasium. I did suffer with a hangover from time to time, but I was always able to ignore the pain. I became quite proud of my weight loss and took great pleasure in showing my friends how roomy my clothes had become. Even so I could still pinch an inch or two of fat around my stomach and worked hard to try to get rid of this.

One day after work I went to the gym as usual and easily completed my three sets of pull-ups during my warm-up. I moved over to the running machine and stood ready on the treadmill. I saw and heard several other keep-fit enthusiasts talking about my high level of fitness and I looked up at a television screen that had the national news showing on it. The reporter referred to Sierra Leone and the successful achievements of the Royal Marine Commandos deployed there. My face shone with pride and I was glad to be wearing a T-shirt that displayed the Royal Marines logo.

I placed my headphones over my ears and clicked the play button on my Walkman. A song called 'The Boys are Back in Town' by Thin Lizzy played out. The treadmill started to accelerate and I quickly built up a good pace. The record reminded me of a lot of my former Marine colleagues whom I used to socialise with down in Plymouth's Union Street. Whenever we returned to Plymouth from deployments abroad, we found that local civilians had started gathering in the pubs and wine bars that we used a lot. When we returned, we literally used to throw them out. This record reminded me of those times, when the boys were back in town.

My pace was fast as I powered on through my normal 20-minute routine. I still felt that I had a lot more energy to put into my running and pressed the treadmill speed button until it reached maximum. I fought hard to draw in as much oxygen as possible and felt the sweat teeming down my face onto my soaking-wet shirt. I still wanted to go faster, so I started lifting my knees up higher, which required more effort. The running machine started to make loud squeaking noises as I pounded away and the many keep-fit enthusiasts who surrounded me watched as I matched the speed of the whirring machine. Suddenly I felt something give way in my left knee and I quickly jumped up from the spinning belt, planning to land with my feet on either side of it. However, my momentum carried me forward and I hit the front of the machine with a hefty bump, causing it to tilt forward and then to bang down heavily onto the floor. The power that drove the machine instantly cut out, causing the treadmill to stop dead.

I stepped off the machine and sat down on a nearby bench. I bent and straightened my left leg and it felt very stiff. I tried walking about but had to drag it as I walked. I was dismayed and knew that the fitness display that my ego had produced had resulted in a serious injury. A few people asked me if I was OK and I told them that I was. I still felt determined to finish some more of my workout and moved onto the punch-bag. As I moved around it and threw a few combination punches, I kept feeling the stiffness in my leg. Initially I chose to ignore it for a bit longer, but then I started experiencing a searing pain. It became so bad that I knew I had no choice but to stop.

That night I limped home feeling somewhat depressed. My level of fitness was something I always took pride in and I was extremely worried that I had undone the good work of my knee operation.

'What's the matter with you, Steve?' asked Anne curiously as I limped in through the doorway. 'What have you done to your leg?'

'I don't know, Anne. I was running as fast as I could on the running machine and felt a searing pain in my left knee.'

'Is that the one you had the operation on after you came out of the Marines?'

'Yes, it is,' I sighed deeply.

I originally injured my knee in the late '80s whilst the Marines were doing a daily exercise routine on board a Royal Navy ship called HMS *Intrepid* off the coast of Norway. The sea was fairly rough that day and we found exercising difficult because the deck of the ship was rolling up and down on the waves. At one point we did a tuck jump, bringing our knees up to our chests. At the same moment the ship rose on a wave and the deck surged up to meet us halfway through our descent. The collision of gravity and body weight against the unyielding rising deck caused the cartilage to tear instantly in my left knee. I got permission to break from the exercise session and went to see the doctor, who gave me some anti-inflammatory pills. The knee continued to bother me when we returned to the UK so I went to see the unit doctor, who also gave me some anti-inflammatory pills and refused to excuse me from physical activities or guard duties. I learned to ignore the pain and soldiered on, but this did continue to greatly trouble me right up until the operation after the car accident in 1990.

On the advice of a friend I tried to sue the MOD for medical negligence a few years after leaving the Marines. I sought the services of a solicitor at my own cost and they requested my medical documents. Unfortunately there was a timescale in which any claims for medical negligence had to be placed after a serviceman left the armed forces. I would have been inside the timescale if the MOD had sent the relevant documents out in time, but I received the wrong documents on several occasions and eventually the allotted time was exceeded and my claim against them became null and void. I later learned that I should have sought the services of the Royal British Legion, because they not only represent the welfare of both current and ex-servicemen, they also do this work free of charge.

The very next day I took the day off work and went to see the local doctor. When I walked in, he smiled at me.

'Hello, Steven. How are you? Are you keeping all right?'

'If I was keeping all right, I wouldn't be here, doc,' I answered sharply.

The doctor saw the funny side of my answer and just laughed. He took hold of my knee to do some muscle tests on it.

'Does that hurt, Steve?'

'No, doc.'

Then he twisted it another way. 'Does that hurt, Steve?'

'No, doc.'

He looked at me with a frown on his face. 'Your knee is badly swollen, Steve. It should be causing you pain.'

'It does cause me pain, doc.'

He frowned again. 'Then why do you keep saying it doesn't hurt?'

'Because I can accept the pain.'

The doctor put my leg back down and scratched his head. For a moment he just stared at me and then he reviewed my medical records.

'I see you're an ex-serviceman, Steve.'

'Yes, I'm an ex-Marine.'

The doctor grinned and nodded his head up and down slowly as if suddenly coming to an understanding.

'I don't want you to tell me if you can accept the pain, Steve. I want you to tell me if you feel any pain.'

'Oh. OK, then. It all hurts.'

That evening I sat with Anne watching the television and the news. Again the Royal Marines came onto the screen and I suddenly realised that I wasn't even an ex-Marine any more; I was merely a former employee of the Royal Marines. I'd kept my physical training going because I still believed that I needed to maintain a peak level of fitness. Unfortunately, at the expense of my left knee, I'd realised too late this was no longer required.

CHAPTER TWENTY-ONE

STRESSED OUT

By April 2001 my aggressive nature had somewhat mellowed and my energy went into enhancing my professional qualifications even further. Consequently I was employed as an IT operations manager by a large corporate organisation working in Leeds. The project was sizeable, to say the least, and encompassed an IT service that was used by 80,000 people across the UK. It was said to be a highly pressurised job and consequently I was paid a rate of forty pounds per hour.

When I arrived at work, I was introduced to the team, which consisted of ten people, all of whom were highly qualified and very professional. The original operations manager was off sick with a stress-related illness and had been absent for over six months. During the first week I realised that the team needed pulling together because they had become unused to being managed. Consequently they tended to pick their own tasks and do their own thing.

Initially I held a team meeting and set about evaluating the skills and workload of each team member as well as familiarising myself with how the whole computer-network process fitted together. The job soon proved to be ridiculously busy and I began to understand why my predecessor had suffered a breakdown from an overload of stress. I had to attend meeting after meeting, my phone rang constantly and numerous people were constantly approaching me with work-related issues. Outside of work I carried a paging device that was used to contact me in the event of any interruptions to the computer network's service. It bleeped frequently and I had to utilise all available engineers to work on the trouble spots at all times of the day and night.

At first I chose to stay in Leeds overnight in guest-house accommodation because I was so busy, but a problem with my next-door neighbours soon altered that. We lived in a four-bedroom detached house on a large open-plan estate near the sea. We got on fairly well with the set of neighbours on one side of us – Gavin and his wife – and very well with Brad and Alison on the other. Our houses were right at the entrance to the estate and we experienced all the through traffic of the local residents. The traffic worried Anne and myself at times and we were afraid of letting our children play on the front garden in case they ran out onto the road and suffered a fatal accident. We also had to endure the many dog owners in the area allowing their pets to foul our gardens each day and night as they took them for a walk. This sometimes annoyed me and on a couple of occasions I picked up the fresh dog dirt and threw it at the owner. It was a very direct approach and it seemed to achieve the desired effect.

To combat the issues of through traffic and dog fouling I decided to have a wrought-iron fence installed, complete with ornamental arrowheads. Prior to the erection of the fence I discussed it with both sets of neighbours and they amiably told me that they really didn't mind. Following this I went ahead and commissioned the workmen to build it.

After a couple of hours the front section of the fence was assembled and put in place. Anne looked at it through one of the upstairs windows. It looked fine and the gold arrowheads gave it a look of elegance. Suddenly she saw Gavin's wife shouting angrily at the workmen. She appeared to be expressing displeasure about the location and height of the fence so Anne went outside to ask what the problem was. The neighbour refused to give a reason for her resentment and hurled a barrage of abuse at Anne before disappearing back into her house. The workmen seemed unflustered by the abuse and stuck with their intended task. Consequently they finished the job a few hours later.

Anne telephoned me at work to inform me about the situation and I travelled home as normal on the Friday evening. When I arrived on my front drive, I parked my car in the garage and went next door to try to resolve the bad feeling about the fence. I calmly knocked on the door and waited for an answer. A few seconds later Gavin appeared at the door. He was usually a fairly easy-going type of guy who generally chose to keep himself to himself and mind his own business. He was a tall middle-aged man with thick black hair and big broad shoulders.

'What do you want?' he snapped viciously.

'I've come to talk about our fence with you. Is there a problem with it?'

'Yes, there bloody is!' screamed his wife from behind him.

'What do you mean?' I asked genuinely, because I was keen to find a way of resolving the issue.

'The arrowheads are too high,' said Gavin.

'They have to be that high. Otherwise someone could fall on them and they'd be dangerous,' I explained to them.

'It makes the outline of your house stand out,' screamed his wife. 'That makes my house look small.'

I stared at her with a feeling of disappointment as I realised the real reason for her initial resentment and ongoing anger. I immediately knew that I was wasting my time trying to find an amiable solution and vented some of my own frustration on them.

'The only thing that's small, sweetheart, is your bloody mind,' I snapped. 'Why don't you go back into your rabbit hutch and calm down?'

'Cheeky bastard,' growled Gavin. 'That fence is an inch on my land and I want it moving.'

I grinned at him. 'Are you taking the piss or what?'

'No, I'm not. It's an inch on my land and I want it moving,' he repeated.

'I'll tell you what,' I answered calmly. 'I'll move it, but not one inch. I'll move it six inches and if you put any paving stones or anything near it, I'll smash them with a hammer.'

'Go away and don't come back to my door,' snapped Gavin and he slammed the door shut.

I went back into my own house to tell Anne about the reception I had received from the neighbours and discussed the problem with her at length. I felt very disappointed with the attitude of the neighbours because I did ask them first about the fence and they approved.

The weeks that followed were very uncomfortable for Anne in particular because Gavin and his wife just stared at her in the street, as did Gavin's in-laws when they made their daily visit. At first I suggested to Anne that I could pay for another fence to be erected in the neighbour's garden, because I thought this would settle the issue. Anne bluntly refused and was adamant that it was a materialistic matter and something we would refer to as a 'keeping up with the Joneses' issue; e.g. you've got a blacker cat than I have or your house is bigger than mine.

A few days later I stuck to my guns and recalled the workmen to move the fence six inches at a cost of several hundred pounds to myself. Gavin and his family continued to ignore Anne and myself and cast a few insulting remarks when passing us now and then as they walked into their household. After a while this started to depress Anne so I decided to travel to and from work each day instead of staying in a hotel room. This was a round trip of 160 miles on top of my very busy job.

The additional stress started to cause me a lot of restless nights so I started physical training once again to help me to sleep better. Obviously I couldn't do any running exercises because of my knee injury so I put together a circuit of other physical exercises and did them in my garage. These consisted of sit-ups, burpees, squat-thrusts, press-ups and dorsal exercises. I sequentially moved from one exercise to the next and did them in sets of 20, totalling 200 exercises per circuit. After each circuit I rested for one minute and then started again for a total of three circuits and six hundred exercises. After I finished circuit training I worked out on my punch-bag for ten or fifteen minutes. It was a good way to finish my training and also a good way to vent my growing anger.

Whilst we were sat in the garden one sunny afternoon, we saw that our other neighbours were having a barbecue in their garden. These neighbours were called Brad and Alison and were about the same age as us. We'd got on quite well together over the years and had occasionally invited each other into our homes for a social evening. Normally this went very well, except we constantly had to listen to Brad telling us all about how great a soldier he was because he was in the Territorial Army (TA). I never mentioned the Marines to him and realised what I must have sounded like over the years when I harped on about my military career. Nevertheless I found him quite entertaining.

Later that afternoon Brad and his wife leaned over the back-garden fence together and waved at us. Brad was a short, chubby man with curly hair and Alison was of similar build with short ginger hair.

'Hi, Steve,' shouted Brad. 'We're having a barbecue with some friends. Do you want to join us?'

I looked at Anne and she nodded her head to acknowledge that she thought it was a good idea.

'Yes please, Brad. We'll be over in a few minutes.'

I quickly pulled a few bottles of wine out of our wine rack and we went next door and joined the company. We weren't familiar with the other guests so we just mingled in after a brief introduction. The beer was plentiful and flowing but we chose to stay away from the barbecued food because of the state of the grill that the food was being cooked on. It was heavily rusted and covered in several months' worth of fat and meat stains from previous barbecues.

After sunset all of us were sat on the garden chairs around a couple of wooden tables. Two large umbrellas were extended above us, blocking out some of the light of the bright full moon. Brad was sat next to me and appeared to be very drunk. He was dressed in a small pair of shorts and a T-shirt, with a baseball cap on his head. He was facing my wife. I watched him as he tried very hard to catch her eyes with his own. He appeared totally oblivious to the fact that I was sitting next to him as he continued to try to get her attention. Anne carried on conversing with other people and occasionally looked around at the company. She saw him looking at her and looked away from him. This didn't deter Brad and he pulled his chair further away from the table to expose his shorts. Then he lay back in his chair and placed one of his hands over his groin area. He used his other hand to play with his baseball cap as he continued to seek an exchange of glances from Anne. For the first time in over a year I had an overwhelming urge to burst into violence. However, I had enough sense not to explode and make a scene in front of everybody. I leaned forward and whispered in Brad's ear, 'Why do you keep staring at my wife?'

Brad didn't answer. He just smiled and continued to seek Anne's attention. This made my blood boil even more. So I whispered into his ear once again.

'If you don't stop staring at my wife like this, I'll bloody strangle you.'

He looked at me and looked back at Anne once again. It was obvious that he was now making her feel uncomfortable because she held her wine up in front of her face so that it disrupted his line of vision.

I casually shuffled my seat forward so that I was sitting between Brad and the rest of the company and I leaned back and grabbed a tight hold on his windpipe with my thumb and forefinger. I continued to face towards everybody and could feel Brad choking under my grip. As he struggled, I held him firmly in his seat. I was very surprised that nobody noticed what I was doing but the visibility in the garden was very poor now because the moon had shifted behind some clouds. To finish with Brad I leaned back and pushed him to the ground without looking in his direction. His chair tipped over backwards and he fell onto the grass below, where he started to cough and splutter.

'Brad, what on earth are you doing?' screeched his wife Alison. 'You're drunk again. Get up now,' she commanded, with a look of embarrassment on her face.

Brad got onto his feet and continued to fight for his breath. He looked at me briefly and then at his wife. 'I'm going to bed,' he slurred and staggered off.

The next day I saw Brad working in his garage. I still felt very angry towards him and followed him in to have a word. When he saw me, his face dropped.

'Steve, I'm sorry, mate. One of the guests told me that they saw what I was doing. I'm sorry, mate. I had too much to drink. I really don't know what I was thinking.'

I looked deep into his eyes. I still felt angry towards him, but had enough control to settle this issue with my voice and not my fists.

'Fair enough, Brad,' I snapped, with a hint of aggression. 'But if you come anywhere near me or my family again, I'm going to rip your fucking head off.'

An hour later I looked out of the living-room window and saw an estate agent placing a 'for sale' sign in Brad's garden. Good, I thought. I'll be glad to see the back of him.

Meanwhile the saga with the other neighbours continued as they bombarded the housing-estate builder's planning department with letters about the height of my fence. I discovered this when I also called the builders with an enquiry about the border between our houses. The builder told me that he thought our neighbours were pathetic and he finished with 'tell them to get stuffed'.

In the weeks that followed, Gavin and his family continued to maintain the tense atmosphere between us. At one point we thought about moving house and travelled around other parts of the town to see if we could find something suitable. Then we debated how much it would cost for us to move.

'It's going to be very expensive to move, Steve,' sighed Anne. 'But it would be a lot better than putting up with these neighbours.'

'Hhhmmm,' I murmured as I thought about how hard I'd worked over the years to buy the house we owned and to pay off most of the mortgage.

'What do you think, Steve?'

I looked at Anne. She was my best friend and a great wife and doting mother. She didn't deserve to be treated like this.

'I've changed my mind, Anne.'

'What do you mean you've changed your mind?'

'We've worked hard to live in this house. I've worked all over the world through thick and thin and we've spent years apart.'

Anne didn't answer. She just looked at me with tears in her eyes and nodded. I held her in my arms and cuddled her.

'Don't worry, sweetheart,' I said softly. 'I'm going to turn this around.'

From then on I went out of my way to exchange glances with Gavin and his family. I literally stopped in my tracks when I saw them looking at me and I held their gaze until they put their heads down and scuttled inside. I even stood in my back garden and stared at them through their kitchen window until they closed the blinds. I also raised the net curtains in the living room and stared at them every time I saw them passing. Eventually they stopped staring at us altogether and chose to keep their heads down whenever they passed us.

Late one night I climbed over their fence after dark and sat quietly beneath their dining-room window. They were sat only a few feet away and I could hear them talking about us. Gavin looked very angry.

'If he stares at us once more, I'm going to rip that fence out of the ground and smash it over his head,' snapped Gavin, banging his clenched fist down on the table.

I felt so angry towards him that I thought about kicking his back door open and dragging him outside to vent my anger on his skull. Then I thought about the charges that could be brought against me if the police were called and decided to bide my time.

The following weekend I was working out on my punch-bag in the garage. The weather outside was warm and mild so I kept the garage door open to give me some fresh air whilst I trained. I stopped for a breather and looked outside, where I saw Gavin walking past with his wife. He looked in my direction.

'This is what you're going to get!' I shouted and started punching the punch-bag wildly.

Gavin didn't reply and just hurried past and went into his

house without a sound. I was furious and continued to throw many combinations of punches at the bag. Shortly afterwards I went into the back garden to do some stretching exercises. Whilst I was there, I noticed some movement through Gavin's kitchen window so I leaned over the fence to stare at them. Gavin glared back at me. He snarled and gritted his teeth before rushing out through the back door towards me. He wasn't aware of it but he was playing right into my hands.

'STOP FUCKING STARING AT ME!' he screamed, with saliva dripping from his mouth.

'RIGHT. GET OVER THE FENCE NOW AND I'LL FIGHT YOU IN THE GARDEN,' I growled back at him, with immense aggression and fury.

Suddenly he seemed to stop dead in his tracks and the anger quickly drained from his cheeks. He stood looking at me with his mouth half-open.

'I, I don't want to fight with you, Steve. I'm not bothered about your fence. It's my wife. She's jealous because we can't afford one.'

'Well, I suggest you sort your wife's attitude out,' I told him.

'Yes, Steve, I will,' he replied in a timid voice and disappeared back inside his kitchen and closed the door.

A couple of hours later I was washing my car on the front drive when I saw an estate agent pull up in a van and erect a 'for sale' sign at the front of Gavin's lawn.

Back at work the pressures of the job were constant and the stress of it all continued to affect my sleep pattern. The project director informed me that the original operations manager was recovering well from his stress-related illness and was planning to return to work. He told me that this man was called Kenneth and he wasn't confident enough yet to come into the workplace and wanted to arrange for me to meet him for lunch in a nearby public house.

I was only too happy to oblige. The pressure of the job was immense and relentless. At least when he returned it would lighten my workload and make things a little easier, I thought. Kenneth called my work telephone extension and introduced himself. He congratulated me on managing to stay on top of things, but I assured him that the pressure was taking its toll on me. He sounded like a pleasant guy and asked me to meet him for lunch that very same day.

When I entered the public house, I saw him straight away because he'd told me he was wearing a light blue coat and nobody else in the room was wearing one. He saw me approach and smiled at me. Kenneth was in his mid-50s and had short black hair combed across his forehead.

'You must be Steve?' he said, holding his hand out to shake mine.

'Yes, that's me, and I guess from your blue coat that you're Kenneth.'

'Yes. Please have a seat and I'll buy us some lunch.'

The initial conversation with Kenneth was warm and friendly, but after a while he wanted to know what qualifications I had, where I'd worked previously and how I'd managed to cope with the pressures of the job. I felt confident as I told him about my qualifications and experience but he didn't seem too happy when he realised that I was more qualified than he was. He also asked me what the biggest challenge was that I'd faced whilst holding this position. I told him there were many, but one example was managing a situation quite well when we lost total power to the whole five floors of our building. The more I told him about how well I'd managed a number of situations the more uncomfortable he seemed to become. After lunch he asked me to arrange to invite him back into the workplace and to organise a visit to each department to reintroduce him as the operations manager. Although he made me feel uncomfortable during our meeting, I agreed to do this because I really needed some help with my workload. The agreement we both made with the project director was that we would work together and split the tasks assigned to me. Initially he returned for two days each week and said that he wanted to break himself in gradually.

I watched him as he carried out his management duties and at first I treated him with respect for his level of professionalism. However, after a couple of weeks he insisted on coming back full-time and started to take more and more of my tasks from me. In meetings with other managers he insisted that he was the operations manager and that I had just been standing in for him. This was quite true but I found it condescending because of the way he put this across to them.

Next he insisted on running all the meetings that I normally chaired and even started to make facetious comments about me to the rest of the team, who at times looked embarrassed by this. Ken said he also wanted to hold one-to-one meetings with me, commencing straight away. A few minutes later we sat alone together in one of the meeting rooms. I felt nervous as I sipped a cup of hot coffee and waited in anticipation to hear what he wanted to say.

'Right, Steven,' he said, looking me straight in the eyes. 'Let's both make sure we understand something here.'

'What's that, Ken?' I asked with interest, but felt as if I knew what he was going to say.

'I'M THE OPERATIONS MANAGER!' he screamed, pointing at me. 'ME, NOT YOU.'

'OK, Kenneth. You don't have to shout,' I replied quietly. 'I have no problem with that.'

'Good. Just as long as we understand each other clearly,' he said with a straight face.

He then opened his task book and asked me to give him a progress report on the items that had been assigned to me. He snarled and struck a line through each task with his pen as I told him each one was completed.

Overnight the job turned into a nightmare and the days and weeks that followed were repetitive. At one point I discussed the situation with the project director, who told me that I needed to continue to give Kenneth my support to help him to get over his illness. Kenneth's attitude towards me was at times aggressive and he seemed to thrive on knocking my confidence down. He also started to drink heavily on a lunchtime, which often made life almost unbearable. The engineers on my team sympathised with me and told me that they didn't know how I managed to put up with his attitude.

On top of this I found that the long car journeys home were starting to get on top of me and I was beginning to actually dread the return journey to work the following day. My initial answer to these new pressures was to start drinking on work nights. I knew it wasn't the right solution, but I did it anyway.

On a weekend I drank even more, to the point of actually passing out. One Sunday morning I awoke early and sat in the kitchen eating my breakfast with Anne.

'Steve, you've got to stop this drinking,' she pleaded. 'You're drinking far too much. You look terrible at the moment.'

'I feel like shit,' I replied and went upstairs to go on my computer and surf the Internet to try to find another job.

Whilst I was looking through various websites, I felt a dull burning pain in my diaphragm. Suddenly the computer started to flick through the Internet pages at great speed. It was as if someone had put the world outside my head on fast forward. For a moment I felt confused. I had a strange sensation of standing next to the bedroom door looking at myself a few feet away on the computer. I could see myself holding my diaphragm. What was happening to me? Had I died and come out of my body?

I gasped for air and was once again sat in front of the computer screen with both hands on my chest. I took a few deep breaths and got up to go downstairs. As I entered the living room, I seemed to keep jumping out of my body and looking at myself. I feared I was about to die.

'Anne, Anne, I don't know what's happening to me. I seem to keep coming out of my body. I think I'm going to die.'

'You look terrible, Steve. Sit down and rest yourself,' she said anxiously.

The doorbell rang and Anne rushed to answer it. It was my brother Peter, and Anne invited him in and told him about the state I was in. Peter wasted very little time. He persuaded me to get in his car and drove me straight to hospital.

I must have looked terribly ill when we entered the reception because the nurse rushed me straight into an empty casualty room on a hospital trolley and pushed an oxygen mask over my face.

The nurse was familiar to me because I knew her from my mid-20s when I was still a Royal Marine. She was the mother of one of my friends. I sucked hard on the fresh oxygen and tried to settle myself down. I told the nurse about my out-of-body experience and that I thought I was going to die.

'I'm suffering from stress,' I told her. 'That's what's causing this: too much stress.'

The nurse frowned at me and stood with her hands on her hips. 'Too much stress my arse, Steven. More like too much bloody drink.'

'Ha ha,' laughed Peter. 'Sounds about right to me.'

The nurse left us alone for a while and Peter pulled up a chair next to my bed and talked to me. It was a strange conversation because I really did think I didn't have long left to live. All I wanted to talk about was the fun and happy memories we had of the times we'd played together as children. Peter didn't seem flustered about my medical condition. Instead he chose to look through a drawer of other patients' medical records. He flicked through a group of files and pulled one out to look at.

'Hey, I knew this guy,' he whispered to me. 'He died last week. I think you knew him too. He was about the same age as you.'

I frowned and looked at Peter as I pulled the oxygen mask from my face. 'It's not quite what I want to hear at the moment, Peter.'

Peter laughed and put the file back into the drawer. He looked at his watch. 'Bloody hell, it's ten minutes to nine. *Auf Wiedersehen, Pet* is on the TV in ten minutes.'

'So?' I answered, lifting the oxygen mask up once again.

'Well, I know you look like shit, Steve, but it's the last in the series. I'm off to watch it. I'll be back some time after ten o'clock,' he grinned and disappeared through the doorway.

'Bastard,' I shouted after him and took in a few more deep breaths of oxygen.

The next morning I woke up in a hospital ward and still felt disorientated. I didn't need the oxygen any more and was told by the doctor that my illness was short-term and had been caused by drinking excessively. He said the out-of-body experiences were probably the result of my body's chemistry getting all mixed up.

'What are you in for, mate?' asked a man in the bed next to me.

'Too much to drink, I think,' I replied.

'What about you?'

'Oh, I've got some sort of infection in my bollocks and they've swelled up like footballs.'

A doctor who came to speak to this guy interrupted our conversation. He stood opposite him with a clipboard in his hand.

'Can you take away the pain and leave the swelling?' said the patient, and the doctor and I started laughing.

'Wise guy, uh?' he smirked, and walked away.

A few minutes later the other patient was using the mobile bedside phone. I could hear him talking to his wife.

'Don't worry, darling,' he said. 'Everything's going to be OK and I'll be out soon.'

He said this just as the doctor appeared at the end of his bed once again. He held a huge needle in his hand, which was full of fluid. He held it up and stood looking at it.

'Mr Jones,' he said.

The patient nodded his head and the colour seemed to drain rapidly from his face. He looked terrified.

'I'll have to go now,' he cried on the telephone and put down the receiver.

The doctor flicked the needle and looked at Mr Jones. 'This is for him,' he grinned and pointed to another patient at the end of the ward.

I burst into laughter, as did the rest of the patients in the ward who had been listening. Mr Jones said he didn't think it was very funny but we all knew the doctor was getting his own back for the patient's 'leave the swelling' comments earlier.

When I returned home from hospital, I got a telephone call from an old friend of mine who was still serving in the Marines. His name was Diz. He was a tall well-built guy with a thick walrus moustache. He'd been in the Royal Marines for about 18 years now and was ranked as a sergeant-major. He was based in a top-secret NATO base called HMS Warrior on the outskirts of London and was in charge of the Royal Marine security detachment that guarded it. Diz had been one of my best friends during my military service and had endeavoured to keep in touch with me. I told him that I was returning to work soon and would be driving down to visit a data centre that was fairly close to the NATO base. Diz insisted that I should take the opportunity to visit him and I told him that I would.

As I prepared to leave home that day, Anne came rushing out. 'Steve, don't drink too much and keep out of trouble,' she told me with a worried look on her face.

'Anne, I've been out of the Marines for nearly twelve years now,' I sighed at her. 'I won't drink too much and I won't get into any trouble.'

'Steve,' she smiled. 'We've been together a long time now. Please be careful.'

'Don't worry, Anne. I'll behave myself,' I replied, trying to reassure her through the open car window as I drove off.

CHAPTER TWENTY-TWO

REUNION – WARRIOR

'Hey, Preecey. It's great to see you at last, you fucker,' shouted Diz as I casually walked past the armed Marine sentry and through the main gates of the NATO Allied Commando Channel in Northwood, which is also called HMS Warrior.

I hadn't seen Diz for a number of years now. He still looked to be in good shape but I noticed his short dark hair was now short grey hair and that he'd put a little weight on around his cheeks since the last time we'd met.

'Yo, Diz. How the fuck are you?' I grinned broadly.

'I was good, Steve, but now you're here, I'm even better,' he replied as he gave me a big hug and patted me hard on the back.

'I see you've gained a few pounds, Diz. Are they feeding you well?'

'Yes, very well. The extra few pounds are from good living.'

'Yeah. You look like you're living good.'

'Yeah. Damn good.'

I looked around the front of the GHQ building where the Navy and the RAF carried out their administrative work. The buildings were high and reminded me of a time when we were practising abseiling from them. I was generally pretty good at abseiling and confident enough to run and jump off the top of a 50-ft building and just pull the rope once before I hit the ground. Experience had taught me how to judge the latest time to apply the brake before hitting the ground so that the stretch of the rope would slow me down just enough for a comfortable landing. I performed this successfully and raised my arms to allow the rope to whip through my karabiner and into the air. Out of the blue came the Marine detachment officer. He was one of those guys who always had to go one better. I personally didn't like him. I once played him at squash and every time I scored a point he told me how lucky I was and every time he scored he told me how good it was. Anyway, on this occasion he saw my descent and wanted to outdo me. He clipped onto the rope and jumped outwards into the air. As he came towards the ground, I knew he would try to brake once like I'd done. He did this, but he did it too early and the rope pulled taut and swung him back towards the building. The lower part of the building had an underhang that housed huge rubbish bins. The rope swung him straight towards them and we all held our breaths as he disappeared into one. Seconds later he climbed out and brushed himself down.

'Well, gentlemen, that was pretty cool, I thought. Just as I planned,' he said.

We all stood amazed that he didn't hurt himself and watched him dusting himself down and then looking at his watch.

'Well, that's about all I've got time for. I must dash,' he said seriously.

As he disappeared around the corner, we all followed him and looked on as he began to limp. After a couple of strides, he clutched his wounded leg, revealing the true result of swinging into that bin. Obviously he didn't want to lose face in front of the men!

'Come on, Steve. The Marines are going to war tomorrow. Let's get pissed,' Diz grinned, rubbing his hand through his short-cropped hair.

He took me into the senior ranks' mess on the base, where the beer was cheap and plentiful. The year was 2002 and the Royal Marines were about to play their part in liberating Afghanistan. The NATO base was one of the places that the war would be monitored from.

We sat in the quiet bar and drank a few cold beers whilst we laughed and reminisced about some of the funny antics we used to get up to when we served together. Diz said they were his most enjoyable days as a Marine because his seniority as a sergeant-major now meant that he couldn't become too familiar with the men and had to spend a lot of his time alone.

Two hours later we called a taxi and went into the local town of Northwood to socialise in the wine bars. When we arrived, I noticed that times had changed since I had last been into Northwood between 1986 and 1988 during my service at the NATO base. The then-old wine bars were now new refurbished wine bars.

Socially Diz hadn't changed one bit. He was still living in the fast lane and was drinking his beer like there was no tomorrow. I made a determined effort to keep up with him but he just laughed and continued to pour it down his throat as if he was pouring it into a bottomless pit.

Earlier in the evening I'd telephoned a former Marine colleague called Rick Andrews and asked him to come along to meet us for a couple of beers. Rick was renowned for his hugely powerful and muscular build during our time in the Marines. We used to joke that he had muscles in his piss. When he'd first left the Marines, he initially worked as a debt collector and, believe me, if he knocked on your door, it was as good as a call from the reaper. Several years later he set up his own weightlifting gym and progressed into the professional world of power-lifting. He was a special friend of mine whom I fully respected.

Rick was busy in his gym when I called him and he said he would try his best to make it. Consequently I kept looking towards the entrance for his arrival. By 10.30 p.m. he still hadn't shown up and I was beginning to feel a little disappointed because I was really looking forward to seeing him again.

Diz patted me on the back. 'Come on, Steve. Stop watching the door. Rick isn't going to show. Here, get this down your neck.'

He passed me a strange concoction of a drink, which I consumed with very little thought. Then the entrance door opened and Rick walked into the bar. His huge muscular physique made practically everybody in the bar turn around and look at him. Some of them gasped in amazement at the size of his biceps, which bulged out of the sleeves of his T-shirt. Instantly I felt elated and held out my hand to give Rick a firm handshake. He did the same and almost crushed my hand as he shook it.

'Good to see you, Steve, mate,' he grinned. 'You look pissed.'

'I am pissed. This big gorilla has been pouring the ale down his neck like there's no tomorrow. I don't know what that last drink was, but it feels like my head is on fire,' I hiccupped, and Rick laughed as he shook Diz's hand too.

We sat together and talked for a while. Rick was a great friend of mine and I was absolutely delighted to see him. I had some good memories of the time we'd served together and also some of when we worked together in a nightclub in London. Rick told us that he still did nightclub door work from time to time, just to keep his hand in.

'So what's the worst thing you have ever had to do to a violent drunk on the doors, Rick?' Diz asked him.

'I was once attacked by a guy who was high on drugs. He punched me hard in the face couple of times so I hit him hard several times in the ribs.'

'I bet that stopped him,' I commented.

'No, it didn't,' said Rick, shaking his head. 'I actually broke several of his ribs, but he still kept coming at me because of the drugs he was on.'

'Bloody hell,' exclaimed Diz. 'What did you do next?'

'I pulled one of his eyeballs out of its socket.'

His comments sent shivers through our spines. We knew that he was being deadly serious.

'Did the police get called?' I asked him.

'Yes they did, and believe it or not I actually got away with using the minimum amount of force necessary to control the situation. The moral of the story is drugs are for losers.'

All of us looked at each other and nodded our heads in agreement.

Rick generally didn't drink alcohol and ordered a soft drink. I knew this was because of his dedication to power-lifting and also because he knew he could be extremely dangerous towards anyone who got in his way if he'd had too much to drink. None of us ever questioned this and respected him fully for his choice.

At the end of the evening Diz and I opted to go for a meal at a nearby Indian restaurant and put the idea to Rick. Unfortunately he declined the offer and explained that it would be detrimental to his training diet. We bid him goodnight and made our way to the restaurant, where I quickly ordered a couple of bottles of expensive champagne to go with our food. Diz thought it was his lucky day because I told him to order anything he wanted from the menu and that I was going to cover it.

After we drank the second bottle of champagne, I ordered another, but Diz changed this to a bottle of house wine, explaining that he didn't want to abuse my kind hospitality. By the time we'd finished it, we were very drunk and both decided it was getting late and time to call an end to our evening. I paid the bill and we made our way outside and walked to the end of the street.

The hotel I was staying in was in a different direction than the NATO base so I shook Diz's hand and said goodbye. We were both slurring heavily as we spoke and I felt myself starting to lose consciousness. My hotel was about a mile away so I started to run in an attempt to get there before I passed out. I looked left and right as I stepped off the pavement to cross the road. Suddenly my ankle buckled violently as it came down on the edge of the pavement and the gutter, and a sharp pain shot through it. Momentum caused me to fall hard onto my knees and then forward into the gutter. As I made impact with the ground, my jacket flew up onto my back and shoulders and a couple of items came loose from my trousers' back pockets and hit me on the back of the head.

I paused momentarily to catch my breath and focus on the area around me. Thankfully there was no traffic coming from either direction and the street was quiet. I searched through my pockets to see what had become dislodged from them and realised that my mobile phone and wallet were missing. I spent about 15 minutes looking around the nearby parked cars, but they were nowhere to be seen. Eventually I gave up because I was starting to lose consciousness once again. I tried to get back on my feet, but couldn't put any weight on my ankle, which was causing me a great deal of pain. I looked up the quiet street and could see my hotel in the distance. My only hope was to crawl there on my hands and knees so I started to shuffle along on them. My knees were painful because of the fall but after a few minutes they became hot and the pain seemed to fade. I don't know how long it took me to get to the hotel doors but eventually I made it and crawled inside. I could hear someone snoring gently from behind the reception desk. At first I was going to haul myself onto the desk and ask for my room key, but then I remembered I had taken it out with me and I managed to locate it in one of my coat pockets. I crawled along the corridor and soon arrived outside my room. I put the key in the lock, opened the door and crawled inside. By this time I felt a great sense of relief that I'd made it back and I climbed onto the bed, where I immediately fell into the state of unconsciousness I'd been fighting against.

The next morning I awoke around 7 a.m. The room was light because the sun shone in brightly through an open window, which also let in a cool fresh breeze. My head ached and my hands and knees were covered in blood, which was also all over the bedclothes. I shuffled off the bed and stood up. My ankle was causing me a great deal of pain so I pulled up my trouser leg and rolled down my sock to have a look at it. Shit: it was swollen and heavily bruised.

My body ached all over from the alcohol I had consumed so I sat down in a nearby chair to try to recollect my journey back to the hotel. I remembered losing my mobile phone and my wallet and was determined to go and find them before somebody else did. I had no money in my pockets but remembered that I had left my credit card with the receptionist when I'd initially booked into the hotel. Thank God for that, I thought. That will allow me to pay my hotel bill and cover the extra cost of cleaning of my room.

I got into the shower to clean myself up. My knees hurt badly when the hot water hit my open wounds but I just gritted my teeth and washed them clean. Next I got into a clean set of clothes and limped downstairs to pay my bill. I explained to the female receptionist that I'd had too much to drink the previous evening and had scuffed my knees on the pavement outside. I offered an extra fifty pounds to cover the cleaning costs and she gladly accepted it.

Next I walked down the street I had crawled up the previous evening and searched frantically around the area where I was fairly sure I had fallen. I looked under several parked cars and in and around the nearby gardens. After a while I decided to call it a day and climbed into my car and drove to the NATO base to see if Diz was OK. When I arrived, I saw him standing in the guardroom briefing his men.

'Hey, mate, have you got any ID?' shouted a Ministry of Defence policeman who was standing next to an armed Marine at the main gate.

'It's OK. He's with me,' shouted Diz through a window he had just slid open.

'Bloody hell, Diz. I don't know about you, but I'm absolutely wrecked with all that booze we drank last night,' I sighed as I limped towards him.

'Yeah. Me too, Steve. I feel like shit. Look at my eyes. They're like pissholes in the snow.'

'What have you done to your foot?'

'I fell over when I made my way home last night.'

'Yeah. Me too,' grinned Diz as he raised his Green Beret to expose a large lump on his head.

'I've also lost my wallet and mobile phone in one of the streets. Can you get a couple of the lads to help me to look for it?' I asked him.

'Yes, I can, Steve, but not for long because the Marines have just been sent to Afghanistan and we're on a security state of red alert.'

I nodded my head to acknowledge that I understood what he had said. I knew that all the military bases around the UK would be on a state of red alert by now. Half an hour later Diz and several other Marines were helping me to search around the area where I had stumbled. A few minutes later an old man who lived in one of the nearby houses approached us.

'You lot must be involved in this war with Afghanistan,' he said, looking all concerned. 'Are you looking for explosive devices?'

Diz shook his head and sighed deeply. He looked at me with weary eyes and I knew what he was going to say. 'Sorry, Steve, I'll have to call the search off. The newspapers will probably turn up next.'

'No problem, Diz,' I replied and shook his hand. 'Thanks anyway, mate.'

Shortly afterwards Diz made me a cup of hot coffee in the busy guardroom and told me that he would have to go soon because of the conflict.

'Thanks, Diz. It was a good night.'

'Yeah. A bloody good night,' he grinned. 'I really can't believe you got up so early today, Steve, after drinking those concoctions of alcohol I bought you last night.'

'Believe me, Diz, it hurts a lot more on the inside than it does on the outside,' I answered as I shook his hand and said goodbye.

CHAPTER TWENTY-THREE

NINJUTSU

'I'M THE OPERATIONS MANAGER,' Kenneth screamed at me whilst we sat together in a quiet meeting room.

'Yes, Kenneth, you're the operations manager,' I answered. 'I've told you I have no problem with that.'

Ken's illness and aggressive attitude towards me continued to be a problem and I hated working with him more than ever. My violent days in the workplace were well behind me now and the last thing I was going to do was to beat the hell out of him – although I must admit I certainly felt like it at times. It seemed quite evident to me that Kenneth was still having mental-health problems. Every morning he walked into work with a happy-go-lucky type of attitude; by lunchtime he looked shattered and disappeared for a few beers; and by the end of the day he was always sat by his computer with red blotches all over his face and his mouth opening and closing with no words coming out of it. This might sound like he was totally intoxicated but he wasn't, because he ended up in this state every day whether he drank at lunchtime or not.

One of the annoying things I hated about this guy was that he always tried to disagree with my management observations and decisions. Even the blatantly obvious sometimes eluded him. An example of this was that the network we supported across the UK had to be available 24 hours a day, 7 days a week and 365 days a year. To support this requirement during the evening we had engineers available on an on-call basis. One of the engineers was not very happy that the contract staff got paid more than he did. Then a pattern evolved where there were problems with the network every time he was on call. This meant that he got called out and got paid a lot more money. He even started to come into work wearing a thick expensive gold necklace as well as other items of jewellery and new clothes. At first I thought it was just a coincidence but it stood out like a sore thumb because these issues were greatly reduced when he was on his holidays or was not on call. I discussed this with Kenneth and he told me that it was nonsense and that we trusted our engineers wholeheartedly. I asked him if we could check the log files to see if the errors were occurring after this guy accessed the network, but he refused to let me do this. To manage the situation I arranged a series of training courses and sent the engineer on them for a number of weeks. Our network support issues were greatly and tellingly reduced during this period.

Also around this time I had another engineer who had just returned from Manhattan at the time of the 9/11 catastrophe. He hadn't been in the Twin Towers at the time; he'd just been in Manhattan. The engineer was being paid sixty pounds per hour for his work and told me that the atrocities had made him unmotivated to complete his tasks. He said he just wanted to take it easy for a couple of weeks. My answer to this was that he should go home and take it easy so that he wasn't getting paid a lot of money for very little productivity. He seemed shocked when I put this to him and instantly recovered from his ordeal.

The constant stress and strain of work, travelling daily and Kenneth's bad attitude continued to take their toll on me. I was only managing to get a couple of hours' sleep each night and I didn't feel fully alert during the working day. Also I started to get a searing pain in my neck and decided to go and see a chiropractor to try to alleviate it.

'Good morning, Mr Preece,' said the tall middle-aged chiropractor as I walked into his surgery. 'What can I do for you?'

'I've got a burning pain in my neck. I slipped over on the pavement a couple of days ago and twisted myself as I fell.'

'Sounds horrid,' he said.

'Yes, it hurts like hell.'

'What about your limp?' he asked.

'I've twisted my ankle too.'

'OK. I'll carry out some muscle tests first and try and fix your neck and a possible twist in your back. Once I've done this, I'll see what I can do with your ankle.'

I lay back on a soft padded bench and went through a series of tests with him as he tried to pinpoint the cause of the pain. As we did this, he asked me about my background and I told him I was a former Royal Marine Commando. This seemed to amuse him because he said he once served as a physiotherapist in the Royal Navy and was aware of a common problem that Marines seemed to experience with their necks. He asked me to relax with my head dangling over the edge of the bench and then he pulled my head vigorously to one side. A loud cracking noise sounded out from my neck and the pain I'd been in seemed instantly to disappear. Following this he treated my badly sprained ankle and sat down to talk to me.

'OK, Mr Preece, I think we may have resolved the issue with your neck, but I will need to see you a couple more times over the next few weeks. I also think the root of your problem is that you're suffering from work-related stress.'

'But I've got a bad neck and foot,' I said, surprised.

'Believe me, when you've worked in this industry as long as I have, you can see it a mile away.'

'Oh, OK, so what do I do to fix this?'

'Have you heard of the martial art of ninjutsu?'

'No, I haven't. What is it?'

'It's the martial art of the ninja. It's 3,000 years old and I believe it will help you.'

The chiropractor opened one of his desk drawers and pulled a videotape from it. 'Here, take this home and watch it. It's the Grand Master training in Japan. Tell me what you think about it next time you visit.'

Following this I took the video home and watched it with interest. I saw some old man effortlessly throwing people about in a martial-arts dojo. It didn't look like most martial arts because there was no aggression or shouting and screaming. I played it a few times out of curiosity but it didn't really excite me.

When I returned to see the chiropractor for a second time, I walked into his office without limping, because my ankle was much better. He did a little more work on my neck and tugged it until it cracked a few more times.

'Well, Mr Preece, you seem to be mending nicely. What did you think about the martial art on the video I lent you?'

'Not a lot,' I sighed, conveying that I was not impressed with it. 'It looked like nothing to me. It was just some old man throwing people about.'

The chiropractor burst into laughter. He seemed highly amused with the answer I had given him. 'You need to go to one of the local ninjutsu dojos,' he suggested. 'You need to step into their world to understand the true power of the ninja.'

'Look, mate, it sounds like a load of bollocks to me. I used to be a boxer a few years ago and I found that a lot more interesting.'

'No, no, you really need to experience this for yourself,' he insisted. 'This could have an enormous and positive effect on your stress problem.'

'OK,' I sighed, feeling that I would be wasting my time. 'I'll give it a go.'

A couple of days later I followed the directions that the chiropractor had given me and found the dojo inside a small brick-built building. The inside resembled a small sports hall and had a group of padded mats all pushed together in the middle. On my first visit I asked the instructors if I could sit and watch what they did and they happily agreed. As with the video, I watched with interest. However, as they went through their moves, I still couldn't really see what they were doing. What I did like was the amiable atmosphere that filled the room. No one appeared to have an attitude problem and there was no shouting and screaming. At the end of the evening I thanked them for allowing me to watch and accepted their invitation to join them next time.

The next week I decided to attend regularly. At first it was hard work. They told me to relax and showed me how to break my fall by rolling across the floor. For the first month or so I hit the floor like a tonne of bricks and felt totally confused about what they were teaching me. It was totally different to anything that I'd learned before. It was a martial art where strength and aggression were a sign of weakness and unarmed-combat techniques were applied by using your body weight and movement. The instructors, Richard and Bob, were both black belts and they moved with great speed and agility. The two of them were a lot senior in years to me, but this made no difference to their high levels of professionalism and ability. What impressed me the most was their wealth of knowledge and wisdom about life, its energies and nature. They didn't refer to ninjutsu as a martial art; they referred to it as a survival art.

A few weeks later I met and trained under Barty, the most senior of the black belts. He was the sensei (teacher) and was very highly graded as a tenth-dan black belt. He was also highly skilled as a Japanese alternative therapist and probably one of the best in the world in this field. The Grand Master from Japan taught him this powerful therapy. When I first saw him enter the dojo, the atmosphere became electric. His movement and expression of feeling were amazing. He virtually mirrored the Grand Master's physical movements that I had seen on the chiropractor's video a few weeks earlier. I also noticed that the other black belts held him in high esteem and respected his superior level of ability and understanding of ninjutsu. I watched them as they listened carefully to his teaching and guidance. Later, I learned a lot more about him and felt proud to be one of his students. He was without doubt a truly exceptional man.

As the months went by, my confusion diminished and I began to see and understand more and more about this survival art. I could now roll across the floor without the big thuds that I had started with. I learned techniques that would help to defend myself should the situation arise and I learned to disguise them in true ninja fashion. My body became increasingly less stressed and more loose and relaxed than ever before. This helped me to work better and handle situations without feeling so pressured. Kenneth was no longer such a big problem either. I learned to handle his aggression with a cool calmness. This confused him and often made him unsure of what to say to me.

One morning the project director approached me. He told me that he'd been aware of the way Kenneth had been treating me and had hoped that I would be able to work with him to help him to recover from his mental-health problems. However, he'd now decided enough was enough and shortly afterwards he told Kenneth he was out of a job. I suppose I was relieved to see him go, but I did truly feel sorry for him.

That weekend I was cycling along the sea front with my wife. Both of us had small seats attached to the rear of our bicycles and both of us had one of our children sitting in them. As we cycled along, I looked out towards the sea and breathed a few deep lungfuls of fresh air. Suddenly I saw a man cycle past me in the opposite direction with a child sitting in a small seat on the rear of his bicycle. He looked familiar to me and reminded me of a Marine I'd once served with.

Something told me it was him so I pulled tightly on my brakes and came to a halt. I put both of my feet onto the ground and turned around.

'SCOUSE!' I shouted, hoping that, by some remote chance, it would be him.

The cyclist stopped too and turned around. He looked at me for a few moments before turning his bicycle around and pedalling towards me. He stopped opposite me and looked at my face.

'Fucking hell, Scouse, it is you,' I said, feeling elated.

Scouse grinned too. 'Steve. Bloody hell, mate, I don't believe it. After all these years. It's great to see you. What are you doing here in the north-east?'

'I live here, mate. I've lived here for years but I've been working away a lot.'

Scouse was what we called a three-badger Marine at HMS Warrior. Three-badger Marines were men of great experience in the Royal Marines, who were exceptional at their jobs but were not interested in promotion. The three badges were awarded one at a time for each period of four years' service. After 12 years no more badges were awarded. Scouse's military service started in the mid-'60s and finished at HMS Warrior in the late 1980s, shortly after I'd left the base to join the Royal Marines Police. After he left the Marines, he went on to be a personal bodyguard.

As we talked, we both felt surprised to find out that we'd actually lived around the corner from each other for nearly two years. Scouse told me that he'd moved on with his life since leaving the Marines and had never really looked back. He said his last memory of the Marines was when he was about to leave for the last time and the duty sergeant told him that he could be done for trespassing if he didn't leave the premises straight away. It was sad really. Scouse had dedicated his life to the Marines for 22 years and that was his last memory.

Back at the ninja dojo I continued to work hard at learning to stay relaxed when I applied the techniques that were taught to me. I saw the tenth-dan ninja just a handful of times more and spent most of my time training with the two other senior ninjas. After a while I developed a high level of respect for them as I realised that they made age seem like a figment of the imagination.

When we trained, they talked about something called form, which at first I didn't understand. They explained to me that ninjutsu came in many different styles and that their style had been refined by the tenth-dan ninja, whom they said was a genius and that he mirrored the style of the Grand Master in Japan. They said that form was something you could see, like a technique being applied in karate. In their style, though, which was newer than the old 'form' style and was referred to as 'flow', the individual techniques were hidden. They said they used to train with form but had learned to throw it away. I thought I understood what they meant but I wasn't sure.

I also learned about another ninja, called Keith, who used to train with the highly graded tenth-dan sensei some years before.

He had apparently decided to go his own way and put together his own style of ninjutsu based on his interpretation of what the Japanese Grand Master was teaching. Curiosity took me to his dojo and he made me welcome when I entered. Suddenly, I saw someone grinning at me.

'Steve! Hey, how are you?'

'Bloody Nora, Martin,' I grinned as I shook his hand.

Martin was an old friend of mine whom I grew up with as a child. I hadn't seen him for about 20 years and he'd hardly changed a bit. When we were children, we lived next door to each other and were more like brothers than friends. I remembered a time when we stuffed some paper into an empty purse and tied some cotton around it. We placed the purse in the main street and trailed the barely visible cotton back inside Martin's house. When people walked past, they saw the purse and tried to pick it up. We pulled hard on the cotton and the purse mysteriously moved away from their grasp. Some people seemed worried by it and walked away whilst others tried time and time again to pick it up until we yanked on the cotton to pull it hard against Martin's letterbox. Our little game was finally brought to an abrupt ending when a papergirl skipped along the street and kicked the purse like a football. The kick was so hard that the cotton snapped and the papergirl ran off with the purse.

'It's great to see you, Steve. It's been a long time.'

'Yes, it has. I've certainly covered a lot of ground since the last time I saw you.'

'Have you come to train with us, Steve?'

'Yes, if you don't mind,' I smiled, shaking his hand again.

Martin had been training in ninjutsu for around 20 years and was now a fifth-dan black belt. To pass your fifth-dan grade in ninjutsu you had to train with the Grand Master from Japan and take the saaki test. The ninja taking the test would have to kneel in front of the Grand Master, bow and then turn and face the opposite direction. He would remain motionless on his knees. The Grand Master would stand behind him and raise a big wooden staff into the air. In his own time and without warning, he would drive the wooden staff down onto the ninja's head. The ninja was not allowed to move until he could feel the intent of the attacker as he propelled the wooden staff down towards him. To sense this movement the ninja had to use his sixth sense to rapidly move out of the way before the wooden staff hit him. If he moved without the staff striking him, then he would pass the test. If he didn't, then he would fail and would end up with a sore head. The test was thousands of years old and used to be done with a sword instead of a wooden staff. The style of these ninjas was different to that taught by the tenth-dan sensei at the other dojo, but also similar to the style used by the Grand Master in Japan. It was as if both sensei's had taken a different part of the art and refined it to use as their own. Both styles were effectively ruthless and both teachers were in an elite class of their own.

Back at work my contract came to a close and I said goodbye to the friends I'd made. I wasn't disappointed to put that job behind me. It was more something I wanted to forget than a valuable experience. Following this I was offered another job in Liverpool. I wasn't sure if I wanted to take it, though, because it meant being away from home and from my family for at least six months. A man from the employment agency that offered me the job telephoned me at home.

'Hello, is that Steven?' he asked when I put the telephone receiver to my ear.

'Yes. Hello there.'

'I'm calling to give you the details of your new contract in Liverpool.'

'Oh. I'm really sorry but I won't be able to go because my father has died,' I told him.

'I am sorry to hear that, Steve. I'll give you a call in a week or so, if that's OK with you.'

'Yes, please do. Goodbye,' I sighed and put the receiver down.

I felt really guilty about what I'd said to him. I wasn't lying; my father had died, except that he'd died 13 years ago. I was fed up with having to work away from my family all the time. I didn't want to go and decided that I'd now got enough money saved in the bank to take some time off and to chill out for a while. When

I told Anne my decision, she was a little disappointed. This was because she knew our savings would eventually dwindle. We'd seen it happen so many times in the past when I'd been out of work. Nevertheless I was determined not to go and that was that – or so I'd thought until I received a sympathy card from the agent I'd spoken to on the telephone. I felt so guilty when I received it that I telephoned him and told him that I would be happy to start the job a few days later. Before I left I spoke to Richard, who was one of the highly graded ninjas from the tenth-dan sensei's dojo. Richard had short grey hair and was around 60 years old. His fitness and wisdom were phenomenal and I'd begun to respect him and strongly valued his friendship. He told me that he didn't believe in coincidence and that for some reason he believed I was meant to go to Liverpool. Strangely these words appeared to ring true because I found a ninjutsu dojo on the Internet that taught the old-style ninjutsu: form.

CHAPTER TWENTY-FOUR

ENTER THE NINJA

In June 2002 I climbed into my car and headed for my new contract in Liverpool. I got a strange feeling as I returned to the city and drove around the outskirts of the centre, past the Liver Insurance building that housed the famous ornamental Liver birds on its high-rise rooftop. I'd spent so much time there over the years, it was like returning home.

My job was with a huge human-resources company deep in the middle of the city centre. I walked inside the high-rise tower block of offices accompanied by a management consultant from the agency I'd been recruited by. Inside we held a meeting with my new manager, who explained the requirements of the job to me. His name was Paul and he was a tall well-built guy in his mid-40s. Paul was an extremely good manager who never got flustered with problems as they arose and always seemed to be in control of the situation. We got on well right from the word go. Later I learned that he was also a rugby player of 30 years, and this didn't surprise me, because of the size of him.

On an evening I retired to my hotel room, which was situated a short distance from the marina and the infamous river Mersey. The evenings were warm and quiet and I often spent a lot of time just walking along the riverside. I also felt fed up because I was working away from home once again and decided to get the autobiography I was writing out of the cupboard for the first time in nearly ten years. I'd picked it up intermittently in the early '90s, but I decided that 2002 would be the year to finish it once and for all.

After a few weeks I felt it was time to start my ninjutsu training again and I followed the instructions I'd been given over the phone to go and meet my new sensei. I found his house with very little difficulty. I knocked on the door and waited for an answer. Suddenly the door sprung open and a middle-aged lean-looking man with dark hair stood looking at me with a baseball bat in his hands.

'Are you Steve?' he asked. 'Or do I beat the shit out of you with this baseball bat?'

'I'm Steve,' I smiled nervously.

'Good, I'm Mac. Pleased to meet you. I've been expecting you. Please come in and wipe your feet on the doormat.'

Mac asked me about my background and about any martial arts I'd done in the past. I explained to him that I'd spent seven years in the Marines, where I did boxing and jujitsu. I also told him about my training in ninjutsu but he said he wasn't too bothered about that because he intended to teach me his own style. Next I followed him in my car as he drove along to the place where his dojo was located. This was down a quiet alleyway behind a church. My eyes lit up with amazement as Mac opened the door and we stepped inside. The room was fairly spacious yet dull inside because the building had no windows. The floors were padded and the walls were covered in various types of lethal-looking weapons and a multitude of pictures of ninjas. Several sets of heavy wooden beams spanned the width of the ceiling and several different-sized punch-bags hung down from them. At the far end of the room I saw a mirrored wall with hundreds of white candles flickering away in front of it and a large picture of the ninja Grand Master from Japan facing us.

'Good here, isn't it?' said Mac, who had just come out of a changing room dressed in a black ninja suit.

I nodded my head and stood in line with a large group of ninja students facing Mac and the picture of the Grand Master. Mac dropped to his knees and the rest of the class followed suit. He gave me a brief introduction to the rest of the students and clapped his hands to signal the start of the lesson. This was the real beginning of my lessons in the concepts, principles and techniques of this mystical survival art that stretches back thousands of years, through feudal Japanese masters to ancient Chinese monks. It was very different from what I'd been taught previously.

The sensei had an understudy who assisted him with the training. He too moved with great stealth and agility and showed exceptional ability in his teaching. He also taught his own class on a different evening, which I joined. This was a mixture of adults and children. At first I felt a bit silly training with the children but soon realised that it was beneficial because they helped me to learn basic body movements in the form of katas. The fact that I was willing to listen to them pleased Mac and he told me that we were all teachers. If at any point I put a foot wrong with my movements, the children would shake their heads slowly. Then they would show me again and again until I got it right, at which point they would nod their heads and smile at me. When I became well versed in the katas, I helped to improve the children's techniques in turn and felt really pleased when I was told that they liked and respected me.

Back in the twice-weekly adult class I learned countless unarmed-combat techniques and our sensei taught us sword and stick fighting. He was truly a master in this field in his own right. The other students were reliable and amiable and a pleasure to train with. Between us we soon became good friends and developed a camaraderie and a sense of belonging. For the first time in a lot of years I could see beyond my past career in the Marines and felt like I'd finally found something else to believe in.

During training there was a lot of emphasis on physical fitness and a varied amount of unorthodox training techniques. Some of these involved repeatedly punching wooden boards that were wrapped in rope until the skin hung from our knuckles, and thrusting our open fingers hard into buckets of sharp sand and pebbles. Blood poured from open wounds in my hands when I did this, but like the other students I accepted it and just got on with it.

When I wasn't training or at work, I continued to work on my book. There was a personal story I wanted to tell. At the age of 18 I completed my nine-months' basic training and was posted to my first commando unit. During my first night in the accommodation block, an older Marine whom I'd never seen before burst into the room and beat me senseless for no apparent reason. When his colleague dragged him off me, he said, 'He has to learn. He has to learn.' This was my introduction to the lifestyle of some of the Marines at that time: violence and excess came with the territory, and if it happened to you, you kept your mouth shut and didn't report it. I spent the rest of my career embracing this mentality, both in the barrack-rooms and on the street. I wasn't afraid and never hesitated to use violence against people who offered it to me. Like many others at the time, I gained acceptance and earned respect amongst the Marines by using my forehead and fists. Eventually my fighting led to a court martial, but thankfully I was acquitted. My story was without doubt an untold story, but one that needed telling if I was going to move on with my life. That, combined with my ninjutsu training, was now helping me to do this.

Incidentally, I later learned that there was also a personal element to the beating I'd received, albeit a very tenuous one. On my first day at 45 Commando I'd bumped into a Marine who had passed out of training a couple of weeks before me. We were never friends and he called me a sprog. This was a term used for a young Marine who was fresh out of basic training and knew very little about true Marine life (also referred to as a 'bit of skin'). I was a sprog but I told him that he was too, which annoyed him. Unfortunately for me this wasn't the story he told this older Marine, who had previously returned from the Falklands War. He told him I'd been gobbing off that I wasn't a sprog. The experienced Marine wasted no time in teaching me some respect. I settled my score with the pathetic sprog a few years later, when I'd fully found my feet, and I also caught up with the older Marine who'd beaten me, and returned the compliment.

I sat with my wife and children at home one Saturday evening and drank a couple of bottles of wine. It was late but I wanted to telephone Richard to tell him about my training.

'Hello,' said Richard as he answered the phone.

'Hello, Richard, it's Steve. How are you?'

'I'm fine, Steve. How is your training going?'

'It's going great. This is the type of stuff you need to incorporate into your training classes.'

'No, Steve,' Richard laughed. 'You're learning form. When you return from Liverpool and come back to train with us, you will have to throw the form away.'

'But I'm training very well now. I'm getting really good at this,' I sighed.

'Yes, and that's good, but your training will really begin when you return. We left the form behind a long time ago, Steve, and moved on from it. You will do this too. Enjoy the form, Steve. It's a great journey. Remember, form is a series of movements used to deploy a technique. When you throw away the form, the technique will be completed in one move and will not look like a technique. It will be formless. Do you understand what I'm explaining to you, Steve?'

'I . . . I think I do, Richard,' I answered before we said goodbye.

Back in Liverpool I continued to work hard at my ninjutsu training. My fitness level had risen sharply and I began to feel good about myself. My writing was also making good progress and I was finally approaching completion of my autobiography. One part that I found difficult to write was the chapter about my childhood. My father hadn't been the best man in the world; nor had he been a good husband to my mother. When I wrote this chapter, I found myself drinking heavily and occasionally bursting into tears. I did this once during a night out on the town with my boss Paul and he just told me to let all my emotion come out.

After I'd been training for five months I became fairly well versed in the techniques I'd been taught and wondered if this martial-arts stuff would work in a street-fight situation. As fate would have it, I soon got the opportunity to find out.

It was a cold wintery night in Liverpool and a frosty wind made me shiver as I walked through the door of a local public house. It was a Wednesday, which was normally a ninjutsu training night for me but I'd decided to reduce my training from eight hours a week to four. Inside, the bar was fairly quiet, apart from a few old men who sat by a warm cosy fire sipping their beer. I purchased a pint of beer and sat down next to them.

'All right, mate?' said one of them. 'Have you popped in for a few beers?'

'Yes, I have, thank you. It's bloody freezing outside.'

'Come and sit near the fire with us, mate. It'll warm you through,' he smiled.

I joined the old men and sat with them next to the fire. They were a friendly bunch and they talked about the problems created by the youths of today. I listened with interest as I found their conversation to be meaningful and constructive. Suddenly I felt a cold draft on the back of my neck and heard somebody walk through the doorway behind me.

'Hello, John, mate,' one of the men said to an old man who stood by the fire to warm himself.

The old man didn't answer. He just nodded his head as he removed his cap and coat and a scarf that he'd wrapped around his face. He purchased a pint of beer and sat down next to me. I shivered because I could feel the cool air from outside coming off his body.

'Cheers, young man,' he gestured and drank from his beer glass.

I frowned as he did this because I noticed that he had a badly swollen black eye and a badly bruised cheekbone.

'Bloody hell, mate, what happened to you?' I asked him.

'He was mugged a couple of days ago,' one of the other men answered. 'Down by the docks.'

'Did the police get them?' I asked, feeling concerned.

'Don't be silly,' the old man answered. 'This kind of thing has happened to a few of us around here. You have to stay away from the edge of the docks because the youths down there mug you.'

'Do they pick on old men?'

'They pick on anybody who's daft enough to venture their way. They mug them and kick the crap out of them like they did to me,' he sobbed.

'Don't worry, mate,' I said to comfort him and I saw that his eyes were full of tears.

The old man drank his pint down and put his hat, scarf and coat back on and bid us goodnight. The three elderly men told him to take care of himself as he briefly waved and left the pub.

'Those bloody youths piss me off,' said one of the men. 'One of these days they'll pick on the wrong person.'

'Yes,' they all agreed and drank their beers.

After a few more beers I decided it was time to leave and fastened my coat up before saying goodnight to the old men.

'Goodnight, young man. Mind how you go,' one of them said.

'Yes, and stay away from the edge of the docks,' said another.

'Listen, guys: one of these days those youths really *are* going to pick on the wrong person,' I grinned. 'When a stranger walks into a pub and you say hello, you take him at face value. What you don't know is who he is or what he's really like. Do you understand what I mean?'

'We're not sure, my friend, but we think we do. Take care of yourself,' one of them said as I walked out into the dark cold night.

It felt even colder now. Maybe the temperature had dropped a little more or maybe the alcohol I had consumed had reduced my body temperature. I staggered slightly as I walked towards the docks. This made me wonder if I was doing the right thing. Bollicks, I thought. I want to know if this ninjutsu stuff works. As I neared the docks, I saw three youths standing together around a small fire inside a rusty oil barrel. They were all wearing woolly hats and were stood looking in my direction with their hands in their pockets.

As I approached, I saw them put their heads down and stare

into their fire. They didn't seem the least bit interested in me as I walked past.

'Hey, woolly back,' a voice said behind me. 'Hey you. I'm talking to you, mate.'

I stopped and slowly turned around. I recognised the name he had called me as a term used in Liverpool to describe someone who lived on the outskirts of the city. A cold wind blew in my face and caused my eyes to water. I saw that the three youths who had been standing around the fire were now just a few feet behind me. One of them had a stick in his hand and was wearing a yellow padded jacket.

'Give us your money now, woolly back, or I'll beat the fucking shit out of you with this stick,' one of them threatened.

'You can't beat me up; I'm not an old man,' I answered in a firm voice.

'You what?' one of them exclaimed.

'I said fuck off.'

'Let's do him now,' one of them shouted as he ran at me and grabbed a tight hold on my jacket.

I grabbed a hold of his hand lightly and twisted it in towards his body in one swift move. His arm locked tight and he squealed. Another came running at me from the side but I quickly reacted by thrusting the body of the youth I had hold of hard into the oncoming assailant. Their heads clashed and they both cried out in pain. The third youth ran at me with the stick in his hand and swung it hard towards me. I released the arm lock I was holding and rapidly ducked to avoid the oncoming blow, which swished just millimetres from my face. I moved towards him and felt for something to get hold of. I sensed he was swinging the stick again so I resorted to old faithful and swung a forceful head-butt hard into his face. His legs buckled and he fell back and onto the ground. The three youths started to run off in different directions and were soon out of sight.

Then all was silent apart from the fire in the rusty oil barrel that was crackling away. The cold wind made my spine shiver so I stood by the fire for a while to warm myself. I felt quite pleased as I made the short journey back to my hotel. That's the type of justice those bastards need, I thought.

The next week when I entered the pub, I saw all four gentlemen sitting together.

'Come in, young man, and sit with us,' one of them said. 'It's warm by the fire.'

'It's cold tonight,' I said with a warm glowing smile on my face.

'Yes,' one of them answered. 'We hear there was a vigilante walking the streets causing heat last week.'

'Sounds interesting,' I answered. 'Is it somebody you know?'

'No. When you meet strangers these days, there's some questions you just don't ask,' one of them said.

We all nodded and laughed together as we warmed ourselves around the hot fire. The old men refused to let me buy a beer that evening and I walked home peacefully past the quiet docks wall area.

Back in the dojo we learned about the history and traditions of the ninja and were introduced to more lethal weapons that were used by them on the battlefield or during enemy-infiltration operations. I recognised a lot of their stealth tactics from what I'd been taught in the Marines and was amazed that the ninjas had been using them hundreds of years ago. The training was so realistic at times that I felt as if I'd been cast back in time to the battlefields of the ninja and the samurai and, if anything else, the whole thing was a fantastic experience and a great adventure.

During my last couple of weeks in Liverpool I put the finishing touches to my autobiography and lent it to an old friend of mine who was a former Royal Marine during the 1960s. After he read it he made a request that I add a forces myth to it. The old story he wanted me to add was about a recruit standing on the parade square. A regimental sergeant major (RSM) pokes him with his pace stick and says: 'There's a piece of shit on the end of this stick.' And the recruit says, 'It's not on this end, sir.' Then the RSM beats him with his stick. I thought about the request for a day or two and told him that I would add it for him.

Why not, I thought: the rest of the book describes exactly what I did and experienced in the Marines during the '80s, so one funny episode which may or may not have happened before I joined couldn't do any harm.

Next I lent it to my mate Scouse, who also joined the Marines in the 1960s and served with me in the 1980s. It was quite amusing that I was now working in Liverpool during the week with Scousers and travelling home on a weekend and visiting my mate called Scouse too. He read the book and told me he thought it was great. He said it brought back a lot of good memories for him and gave him a sense of belonging. He also said that he thought the book would cause a lot of controversy amongst former senior ranks who would not like this side of the story being told. However, this was my story and I was adamant that I was going to tell it. Obviously this was dependent on a publisher accepting it so I began my search for one that published this type of book and consequently sent it off to Mainstream Publishing in Edinburgh.

When I left Liverpool for the last time, I bid goodbye to Mac and his fellow teacher and all the other ninjutsu students, not forgetting, of course, to say goodbye to the children. Lastly I said goodbye to my boss, Paul, whom I knew would be a good friend for the rest of my life. I felt a little sad as I drove away. It was a great place, which held so many memories for me, and I found the majority of people there to be realistic and down to earth. I'll be back one day, I thought. I love Liverpool. It's a great city.

CHAPTER TWENTY-FIVE

AIKIDO

'Welcome back, Steve,' said Richard, holding his hand out to shake mine.

'It's good to be back. I've learnt so much about ninjutsu.'

'You've learnt so much about the form of ninjutsu,' interrupted Bob as he fastened his black belt around his waist. 'Now you need to throw it away.'

The tenth-dan ninja arrived a short time later and also welcomed me back. He didn't seem too pleased about my newly acquired skills and also told me that I needed to throw the form away. I knew that he certainly practised what he preached, as his techniques were always hidden inside his movements. He made the most lethal of moves look like nothing and could disguise his techniques so well that it looked as if he was actually trying to help an assailant when really he was suppressing them. To him it must have been disappointing that I'd come back from Liverpool with something that he'd moved on from many years before. I knew I had to lose the form, but this was never going to be easy. If I applied a technique in two or three moves, I had to learn to apply it in one move. When a movement stopped, I had to keep it flowing, and most of all I needed to learn to unbalance my opponents before I applied my techniques.

On the work front I was offered a project-management position for a pharmaceuticals company in Manchester. The project was huge and had a budget of ninety two million pounds. It meant travelling away from home again, which I again wasn't too happy about. Nevertheless I still had to support my family so I willingly accepted the job. The complex I worked in was state-of-the-art stuff with no expense spared on buildings or equipment. It was generally a great place to work, where the majority of employees were scientists. Some of these people also practiced martial arts, which came in the form of aikido.

Aikido is a modern Japanese martial art unique in its synthesis of classic forms with a well-defined spiritual base. Like ninjutsu it is non-competitive and practiced without the need for aggression. The practitioners in this art moved with a flow when they applied their techniques. This was the same flow that I had to learn in order to throw away my ninjutsu form. Naturally it was a logical choice for me to join the club straight away.

The aikido senseis I met were very amiable and professional people. They made me feel comfortable straight away as they welcomed me to train with them in their dojos. The art of aikido was both form and formless, but it was still very different from the formless ninjutsu I'd learnt back home. I was literally starting a new style of martial art from the beginning for the third time. Initially it was like learning the form in Liverpool because I needed to learn the set movements and techniques that were required as part of the grading system. This at times I found very confusing because I couldn't always remember all the required movements. The more experienced senior grades knew all the techniques and moved well with an impressive flow. They demonstrated the techniques first and then worked hard between them to pass their skills and knowledge on to the rest of us. What I noticed and liked as I trained with them was a great feeling of peace and harmony that seemed to flow like the movements amongst us. After a while I began to gain a better understanding of the art and started to get a basic understanding of the principles needed to apply it.

Most nights after training we went to the pub for a few beers. It was a regular activity that I enjoyed because the people I trained with were so friendly and were a pleasure to know and socialise with.

Whilst I was working in Manchester, my curiosity led me to read up on the energies of the body. These energies are referred to as chi by the Chinese and ki by the Japanese. In the Western world the majority of people would pass the theory off as a load of rubbish but these energy points are the same energy points used in acupuncture. Initially I thought the energies were a load of hocus-pocus, but the more I learned about them the more I began to understand them.

One night I was sat reading about the energy points in the body and nodded my head as I suddenly realised that Westerners had difficulty believing in them because they couldn't see them. My mind cast back to the highly graded ninja back in the north-east. Bloody hell, I thought, as I finally began to understand the potency of formless ninjutsu, the sensei is a genius. I realised that he had incorporated the healing therapy into the martial art to the extent that he and his pupils had the ability to force the human body to trust their touch and to allow them to penetrate its defences without it being able to resist them. It was so advanced that you couldn't see what they were doing without them teaching you their ways. It was similar to my newly found perception of the energies. You couldn't really see its power; you needed to feel it.

The book I was reading also referred to the highest level of energy, called the kosmos. This is what we in the modern Western world would generally refer to as God. This made me think about the church that I went to when I took my children to get baptised. Jesus Christ came in the form of a human being so that we could see him and believe in him. Undoubtedly if we couldn't see him then we wouldn't believe in his existence. That night was a great night for me. Suddenly my understanding about form had been cemented in my thoughts. Now I knew why Richard had told me that I had to lose the form. I needed to do this to advance in my training.

Several months later I was offered the opportunity to go for an interview for a permanent management position near home with a huge global corporate company. It was a dream come true because I was fed up with spending so much time away from my family. I was being well paid for this, but money couldn't buy the time back with them. If I got the job, it would also mean that I could continue to train under the great sensei and advance my skills as a ninja.

After attending three consecutive interviews with the company, I was delighted when they offered me the position, as were my wife and children when I informed them. A couple of weeks later I said goodbye to my work colleagues and fellow aikido students and teachers and joined the company as a senior technical operations manager. I was pleased with my new position. It wasn't as senior as some corporate positions I'd held in the past but I wasn't bothered because I was going to work each day and then coming home each evening to see my wife and children. It was, as far as I was concerned, a damn sight better than going back to a lonely hotel room each evening and travelling home each weekend.

My ninjutsu training started to improve too, and the elite senseis from both ninjutsu dojos welcomed me with open arms to train with them once again and to work at throwing away the form of ninjutsu. I also spent more time with Richard, who continued to be a very special friend. I frequently visited him at his home, where we talked about my violent past and more importantly about the philosophy of ninjutsu. I listened carefully to his advice and the great wisdom that he and the tenth-dan ninja taught me. My journey into the world of the ninjas had dramatically changed my outlook on life and for the first time in years I really felt in control. The fire that had burned inside my spirit for so long seemed to be more subdued now and I became well versed in handling difficult situations calmly, without any sign of aggression or frustration. Additionally I began to cherish the time I was able to spend with my family. They were fed up with my working away all the time and seemed a lot happier now that I was with them every day.

My run of good luck continued, as Mainstream Publishing sent me a letter to tell me that they wanted to publish my book.

I felt really pleased with the news, but was unsure what to call it. Initially I thought of the old Marine saying, 'Tell it to the Marines', but found that this had been used before. I thought long and hard about the contents of my book and the fact that it was different from most stories soldiers had to tell because it was a personal story about friendships, enmities, drinking and fighting amongst the ranks. Consequently, I decided to call it *Amongst the Marines*, with a subtitle of *The Untold Story*.

Once I received a copy of the printed book, I felt nervous and unsure of whether I still wanted to tell my story. However, by this time I knew I'd written it to move on from the past, so I had to go through with it. I knew this was the right thing to do.

CHAPTER TWENTY-SIX

WE'RE IRA

'Good morning, Steve,' said Colin. 'Are you coming with us for a night out in Newcastle tomorrow?'

Colin was a fellow project manager. He was a tall stocky man with short wavy blond hair. He had organised a night out for all the project managers that worked as part of the company's IT management team.

'I've been working away from home for years, Colin. I rarely go out socialising these days because I like to spend my spare time with my wife and children.'

'Oh, come on, Steve. It'll be a good way to get to know all the other guys. Don't be the odd one out. All the other managers are coming.'

'I live a good distance away from Newcastle city centre. It'll cost me a fortune to get home in a taxi.'

'No problem there, mate. The company is paying for all of us to stay in a hotel. They're paying for everything. All the food and drink is going to be free.'

'Sounds inviting, Colin. Maybe I will come.'

'Good. Don't miss it; it'll be a good night,' he finished and patted me on the back before walking out of the room.

I wasn't sure whether to accept the invitation because I knew Anne wanted to spend our spare time together. I also knew she wouldn't be too pleased if I told her I was going out for the night because she knew there was still the potential for me to get into trouble once I was under the influence of alcohol.

When I got home that evening, I mentioned the night out to her and she reluctantly agreed to let me go without argument because I said that it would be a good opportunity to get to know my new work colleagues. The children didn't look too happy about the idea either as they looked at me with sorry eyes.

'What's the matter, sons?' I asked them with feigned surprise, but really knowing the answer.

'We don't want you to go, Dad. We want you to stay with us.'

For a moment I felt like deciding not to go for the night out, but I was keen to socialise with my new colleagues because I thought Colin was right, in that it would be a good opportunity to get to know them all.

'Don't worry, my lads. I'll see you the following day. It's not like I'm working away for ages, is it?'

'We know, Dad,' said Gary. 'But we don't like you staying away from us any more. We want you to stay at home with us.'

'Don't worry. It'll only be for one night. I won't make a habit of it,' I smiled as I packed my things into a bag to go training at the tenth dan's ninjutsu dojo.

When I got there, I shook hands with the sensei and all the other ninjas. Richard shook hands with me and gave me a hug. He was always a great friend. At times he had almost been like a father to me, which I appreciated because he'd always been there when I needed him. Sometimes this had been at various times of the night when I had consumed vast amounts of alcohol and needed someone to talk to, and other times I'd gone round his house to visit him. I had changed a lot over the years, especially since I had entered into the world of the ninja. Richard had a lot to do with that change and truthfully I will always be grateful for this.

The sensei started the lesson and used Richard as his would-be assailant. Richard threw a hard punch towards him, which he swiftly dealt with by throwing him powerfully to the floor. Richard rolled forwards and practically moulded with the ground as he rolled across it and ended up back on his feet. He smiled as he did this. He, like the sensei, made the most difficult of movements look easy.

The sensei called me onto the floor next. It was a free-for-all in that I could throw anything at him that I wanted. I knew his ability was exceptional and for some reason he referred to my background as a boxer and asked me to attack him as one. I was sceptical about his request because I'd once heard about the Grand Master of ninjutsu taking the arms away from a boxer. Nevertheless I quickly adopted a boxing stance and blocked the oncoming onslaught of blows. Suddenly his attack movements seemed to strike me in slow motion on the lower part of my forearm. After he did this he stopped still and smiled at me. Then he casually stepped back and sat down as if he was waiting for something to happen. For a moment this puzzled me, because I was still standing in a boxing stance waiting for him to throw a few more blows at me. Suddenly my right arm started to give way and for some reason it strangely fell weak and limp by my side like a loose piece of meat. Initially I felt a little dismayed, but I'd always known he was more than capable of this and was mirroring the Grand Master's movements from the stories I'd been told about disarming a boxer. Ultimately he was my teacher and I respected him. If he hadn't done this, I would never have believed it possible. He was without doubt an exceptional man and, as they say, the proof is in the pudding.

Afterwards, on completion of training, I stood talking to him whilst he massaged my arm muscle to put some life back into it. His knowledge of human anatomy was immense and I don't think there was a single thing that existed inside it that he wasn't aware of. As he massaged my arm, he smiled at me.

'You're welcome to train with me in Japanese healing therapy if you want to, Steve,' he said.

My eyes lit up. I already had great respect for my sensei, but to be accepted to study with him as a practitioner was a great honour. I knew a condition of doing this was that my heart had to be pure. This was an unwritten rule and to be honest I really don't know where it came from. Even so I was given the invitation and felt very proud and pleased with myself.

That evening I went to bed happy. I knew after all these years I had finally made the transition from being an aggressive serviceman to a normal respectable citizen and an everyday accepted member of the public. At last I was just another person walking down the street without somebody crossing the road because they saw me approaching. I looked at Anne, who was fast asleep on the other side of the bed, and felt proud of her. She had stayed with me through thick and thin over the years and understood me better than anyone. Truthfully, apart from my mother, she is the only woman I have ever really loved. I knew I was very lucky to have a wife like her.

The next evening I met up with my work colleagues and we drove into the heart of Newcastle city centre, where we booked into the hotel. The interior was nice and plush and my room was spacious, with a double bed and nice furniture. I quickly unpacked my belongings and showered before meeting the other guys in a bar downstairs. The lounge had a green carpet with white wallpaper and gold fittings. There were rows of small tables with several chairs placed around each of them. Firstly we all drank a beer in the hotel bar before heading off to another pub where we had arranged to get some food.

This pub was small and dingy inside, with red walls and a low ceiling. There was a warm fire burning which gave off lots of heat, making it feel nice and cosy. Throughout the night I mingled with my work colleagues and generally felt content with their conversation and enjoyed their company. The beer was free as well as the food and we all drank plenty. Somehow I ended up drinking with two different sets of people and consumed a mixture of beer and spirits. Later, when the pub closed, we headed back to the hotel with the intention of taking advantage of the late bar that was available in the lounge. This would be open until the early hours of the morning.

When we arrived, we occupied three sets of tables and chairs next to the bar, where we started to crack jokes and exchange good-humoured banter between ourselves. Suddenly two men sat on the vacant chairs amongst us. Both of them were aged around 30 and looked physically fit, as if they were training, or had been trained, for something. One of them had short-cropped brown hair and the other had a skinhead.

'What are you lot doing here?' asked the skinhead in a very broad Northern Irish accent.

I stared at them as Colin told them that we all worked together and were staying at the hotel for one night only. Personally I felt a little annoyed about their intrusion into our company but was fairly sure that their intended targets were a couple of our colleagues, who were females.

'We're from Belfast, my friends, and we're just here for one night too,' said the Irishman with the brown hair. 'Do any of you lot want a drink?'

We accepted their kind hospitality and drank the beer they bought us. After this I went to the bar to purchase another round to return the compliment. When I got back, the Irishman with the short-cropped hair walked over and sat next to me. He had a big grin on his face and stared deep into my eyes.

'I've been told you're an ex-Marine,' he smiled, putting his hand on my shoulder as I placed the beer tray I was carrying down on the table.

'Yes, I was in the Marines. I served for seven years. I've been out a long time now, though.'

'I fucking hate Marines,' he snarled, making me feel threatened and uncomfortable.

'Here. I've just bought you and your friend a beer. Drink it and chill out. I'm not looking for any trouble,' I assured him.

The Irishman leaned over and whispered in my ear. 'Do you know who we are, my friend?'

'I have no idea, mate.'

'We're IRA and I'll tell you what, my friend . . .'

'What?' I asked with a big sigh.

'We're going to fucking kill you tonight.'

Suddenly the Irishman's words created a worrying situation for me. I looked around for the door just in case I needed to use it quickly.

'Don't bother running, my friend. We're both armed and will

shoot you dead if you do,' he threatened, patting one of his pockets.

One of my colleagues called Tony heard what the Irishman had said to me and came and stood next to me. He knelt down and whispered in my ear.

'Steve, I heard what he said to you. I'll back you up if there's any trouble, mate.'

'No,' I replied and shook my head. 'Don't get involved. This is something I'll have to sort out myself.'

'No, Steve, I'm going to back you up,' he continued in a determined voice.

I appreciated his willingness to help me, but I didn't want to draw him into this dangerous situation.

'No, Tony I don't want you to. Go and sit back in your seat,' I insisted.

Tony shook his head and stared wildly towards the two men who were sat grinning at the two of us.

'Look, Tony, if these men are who they say they are, they won't punch you, they'll fucking shoot you. So go away and leave me to sort this out.'

Tony looked angry, but I wasn't sure if he was angry with me or with the two Irishmen. He sat down in a vacant chair opposite and was joined by Colin, who came over to find out what was going on.

The brown-haired Irishman stood up and told his friend he was going to the bar to buy a round of drinks. As he passed me, he spoke briefly to me.

'You're fucking dead tonight, Marine,' he laughed.

For a moment I sat and thought about what he had said. If he was a member of the IRA, he wouldn't have told me, I thought. Then another man entered the bar and sat next to the skinhead. I leaned over and shook his hand.

'Hello, mate. Are you and your friends RUC?' I asked, feeling that I already knew the answer just from their appearances.

'Yes, mate. We're here for a night on the piss,' he answered as his colleague returned from the bar and passed him a pint of beer and sat between us.

I reached inside my pocket and pulled out my mobile phone. I proceeded to dial a number and put the phone to my ear.

'Are you calling a hearse, Marine? Because you're going to need one,' the brown-haired man said.

'Hello, Diz, it's Steve. I've got a couple of Irishmen threatening me in a hotel bar. Can you come round with a couple of the lads to help me sort it?'

'What?' Diz exclaimed in a state of confusion. 'Is that you, Steve? It's two o'clock in the morning, mate, and I'm 300 miles away at home in bed. Are you winding me up?'

'Right, I'll see you in 15 minutes. You know which hotel I'm in,' I said and switched the phone off and pushed it back inside my pocket.

'You don't worry me, Marine,' he grinned. 'You'll be dead before your friends arrive.'

'Look, mate,' I snapped. 'I know you're not IRA, you're fucking RUC.'

Suddenly the alcohol I had consumed throughout the evening took hold and my temper leapt up like a burst of fire.

'I'm going to fucking kill you, bastard,' I screamed wildly at him.

'Steve, leave the bar and go to bed,' interrupted Colin. 'You've had too much to drink.'

I knew Colin was right, but I was angry, very angry, towards this man. After all he had threatened to kill me. I contemplated hitting the man but fought hard to control my aggression. Suddenly Tony chirped up once more.

'I'll back you up, Steve. We'll take them on together.'

I frowned at Tony. I really didn't want him to get involved. I moved to tell him to stay out of it but my pressing anger caused me to shout, 'Go away. Go to bed now!'

Tony remained hesitant but I was adamant that I didn't want him to get involved and continued to shout at him, which made him angry towards me. I used his anger to channel him out of the bar.

'Get outside now,' I screamed at him.

'Come on then,' he snarled back and hurried towards the door.

I followed him out along with Colin, who seemed content to get the pair of us away from the now subdued Irishmen. Outside we began a screaming match and I vented a burst of aggressive shouting towards him, which seemed to calm him down. I had no intention of fighting him; I just wanted to frighten him so that we could resolve the situation. After this we sat and talked for a while and my two colleagues told me that they were concerned about my safety in the bar and that they wanted me to calm down and get off to bed. I knew they were right so I retired to bed a short time later.

The next day I was summoned by two senior managers at work who wanted to discuss the events from the previous evening. They told me that they were unhappy with the fracas caused the previous evening and also that they were concerned for my safety. One of them suggested that I may have been suffering from post-traumatic war syndrome, but I assured him that I was not and that all I'd really done that night was shout at a few people. Nevertheless I rightly apologised for my unacceptable behaviour and assured them that it would not happen again. Thankfully they were happy to let it go and told me to forget about it and to get on with my job.

That evening I went to see my friend Richard to talk about the incident. He said the odds of this happening again were one in a million and referred to the situation as a residual aggressive blip because I'd mixed my drinks that night and got too drunk. He was right. The odds of this happening again were very slim and the aggression had burst through because of the quantity of alcohol I had consumed. Consequently I learnt from the experience and realised that I needed to consume less alcohol in the future to ensure I was always in control.

CHAPTER TWENTY-SEVEN

WE'LL ALWAYS BE MARINES

A few weeks later, on Remembrance Sunday 2003, I searched frantically around the house for my Royal Marines Corps tie.

'Anne, have you seen my Corps tie?' I asked desperately, because my home town's remembrance parade was about to start in 30 minutes' time.

'It'll be under your nose somewhere, Steve,' she answered, with a hint of sarcasm. 'Have a look in your wardrobe. It'll probably be amongst the rest of your ties.'

I'd already looked there, but decided to look again just in case. Sure enough it was amongst them and I pulled it out from the pile.

'Have you found it?' asked Anne.

'Yes.'

'Was it under your nose?' she grinned, rolling her eyes at me.

'No, it was tucked away in a jacket pocket,' I fibbed, and Anne smiled and shook her head.

I pulled a Royal Marines tiepin out of one of the drawers and clipped it onto my tie. It was slightly buckled because I'd fallen on it a few years before when I'd drunk too excessively and tried to run home from the pub. As I pulled on my jacket, I smiled at myself in the mirror. I'll be happy if the children turn out like me now, I thought.

Outside the weather was dry and cold and a fresh breeze blew in my face as I hurried down to the war memorial. When I got there, I saw rows of servicemen dressed in their regimental uniforms forming up in preparation for marching in the parade. I looked around the huge crowd of people that stood in the background on the side of the road. Amongst them I noticed my friend Scouse. He, like myself, always stood in the background and mingled with the crowds of people. It's what we preferred to do. I walked towards him and saw him smile when he saw me approaching.

'Hi, Steve,' he said, shaking my hand. 'Bloody cold, isn't it?'

'Yes, bloody freezing, Scouse.'

Suddenly the sound of drums started to beat and the formed-up troops marched towards the memorial. The majority of soldiers who marched past us were made up of the Territorial Army. Their rubber-soled boots thudded as they hit the ground in step.

'Not quite the same as the crunching sound of the Royal Marines' drill boots, Steve, is it?'

I didn't answer. I just smiled at him as I suddenly felt out of place amongst the focused crowd. I don't need to come here any more, I thought. I no longer feel a part of this. Today is the last time I'm coming here.

'There's our lads,' said Scouse, nodding his head towards a group of former Royal Marines who were dressed in trousers and blazers. They were wearing their Green Berets and were marching with Royal British Legion flags along with a group of men who formerly served with the Parachute Regiment.

The parade halted smartly in front of the war memorial and a young Navy cadet marched out smartly from the ranks and halted a few feet away from them. He was carrying a bugle, which he raised up to his lips and sounded a slightly out-of-tune 'Last Post'.

'Not quite like the Royal Marines' buglers, are they?' said Scouse in a quiet voice.

Once again I didn't answer and just smiled at him as the customary two-minute silence followed. Nobody uttered a single word during this time and only the sound of the Regimental flags could be heard as they flapped in the bitterly cold November wind.

Following the silence we looked on and watched the rows of poppy wreaths being laid by a couple of the local politicians and current and former servicemen. We stood and laughed together as the military ranks and former servicemen marched off and out of sight. The large crowd we were standing amongst started to disperse in all directions as the people went about their business. I breathed in a deep breath of fresh air and looked up at the sky. I felt good inside and my mind felt free.

'Let's go and have a look at the Royal Marines' floral tribute, Steve,' Scouse suggested as he rubbed his hands together to get them warm.

I nodded my head and we crossed the road towards the wreaths that were laid out neatly at the foot of the high concrete war memorial. We stopped opposite and Scouse pointed towards one of them.

'There it is,' he said, sounding content that he'd found it quickly.

In the middle of the wreath was a picture of a globe with laurel wreaths around it. It was the insignia of the Royal Marines.

'I loved being a Marine, Steve. Did you?' Scouse asked.

'Yes, I did, mate. It was great at the time. It was a long time ago, though. I've been a civvy for thirteen and a half years now.'

'Yes, me too. I've been out even longer than that. I'm going to have a good drink when I get home. Are you going to do the same?' he asked as he huddled his shoulders to keep warm.

'No, not me, Scouse. I'm going to play football with my two children.'

Suddenly a middle-aged woman appeared next to us. She scanned the poppy wreaths from side to side and looked at the badges and labels on them.

'Excuse me, gentlemen,' she said politely. 'Please can I get past you? I want to see the Royal Marines' floral tribute. My son was a Royal Marine.'

Scouse and I stepped aside and let the woman through. She

knelt down and looked at the poppies. As she did this, I turned to Scouse and shook his hand.

'I'll see you next year, Steve,' he grinned. 'Same time, same place.'

I smiled at him and saw the middle-aged woman stand up and face us. 'My son loved being a Marine, you know,' she said to us.

'We're Marines,' Scouse answered, pointing at both of us. 'We'll always be Marines.'

You might, I thought as I walked away. Not me though, not any more . . .